T0386736

SOMALILAND

A Charging Lion

To face page 205

SOMALILAND

BEING

An Account of Two Expeditions into the Far Interior

TOGETHER WITH

A COMPLETE LIST OF EVERY ANIMAL AND BIRD KNOWN TO INHABIT THAT COUNTRY, AND A LIST OF THE REPTILES COLLECTED BY THE AUTHOR

BY

C. V. A. PEEL

FELLOW OF THE ZOOLOGICAL SOCIETY, MEMBER OF THE OXFORDSHIRE NATURAL HISTORY SOCIETY AND FIELD CLUB, ETC.

DARF PUBLISHERS LIMITED
LONDON
1986

First impression 1900
This edition 1986

ISBN 1 85077 086 7

*Printed & bound in Great Britain
by A. Wheaton & Co. Ltd, Exeter*

I dedicate

THESE PAGES TO THE MEMORY OF MY FATHER,

THE LATE CHARLES PEEL,

OF

THE MANOR HOUSE, NORTH RODE,

CHESHIRE,

A CRACK SHOT IN THE TRUE SPORTSMANLIKE METHOD OF

WALKING UP BIRDS WITH THE AID OF DOGS,

A CLEVER RIFLE-SHOT, AND A SUPERB

FLY-FISHERMAN.

INTRODUCTION

THAT 'of making many books there is no end, and much study is a weariness of the flesh,' I am perfectly aware. At the same time, it seems to me odd that, considering the number of men who visit Somaliland, no attempt has hitherto been made to make a list of the beasts and birds which are contained therein. This want I have endeavoured to supply in the following pages, being perfectly conscious of their many shortcomings, yet hoping they may be of some little use, help, and amusement to the hunters and collectors who may enter the country.

My thanks are due to Captain and Mrs. Cox, Captain Abud, Captain and Mrs. Merewether, and Captain E. Merewether, for their kind hospitality and help on the several occasions when I found myself at the coast town of Berbera; to Major H. G. C. Swayne, for valuable information about stores, management of caravan, etc., before starting from England; and to the following experts in natural history for their kindness and help in naming my specimens: Mr. Oldfield Thomas and

Mr. W. E. de Winton (mammals); Dr. R. Bowdler Sharpe and Dr. E. Hartert (birds).

Some of the incidents in the following pages have appeared in the columns of the *Field*, the *Sporting and Dramatic News*, the *Gentlewoman*, the *Pall Mall Gazette*, the *Wide World Magazine*, and the *Sketch*; and I am much indebted to the editors of these papers and magazine for allowing me to reproduce them here.

Owing to the constant glare of the sun it is extremely difficult to take good clear photographs in Somaliland, and I regret that some of mine have not come out quite so well as I expected.

There is no attempt at literary skill in these pages. They simply record facts taken from my diary, and the reader will readily understand how difficult it has been to avoid monotony when recording my daily life in camp and on the march.

I regret to say that my very large collection of insects, including several new genera and many new species, has not yet been worked out, and is at the last moment unavoidably excluded.

I cannot close this introduction without a word of praise to Mr. Edward Gerrard, of Camden Town, London, who set up all my big game trophies in a most natural and life-like manner.

C. V. A. P.

PEEL FOLD, OXFORD,
1899.

CONTENTS

PART I.

FIRST EXPEDITION.

CHAPTER I.

CHAPTER II.

CHAPTER III.

CHAPTER IV.

PART II.

SECOND EXPEDITION.

CHAPTER I.

CHAPTER II.

CHAPTER III.

CHAPTER IV.

CHAPTER V.

CHAPTER VI.

CHAPTER VII.

LIST OF ILLUSTRATIONS

SOMALILAND

---✶---

PART I.
FIRST EXPEDITION.

CHAPTER I.

ON reaching Aden *en route* to the Somali Coast, where I
proposed making an expedition in search of natural history
specimens, I found nearly all the shops shut, as the big
merchant of the place was having a jubilee. However, I
set to work at once, hired a tailor at 10 a.m. to make me
two suits of clothes, which I got finished the same evening
at the cost of twelve shillings each suit, and routed out a
headman, who proved afterwards to be one of the greatest
scoundrels unhanged, a nice-looking 'boy' or 'butler,' as he
called himself, a syce, or groom, and a fine, strong-looking
shikari, or hunter.

The news of my intentions was soon all over the town,
and my bedroom was besieged from morning to night by
every sort, shape, and size of black ruffianism, begging to
be engaged. The day was ended at last, and I went to
bed, perspiring out of every pore, and endeavoured to sleep.
But night was rendered hideous by the shrieks and howls
of innumerable cats.

Next morning I was up at 5 a.m., and after *chota
hazri* and a hair-cut, I discovered on the shops opening I
was too late for the weekly steamer to Berbera, the Somali
Coast town. On the voyage out I had made the acquaint-
ance of two young officers from Cairo, who were going
across for some big-game shooting, so we clubbed together,
and chartered a steamer to take us straight over with our

1—2

men and baggage. Then came the hard work of the day. As I could not ship my rifles and ammunition as personal baggage, but as cargo only, I had to get them all through the Customs, and also get a permit from the Excise and consular authorities, allowing me to take them into the country. I also had to produce my permission to enter the country personally. During these operations I had to sign and get signed several ' acts of parliament,' go several long gharry drives, and pay a large duty on my goods, which employed me from 7 to 2 p.m., entailing not a little loss of time, money, and temper. However, I had everything settled at last, and got rid of the red tape. The officers who joined me on the ship were more lucky, for they had their tents, ammunition, and rifles lent to them, and their cartridges taken as personal baggage with nothing extra to pay, although the weight far exceeded the regulation three hundredweight.

At length we got on board our chartered cockleshell of a steamer which was to take us to Berbera, but we were obliged to wait two hours before our heavy baggage arrived ; and when it did at last arrive, the careless coolies, in attempting to lift up a case of mine containing eighteen Snider carbines, let it slip slowly out of their hands without attempting to make a grab at it. Down it went with a great splash into the sea. But wonders never cease : up it came again, and was secured by means of a rope. I breathed again! It was so well packed and air-tight that it had floated.

We started at 6 p.m. Oh, the dirt and the smells on that tiny boat! Just as we were fairly under way, the agent of the ship, who was still on board, discovered that half of the Somali passengers had not paid for tickets, nor had they any money for them, whereupon there was a general row, which ended in a free fight, the second officer getting badly mauled by some half-dozen scoundrels ere the captain, a big, burly fellow who was three-parts drunk, rushed upon them, and, hitting out right and left, seconded by our three selves, at length succeeded in pitching all the ringleaders head foremost overboard into a boat, and quelled the mutiny.

The ship proved so small that we were obliged to sleep on chairs on deck. There were no cabins. Dinner was served in a poky little hole below, with a tablecloth more black than white. And, ugh! how dirty the dishes were, and how tough the so-called 'chicken,' and hot the soda-water! On settling myself to try to sleep, I found I could not get comfortable owing to the extremely hard chair and the cold. The vessel pitched and rolled, and I began to get very sea-sick. Every now and then the boat would give a huge lurch, and the water would rush in over the side, half drowning the men who were lying on the lower deck. Anyone could see that she was utterly unfit to be upon the sea, and might go down at any moment.*

Next morning I roused myself to find it Easter Sunday, and began the day with a bad headache. During the morning I amused myself by watching a number of porpoises and dolphins (the former have round and the latter pointed noses). On sighting the ship they would swim up to her and play about in front of her bows, so close to her that they must now and then have been touched by the ship. Two of them would then do a kind of 'Dutch roll' before the ship, their action reminding one exactly of two persons skating together. Thus they would proceed for several miles, occasionally coming up to the surface to blow.

The Somalis kept constantly coming up on deck and praying in the usual Mohammedan fashion. First of all they stood up, crossed their arms over their chests, and touched their foreheads and beards; next they bent down as they mumbled out their prayers; and lastly they knelt down, putting their foreheads between their knees on the ground. They ended this performance by getting up and spitting.

* Since writing the above, some few years ago, I learnt at Aden when I was last there that this same boat, which was carrying Her Majesty's mails, a lot of specie, and a crowd of passengers, not long after capsized, and every soul on board was drowned.

Owing to bad steering and other miscalculations, we
arrived at the Somali Coast fifteen miles out of our course,
and so did not get to the excellent harbour at Berbera
until after sunset, when it was too late and dark to find our
tents and pitch them. However, the Political Resident very
kindly gave me an excellent dinner, and the Resident
Engineer allowed me to sleep under the veranda of his
bungalow, close by a cage containing a fine lioness fifteen
months old. This handsome animal played with one just
like a huge dog, but I discovered that her claws were
getting a bit too long and sharp to be comfortable. She
would lie on her back and embrace my legs with her huge
paws. Her strength was wonderful. She would come up
to me, purring like the great cat that she was, and rub
against me. I generally collapsed on the floor. When
you wanted her to stand up, you lifted her up on her legs
by her long tail, with its black tufted end. She was
beautifully spotted on her belly, like the skin of a giraffe.
Poor Kitty ! I wonder what has become of her. Her portrait adorned the pages of the *Graphic* one day. Kitty
kept wonderfully quiet all night, but the mosquitoes did
not, and I got up when the sun rose with a splitting headache, and spots all over my body caused by the noxious
little pests. In the large camping square I found my tent
pitched, together with several others, for there were no less
than four separate shooting-parties just then in Berbera.
The scene was most animated. Dozens of stalwart Somalis
were walking about in their white *tobes*, and talking in
excited tones, as they busied themselves over their master's
kit. Several camels stood complacently chewing the cud,
and ponies were being cantered about to show them off.
Then began a long day's work : opening all the cases, sort-
ing out all my effects, putting bedding in order, opening
cartridge-boxes, and cleaning guns and rifles. Suddenly
up comes a Customs officer to know the value of my
imports.

' I make you bill, I make you bill !' he said, as he glared

at me with his eagle eye as if I was the biggest smuggler
and Customs swindler out of prison.

Just then the pretty hills thirty miles inland were lost
in black clouds, and distant thunder rolled. The rainy
season in Somaliland had begun. My 'boy' remarked :
'Plenty of rain upstairs'—pointing to the hills. 'Don't
you hear him speaking?'—the latter remark referring to
the thunder.

There were no camels on sale, so I was obliged to await
the incoming of a caravan on the morrow, the owner having
been badly mauled by a lion in the jungle. This made the
fourth white man mauled in the last six months. That
morning I took tiffin in the tent of one of the parties which
had just come in from the hills. It proved a very jolly
meal, the ladies relating amusing anecdotes of leeches in
their drinking water, centipedes in their tents, and tadpoles
in their baths, when encamped up in the hills. One of the
gentlemen presented me with what he called a most efficient
trap to catch small animals. I was soon enabled to prove
its efficiency, for I at once succeeded in catching my thumb.

The gentlemen of the party also had some yarns to spin.
One related how a follower had complained to him of a
terrible swelling in the throat, and a close examination of
his mouth disclosed an enormous leech stuck fast to the
roof of his larynx. One man held the poor fellow's mouth
open whilst the narrator with a pair of pincers out of the
tool-chest extracted the noxious animal, together with a
large piece off the roof of his mouth. He obtained imme-
diate relief !

Seeing a Somali with one arm, I asked him how he had
lost the other, when he related how he had been charged
by an elephant, which impaled his arm with its tusk. The
sahib, after minute examination, again had recourse to his
tool-chest, and having produced his meat-saw, and cleaned
away the flesh with his hunting knife, he sawed the bone
in two. The only words the wretched man uttered were,
'Be quick, sahib ; be quick !'

Shortly after in came the party who had been mauled by a lion. I offered to buy his camels, but he said he was going into the jungle again in a few days if his arm and hand (which he carried in a sling) continued to improve.

For a whole week I was obliged to remain in Berbera getting together my caravan. Camels came in very slowly, and the prices asked were exorbitant. At night it was almost impossible to sleep owing to the heat and the mosquitoes, added to which was the incessant din of the men belonging to the various caravans, who would persist in shouting, talking, and quarrelling, entailing my frequent interference with growls of 'Scutter!' (Go away!) and 'Bus!' (Be quiet!).

At length I collected a rabble of 23 men. There were 13 camelmen, 1 headman, 4 shikaris or trackers, a syce, a cook, a skinner, a 'butler,' and a donkey-boy. I bought a pony at last for 80 rupees, and camel-mats for 25 camels; 12 *harns*, or native water-vessels of plaited bark; 10 long white *tobes* and 75 *merikani tobes* (*i.e.*, cloth made in America and used for barter); native axes and cooking-pots; 2 water-casks holding 10 gallons each, and 2 casks holding 7 gallons each; iron tent-pegs, several bundles of loading rope, 10 turbans as presents for women, blankets for followers, cocoanut-oil for ditto, a sack of onions, a sack of potatoes, 12 bundles of extra candles, 6 coloured *tobes* for Sultans, cartridge-belts for escort, and scores of odds and ends too numerous to mention. When I had put down my 23 packing-cases full of rifles, tent, bedding stores, cooking gear, ammunition, etc., I was informed that 23 to 25 camels would be enough to carry the whole. For my 23 followers for four months I provided 20 bags of rice, costing 157 rupees; 375 pounds of ghee (native butter), costing 170 rupees; and 12 *gosras*, or baskets of dates. Day after day I waited, but no more camels came in. I was enlivened in the evening by a madman, who came round chanting a lot of gibberish and pointing at me, surrounded by a huge crowd of natives, who roared with laughter at every word the poor man uttered.

One day I was going down to the native town to deposit my money with a Mr. Mahomed Hindi, a merchant there, when I trod upon a small thick snake lying in the sand, which it exactly resembled in colour. Luckily, I got off without a bite.

The European compound of Berbera is an extremely picturesque little place. There is a Political Resident's bungalow, an Engineer's bungalow—now turned into a traveller's bungalow—a court-house, a hospital — now getting very short of funds, I am sorry to hear—and a prison. Every day the prisoners march up and down to their various occupations, clanking the chains attached to iron collars round their legs, and attended by armed Sikhs as policemen. Theft and assault were the commonest offences. All the prisoners seemed very jolly, and 'bucked' away to each other, making a great noise. They seemed to have very little to do, plenty of society and gossip, and lots of food. In fact, many men in the town used to steal on purpose to get into such good society.

It was very hot in Berbera until about 4 p.m., when a strong wind sprang up. I then had my pony saddled, and rode out into the desert maritime plain, which extends to the first hills south of the town, some fifteen miles off. This plain is covered with little thorn-bushes about 2 feet high, with an occasional ant-heap of large size.

In the hospital some fearful cases of consumption and starvation are always being treated. The women appeared to be by far the most troublesome people in Berbera, either dying of starvation or beating and scratching the eyes of their friends and relations. Whilst I was there I saw one poor old woman, supposed to be mad, who was extremely aggressive and dangerous, rushing after anyone she took a fancy to, and belabouring him or her with a thick stick. She was at length got rid of, her friends being paid to take her into the jungle on a camel, and leave her in a village

there. I was shown here a disgusting photograph of a
poor boy who, dying of starvation, was making his way to
the hospital, and had in fact got within about 100 yards
of it, when from sheer exhaustion he fell, and was
eaten, probably alive, by a hungry hyæna. He was photographed early next morning just as the hyæna had left
him.

In a week I had bought fourteen camels. One buys a
camel in dollars, but the extraordinary part of the transac-
tion is that one pays for it in rupees. The thermometer
averaged 110° in the sun and 93° in the shade at noon
during my stay at the coast, so you can imagine I was
pretty thankful to get out of the heat. I had now secured
fourteen camels; so determined to start for the jungle on
the morrow, and leave half my baggage behind with my
headman and some of the camelmen to buy the remaining
'ships of the desert.' I paid all my men a month's wages
in advance, according to their custom. As I expected,
there was a great deal of squabbling, one man refusing to
be a camelman, another saying he must be a gunbearer,
and all wanted extra pay because I said I wished to reach
the Shebeyli River, and they dreaded fever. There was
such a row that I could with difficulty hear myself speak.
When at length silence was restored, the men requested I
should buy them a sheep to kill for good luck. I consented
on condition they should not make it a rule to ask for
mutton whenever there was no game to be had. I deposited
my leather portmanteaus and empty packing-cases in the
church until my return.

CHAPTER II.

NEXT morning my store-boxes, tent, guns, rifles, ammunition, all divided as much as possible into the usual 60-
pound loads, were placed upon the fourteen camels, and at
length I started for the jungle, wending my way towards
Hargaisa with thirteen followers. The cook managed to
smuggle in a scullery-boy as an apprentice. I left word
with my headman to purchase another good pony and two
or three donkeys. We made a bad start, as one of the
camels, hearing a tin can rattling about him, commenced
to buck, which ended in my eight-bore rifle and two of
my casks coming to the ground with a crash. However,
nothing was broken, and the camel was made to kneel
down and loaded up again. One camel then began to lag
behind, but eventually reached us soon after we encamped
for the night. We had not gone more than two miles out
of Berbera upon the desert (my pony going dreadfully
slowly, not having touched a blade of fresh grass for weeks),
when my syce spotted a herd of nine gazelle (*Gazella
pelzelni*). They took no notice of our caravan, but when
I dismounted to stalk, they slowly walked off. The ground
was very flat and bare, there being only a few thin thorn-
bushes to cover us, so that we were obliged to stalk them
almost in full view the whole time. However, by walking
upright and encircling them, they allowed us to get within
about 80 yards, when, as I was sitting down to take a

shot, they bounded quickly off. I must confess I 'browned' them, but missed, and passing quickly behind some thorn-bushes, they did not allow me to get in a second barrel. I then rode on slowly until I overtook the caravan, which I accompanied until the sharp eyes of my syce again detected a couple of these beautiful little creatures. I again dismounted, and followed them for about half a mile, but, owing to the flat, bare ground, it was impossible to get near them, and getting out of our course we retraced our steps.

Soon after this I called a halt of the caravan, having marched for two hours and a half, the distance covered being about seven miles. The men seemed to know their work, and each appeared to do something. The camels were made to kneel down in a large circle, when all their burdens were removed, and they were then turned loose to graze upon the tiny bushes close around us.

By-the-by, talking of grazing reminds me that, just before halting, my head-shikari, pointing to a diminutive and sorry-looking plant, requested me to dismount. I thought he had found some rare little specimen, and that he expected me to pick it up and keep it as a precious prize. I asked :

' What is it ?'

He replied :

' Grass ; let pony feed.'

I dismounted, exclaiming :

' Poor pony ! what a supper after such a tiring hot march !'

But to return to camp. What a scene of bustle and action ! No sooner had we halted than the cook's apprentice, having collected wood, placed it in the centre of three brick-shaped stones pointing outwards. In the twinkling of an eye there was a blaze, in another the cook had chopped up some meat and begun simmering it on an iron vessel on the fire. My double-roof ridge tent was up in a jiff, water placed in a bucket for me to wash in, a waterproof sheet spread upon the floor inside the tent, and upon it my indiarubber bath, mosquito-curtain, bed, blankets, shoes, pyjamas—all put ready for me, and everything in its right place, my boy having evidently been butler to white men before. Meanwhile, another large fire had been kindled, and as it now grew dark, the camels, pony, and sheep were driven in close to it. No zareba (thorn fence) could be built, as the thorn-bushes were not big enough. By the time I had had a wash and brush-up, I found an

excellent stew awaiting me, followed by some of the best roast mutton I had ever tasted; this, washed down with lukewarm water, diluted with 'a wee drap of the cratur,' set me in good humour for the long day's march on the morrow.

I was up in the morning at 2.45, and at 3.30 all the camels were loaded, with the exception of one obstinate brute, who still knelt and roared, resisting all attempts to raise him until part of his load had been removed from his back and transferred to another animal. As far as I could

see, not a single thing was left behind, although the only
light we had came from the fast-dying-out camp-fires.
During my stay at Berbera I was troubled very much
with diarrhœa, caused by the peculiar water ; this had left
me very weak and shaky. However, by dosing myself
with opium pills and soda-mint tabloids, I gained strength
every day.

We marched through the darkness without incident
until daybreak, when my syce, as usual, spotted some
gazelle, and after slowly walking after them for a mile
without allowing us to get anywhere near them, I let fly
at them at long range, and missed. The same thing
happened two hours after, when my syce was the first to
find again. During the morning we found two more lots,
but they got away without being fired at. We then
halted, after having marched for four hours, and as I was
utterly dead beat, after some tiffin, I had my bed spread
under an attempt at a tree, and slept till 2 p.m., when we
restarted under the burning sun.

At about 4.30 my syce saw gazelle for the sixth time,
when, after the usual walking, running, and crouching in
full view of them, I got tired, and fired a running shot,
making my third miss for the day. The shot started an
old jackal out of a thorn-bush, where he had been lying
asleep ; but he did not offer me a chance, slinking quickly
away, his nose and brush almost touching the ground.
Coming back to the pony, we started a dik-dik, a tiny little
antelope weighing less than a hare. After this we marched
in silence through deep rocky nullahs, surrounded by small
barren hills, the ground becoming more stony and utterly
destitute of grass. We passed over several dried-up river-
beds, and I had frequent recourse to the water-bottle to
gargle out my parched throat, the heat during the afternoon being terrific.

My shikari's method of stalking gazelle did not appeal
to me. His idea was to walk straight at them until they
ran away, and then run hard to the nearest bush, expecting

to find them just beyond it, but, as a matter of fact, they always ran on until they got behind the next bush, through which they would peep at us. In this way they would lead us on for miles. My plan would have been to crawl on hands and knees—a very slow and arduous task, I admit, upon thorny rocky ground—but the gazelle are then so inquisitive that they *must* stand and stare at the unaccustomed sight of a man crawling along the ground towards them. At 5.30 we encamped for the night, and I went to bed with prickly heat and thoroughly tired out. As we had to get to water, we had to march quickly over this dry, parched-up desert country, although it was extremely trying both to men and animals.

Next morning we marched from 4 till 9.30, through deep nullahs, and for the most part up a gradually ascending slope. Trees began to be visible. When day broke we saw an 'owl' gazelle (*Gazella sœmeringii*), one of the finest gazelles in the country ; but we did not go out of our way to follow him, as the men told me I should encounter hundreds further on. Because I had not my gun out, we saw dozens of dik-dik antelopes, so in the afternoon I fetched it out, and of course saw next to none. There were so many beautiful birds about when we encamped for the mid-day rest that I went after them, and bagged about half a dozen. What a trouble the little wretches are to skin under a hot sun, to be sure !

We restarted at 1, and marched on till 5.30. On the way I saw some enormous black and white spiders. I shot a small bustard, which I skinned myself, as my skin-man pulled all the feathers out of the birds I gave him to do, and had not the faintest idea of the art, although he said before leaving Berbera that he was most proficient.

At 5.30, after having passed several caravans of camels laden with skins, and protected by natives armed with spears, and carrying little circular shields, we reached the first water I had seen since leaving Berbera. There, sure enough, in a dried-up river-bed, was to be found for the digging the precious fluid about 2 feet from the surface of the sand. Grasshoppers, beetles, and spiders ran over my face and bed all night, but, as Grossmith used to sing, ' I am so much enjoying myself I don't mind flies.'

Next morning I awoke to find all my clothes saturated with dew, and my men sneezing and coughing. On getting up at 2.45 the air was intensely cold ; I shivered so much riding through the darkness that I was soon obliged to dismount and walk. About 7 I fired at a gerenook (Waller's gazelle), a pretty red antelope with a very long neck ; but the distance was great, and I missed. I found it impossible to get my shikaris to crawl after game ; small wonder, perhaps, as their legs were bare, and they by no means relished the thorns and stones. On returning from the pursuit of the gerenook, I picked up a very pretty tortoise. Passing several caravans, with numerous sheep and goats, we reached stony ground, covered with huge boulders. On the top of these red rocks were to be seen the curious little tailless rock rabbits (Somali name, ' bona '). These animals, which are a little smaller than an English rabbit, possess a pretty rat-coloured fur, and are probably the conies of the Bible. I brought two of them down from the top of a large rock with one shot. Climbing upon the boulder, and looking down to see where they had fallen, I beheld them just below me. Down I jumped on an aloe plant, thinking, of course, that it would be immediately crushed down by my weight. Not a bit of it ! The plant did not give in the least, and the result was anything but satisfactory, as I fell heavily among the rocks ' all of a heap.'

Soon after a jackal ran across our track ; dismounting, I fired my gun, which happened to be loaded with No. 8, and although the beast jumped high in the air, we eventually lost him. The same thing happened with a dik-dik soon after. Whenever anything large appears I always seem to have dust shot in my gun ; but if a beautiful little bird hovers over my head, I find I am loaded with buckshot. In the hurry of the moment the right cartridge can never be found, and the result is either a wound or a blow-to-pieces.

In this country were to be found enormous ants, which were most interesting to watch. I saw one of these insects carrying off a piece of bread four or five times its own size at a great pace. When he came to a steep place, in order to get it along quickly, he clutched it with all his legs, and, placing himself on his back, literally turned head over heels backwards down the little bank, still clinging tightly to his prize. In this manner he got along with amazing rapidity.

My programme when on the march was : Coffee at 2.30 or 3 a.m., march till 9 or 10 a.m., then unload camels and turn off to feed. Breakfast, and an hour's sleep on my bed under a tree, flies, ants, and insects of all kinds swarming over me the whole time, and birds hopping about picking up the crumbs within an arm's length of me. We fetched up the camels at 1 or 2 p.m., and marched again till 5 or 6, when we encamped for the night, and after a thorough examination of the body for the thousands of noxious insects which crawl over one when asleep on the ground, I made a hearty meal, wrote up my diary for the day, and retired to bed at 8 or 9. At first the smell of the camels all round my tent was intensely annoying, but I soon got accustomed to it. The noise of the men was objectionable, singing and dancing often being kept up till well-nigh midnight. The changing of sentries, the glare of the camp-fires, and the howling of hyænas all helped to keep one awake.

The day before we got to Hargaisa we marched at 2.30 a.m., the morning being intensely cold. I was so sleepy that I actually fell asleep in my saddle, when the pony stumbled over an aloe plant, and I awoke with a start to find it still dark, and the reins trailing on the ground. When day broke, my syce, as usual, spotted three gerenook, and after following them in full view for half a mile, one, a male, lagged behind, and as he stood facing me at 100 yards, I fired at his chest, the ball striking his left shoulder. He whisked round, and was off like lightning. We followed

S–B   2

his blood spoor for quite two miles, seeing him twice, but
being unable to get another shot.

At length, owing to the extreme heat, and as I was
getting very thirsty, I left my head-shikari with one rifle
to follow on the spoor whilst I and the syce wended our
way back to find the track of the camels. We had not
gone more than two miles, when the eagle eyes of my syce
made out two jackals running on ahead. I was out of the
saddle in an instant, and, snatching my rifle from him, ran
to cut them off. As they were in the act of crossing a
dried-up river-bed, I showed my head over a little bank,
knowing well that one of them would stop out of curiosity.
Sure enough, the one behind turned and saw me, stopped,
and stood broadside. He stayed where he had been
standing, when a bullet crashed through him just behind
the shoulder. I had no idea of the beauty of this animal
(*Canis messomelas*) until he lay stretched before me ; a
black back with silvery-gray hairs was varied on his sides
with bright yellow. My tiny penknife was the only
skinning tool between us, so the operation was a lengthy
one.

As we sat skinning him in the river-bed, a band of
natives, armed with most formidable-looking spears, came
up and said ' Salaam ' to me, touching their foreheads.
They were followed by a caravan of camels, donkeys, and
women, the latter carrying the latest fashion in European
umbrellas.

After another long ride we caught up my caravan, and
I was very thankful to get some breakfast. Whilst in the
middle of this repast, my shikari, to my surprise and joy,
appeared, bearing on his shoulder the head and skin of my
gerenook.

As I lay on my bed during the heat of the day, some
vultures displayed amazing daring, sitting within a few
feet of me, and watching the skins drying in the sun. I
also noticed the rhinoceros birds (little brown birds with
red beaks), picking the grass ticks off my pony's neck, legs,

and body. The butterflies of this country were so far
disappointing, but the birds magnificent. In the evening
we saw some gazelle, and just as I was about to pull the
trigger on a fine buck, he bounded off. Shortly afterwards,
as my shikari did not understand the working of my rifle,
which, although a splendid weapon (·450 Express) by
Alexander Henry of Edinburgh, had the old-fashioned
half-cock arrangement with bolts, I took it into my hands,
and essayed to bring it from full to half cock, but, owing
to my fingers being wet with perspiration, I accidentally
let the hammer fall on the nipple, firing the rifle. The
stock caught me in the thigh, and one of the hammers took
a piece out of my thumb, otherwise I escaped without
injury. I am afraid I did not impress my shikari much
with my knowledge of the safety of this excellent weapon.

I was now sunburnt to such an extent that my skin was
peeling right off my hands and face, which was most painful, my shikari remarking :

' You go to become bleck allsame Somali ' (You are getting
black like a Somali).

At length we reached the village of Hargaisa, having
been on the march for five days. This curious little collection of huts lies on sloping barren ground, surrounded
by a zareba, or thorn fence. As we approached the place,
which is about 100 miles south-west of Berbera, we spied
three koodoos, two cows and a bull, and after a most
exciting stalk I fired a long shot, and struck the bull too
far back, and the three galloped over the sky-line. We
followed the blood spoor for some way till we lost it on
rocky ground. So I left two men to try and find it, and
went on.

On regaining the pony, the syce said that the shot had
disturbed two splendid bulls, which we had not seen. The
cows of this magnificent antelope are hornless. Soon afterwards we found the old skeleton of an elephant. Alas ! it
is many a day since the last fell so near Hargaisa. This
place, which was formerly overrun with lions, has now been

denuded of every one, so great has been the influx of big-
game hunters in the last few years. As we wended our
way through the now thick bush, my pony stumbling every
7 yards, my syce began grubbing with his spear in the
ground, and soon afterwards produced an object like a huge
oblong potato, which he broke, offering me some to eat.
The inside was white and juicy, and had a most peculiar
and bitter taste. The Somalis call this root 'lika.'

In the afternoon I caught some butterflies, which I found
few and far between, not nearly so numerous as in Ceylon
or India, where I could often catch them as fast as I could
sweep my net. The temperature here was 95° at noon in
my tent, pitched in the shade. As I was away an hour
looking for butterflies, about a dozen of my men set out
in every direction to look for me, thinking I was lost.
Because I had no gun with me, of course I saw innumerable birds (including some francolin), a hare, a jackal, and
dik-dik antelopes.

Early in the afternoon Sheik Muttar, the swell of
Hargaisa, came to call. He was a nice-looking man with
a gray beard, and said 'Salaam!' on pressing hands. (The
Somali takes one's hand in his, but does not shake it.)
We got along very well, thanks to my interpreter. I
asked him how his flocks and herds were, and he answered
that he had none, and then he asked me how many lions I
had killed, and I said none. Then, after a pause, he asked
for a present, so I rummaged in a box and found six pocket-
knives, and asked him to choose one. He promptly picked
out the best, asked if I was going to give him anything
else, and, receiving an answer in the negative, slowly
marched out of my tent without saying 'Thank you' or
'Good-bye.'

I then went out bird-collecting. In the evening the
man I had left to track the koodoo came in with the head-
skin and skull. He said he had tracked it some ten miles
south of Hargaisa, and had at length come upon it stone-
dead in a rocky ravine. The horns of this magnificent

animal measured in a straight line 37¾ inches, and round
the curves 49½ inches ; the circumference at the base was
10½ inches, and it was 19½ inches between the tips.

Round Hargaisa next day I saw much game, including
a herd of twenty oryx antelope, which passed me, trotting,
at long range ; and as they did not see me, I waited for a
better chance, which, however, never came, as they afterwards got our wind whilst stalking them. I cannot
imagine a finer sight than a large herd of these magnificent and stately creatures trotting by one, shaking their
heads up and down, and whisking their bushy tails. I also
saw some koodoo females with one or two males with poor
heads, some gazelle, which I could not hit, lots of dik-dik,
two of which I killed (the female of these sweetly pretty
antelopes is hornless), gerenook, which I never could get
near, besides some francolin. Two of the latter I killed
with one shot. I skinned one and ate the other, which
proved extremely tasty. Being short of meat (the meat on
a dik-dik being about equal in quantity to that on a hare),
I bought three sheep for the men. After eating them all
in a few hours, they set to work, and sang and danced by
the camp-fires till midnight. One man sang a verse in a
falsetto voice, which was followed by a chorus of the rest
chanting ' Oh, ah ! oh, ah !' in a low and quite euphonious
fashion, clapping their hands and stamping upon the ground
with their feet in time with the chant.

My rifle and gun supplied me whilst at Hargaisa with
most appetizing food. Listen to the menu for the day, and
water, ye mouths : Breakfast at eleven. Porridge, a stew
of francolin, dik-dik antelope, and onion gravy, followed by
fried antelope. For dinner at sunset there were game,
soup, curry and rice, roast guinea-fowl, followed by an
extremely tasty little haunch of roast dik-dik. My cook
was quite an artist, and served up my meals in a manner
which would have done credit to many at home.

At last I shot another gerenook. I got a difficult chance
at one of these wily antelopes as he was standing upon his

hind-legs bolt upright, and feeding on the tender shoots on the top of a mimosa-bush. The distance was 100 yards, and only his head and neck were visible over the bush. The bullet went through his neck, and he disappeared from view. On running up, I found him stone-dead behind the bush. He proved to have a beautiful head, and we set to work and skinned him then and there.

On the way home we found an enormous land-tortoise, which we in turn carried home—a distance of two miles. It was so heavy that I could with difficulty lift it. It uttered the most extraordinary snorting and blowing noises on being touched. I also shot a guinea-fowl for the pot.

My gun and rifle shooting was now fast improving daily. Everyone knows *where* to hit an animal. Anybody with the vaguest notions of anatomy knows where the most vulnerable parts of an animal lie, namely, the brain, the heart, and the spinal column. The question is not *where* to hit an animal, but *how* to hit an animal in the right place. This is indeed a difficulty. One can perhaps hit a foot-square board at 100 yards every time one fires at it. But crawl on your hands and knees for 100 yards, run another 200 yards or more under a temperature of 115°, turn the square board into a little moving antelope, showing but his head and neck, or maybe his rump only, find no rest for your rifle, and be obliged to snap at him, and you'll find you miss him nearly every time at 100 yards. You don't want to know *where* to strike him, I repeat : you want to keep a steady hand after a long run and crawl, a cool head, keen sight, no nervousness, and no drinking the night before ; then, if you are naturally a strong man, you will know *how* to strike your game. One is often hurried by one's shikari or followers. When the game has neither seen nor winded you, take *plenty* of time, get as comfortable as you can and as near as you can, disregarding altogether your shikari's cries of ' Quick, sahib, quick ! Now, sahib, now shoot, shoot !' One's shots are often spoilt by the keenness and overanxiety of one's followers. The best shikari is one who keeps his mouth shut, but his eyes always open. On flat ground there is only one steady shooting position—sit down and rest both elbows on your knees. To kneel on one knee is evidently wrong, as one can then only rest the left elbow, the right having no rest whatever.

I found it best, when going out collecting insects, always to take a man out with a shot-gun, not, however, for the purpose of shooting butterflies—although this has often been done to bring them down when hovering over high trees—but in order to be ready for the birds which are always about when there are many butterflies on the wing. The gunbearer must not be allowed to follow you too closely, or he will invariably get in the way of your sweep with the net. When I missed a butterfly, my shikari always tried to catch it in his hands, or, failing that, would knock it down with my gun. It is needless to add that specimens secured by him were not exactly perfect. My gunbearers had a bad and dangerous practice of walking in front of my pony with my two rifles and gun pointing straight at my head, and all at full cock. I had constantly to dismount and show them what I wanted done. After dinner, when writing up my diary, I always kept a killing bottle by my side in which I used to bottle the numerous beetles, moths, and insects generally which invaded my tent, attracted by the light from my lantern.

One day, when going through fairly thick jungle, we all but walked into an old bull oryx, which was lying in the grass. He jumped up and, with a whisk of his tail and a turn of his huge frame, cantered off before I could get a shot at him.

In the evening a terrific thunderstorm, accompanied by torrents of rain, suddenly burst upon us, and before I could say ' Knife !' a small river was running into my tent, swamping everything. I shouted for the men, and, rushing out, made a ditch round the tent, which effectively drained off the water. All the men, with the exception of a few who

crowded under the outer roof of my tent, got drenched to
the skin, and stood huddled together surrounded by the
camels, shivering, chattering, and shaking for an hour
or so. There is nothing a Somali hates so much as rain,
excepting, perhaps, hard work. No fire could be lighted,
so I had to be content with a cold supper. Before I went
to bed the rain ceased, and beetles and 'bugs' of every
description swarmed into my tent, so that I used my killing
bottle with great effect.

Next morning everyone was coughing and sneezing with
the effects of the drenching the night before. Guns, rifles,
camera, 'bug'-boxes, food, tobes, blankets, and everything
perishable, had been stored overnight in my tent out of
the wet, and the collection of articles next morning almost
prevented me from standing upright inside the tent. A
pretty light-coloured snake was brought to me on the end
of a long stick, which I skinned, much to the astonishment
of the natives, who would not touch it with their hands to
save their lives. They reported that it was a very deadly
creature, many men and camels being killed by it every
year. Just as everything was beginning to dry nicely,
down came the rain again worse than ever. In the midst of
it one of my men arrived from Berbera with the good news
that the rest of my followers and camels were now within
two marches of us. The dried-up river-bed now altered its
appearance. What appeared to be a low wall of water
slowly advanced along the bed, and flowed noiselessly past,
forming a very curious spectacle. That evening I bought
a beautiful donkey for seven and sixpence, English money.

Next morning I went out to hunt for meat, and stalked
in vain oryx, 'owl,' and gerenook. We then lost the pony,
syce, and two gunbearers, and after shouting and whistling
for over half an hour, we retraced our steps homewards after
a very disappointing morning.

On the way home my shikari pointed out what appeared
to be a tiny piece of red velvet, which on closer examination proved to be a spider. The natives called it 'robleh

dah,' and said, and firmly believed, that it fell from the clouds with the rain. We also found some beautifully woven nests made of green grass hanging from the trees, made by a pretty little yellow weaver-bird. We got the news from a stranger on reaching camp that one of the parties which had been at Berbera with me had fired at a lioness, missed her, and hit one of his shikaris, the bullet grazing his jaw and taking off two of his fingers. He had been sent back to Berbera for repairs. At nine that even-

CARAVAN ON THE MARCH.

ing my headman turned up with nine men and the remaining fourteen camels and a donkey.

On May 1 we started from Hargaisa with my whole caravan, consisting of twenty-three men and a boy, twenty-six camels, two donkeys, one pony, and a flock of sheep. We were accompanied by another caravan of four camels, the headman of which craved our protection as he journeyed out of one friendly tribe into another.

Starting at 4 a.m., we marched to a spot called Harbarleh,

seeing on the way the inevitable gerenook and a great bustard, which I stalked unsuccessfully. During that night one of the camels sighted a hyæna, and made a bolt for it throuph our zareba; but as he was hobbled, he was soon recaptured. On seeing him going, all the rest jumped up and stampeded in every direction, stumbling over the tent-ropes, and nearly knocking me out of bed.

Next morning we restarted at four and marched on through the everlasting thick thorn-bush. Whilst being loaded, one of the camels attacked another, getting its head ' in chancery ' under it. He was with difficulty persuaded to rise by repeated blows, the poor brute underneath keeping up a continual roar. However, on being released he was found to be none the worse.

How I hated those early-morning marches before the sun rose ! My pony put its foot into a hole and stumbled every other minute ; my face and hands got scratched by the ' wait-a-bit ' thorn-bushes which it was impossible to avoid in the utter darkness. At length the day broke, and we encountered some small herds of oryx, which were, however, unapproachable, and after several fruitless stalks we regained the caravan in fairly open country.

How glad I was for a change to get out of that dismal forest, through which we had now marched for upwards of sixty miles ! I sat down to breakfast feeling rather cross with the failures of the morning, when an ' owl' gazelle walked slowly past me at 100 yards. Throwing down my porridge-spoon, and snatching up my rifle, I rushed behind a bush, from which I got a pretty shot, the bullet breaking her back and killing her instantaneously. I shall never forget the war-whoops of the natives when she collapsed, and they made a wild rush to *hallal* her. She proved to have a very pretty head. The horns of the females are more slender in build than those of the males.

Some natives, seeing our camp, came up and reported much game on the plain in front of us, and said that they had lost three camels. which had strayed, and the men, seeing the spoor of some lions, feared that they must be after their domestic animals. After breakfast I ascended a small rise in the ground, and what a sight met my eyes—a sight to make any sportsman's heart beat! Below me stretched a vast open plain for a distance of about twelve miles, covered with grass about a foot high, and thinly scattered every 100 yards or so with little thorn-bushes 2 or 3 feet high.

This immense area was literally crawling with game. Here, close below us, was a herd of from seventy to eighty ' owl ' gazelles. Further on slowly walked in Indian file six hartebeest (Swayne's), looking like huge donkeys high in the withers. Further still, among some higher bushes, were to be seen five or six gerenook, females with a single male, every now and then standing upon their hind-legs to crop the tender shoots growing on the tops of the bushes. Beyond these, again, I could discern a herd of oryx quietly feeding.

But look! what are those dark objects which look so much taller than anything else? With the aid of my binoculars I make them out to be three ostriches. Behind them rises a great sea of fog, resembling a huge lake, in which one often sees a mirage. I waited no longer, but, running down the bank, set foot for the first time upon the open plain. We tried the ostriches first, and after walking over a mile or two of grass with huge herds of ' owl ' on right and left, which gazed with curious eyes as we passed by, we neared the huge birds. But before we had approached within a quarter of a mile of them, the ostriches, after lifting their long necks and staring at us for a minute, let us know that their name was ' Walker.' I had brought my pony out with me, hoping to come across lions, which often stray out of the thick cover into the open after oryx, and when gorged are to be found lying in the grass, too lazy to return to the bush. They can then be ridden down and brought to bay. Not wishing to tire my pony out so early in the day, I did not give chase, and the gigantic birds vanished into the mist at a tremendous pace.

I next attempted to walk within range of some hartebeest, but they would not allow me to try a shot. They would stand staring at me at about 400 yards, and just as I sank down to try a shot, with a whisk of their tails they would gallop off. At length I waited for the camel I had brought out with me to carry the meat, should any fall to my rifle. When he came up with us, I got a man to lead him towards the hartebeest, which were now almost out of sight in the haze. I walked close behind him, and had not proceeded far, when, on brushing off some flies with my hand from the camel's hind-legs, he suddenly let out backwards with his huge foot, and caught me full on the shin, nearly knocking me down !

At length, hiding behind the camel, I managed to limp up to within about 300 yards of the hartebeest, which were slowly walking parallel with us. Whenever the antelope turned to the right, and so had their heads away from us, we hit up the camel, turned his course, and made straight for them as hard as we could go ; but directly they turned to the left again, or stood to look at us, we also turned to the left, as though we were going to pass without molesting them.

In this manner we steadily gained upon them, and when they next stood still I sat down behind the camel, which I ordered to proceed without stopping, and when it had passed me I took aim and fired at the nearest antelope. But being shaky with excitement (as I was very anxious to bag one), and tired with my long walk in the sun, I made a clean miss. They galloped off, but stopped soon after. On rejoining the camel, we turned his head after the antelope, and again commenced slowly to walk after them. We were soon again within 300 or 400 yards, and were marching thus parallel to them, when, tired of our company, they suddenly turned to the left and made a dash for it across our path. Calling to the man to turn the camel in front of

me out of the way, I sat down, and, aiming a little in front
of the shoulder of the biggest, I pressed the trigger as he
galloped broadside past me. The bullet struck him right
through the shoulder, bowling him literally head over heels.
The remainder of the herd turned sharp at the sound of the
rifle, and galloped away from me, offering a poor chance.
With a tape I always carried in my pocket I measured the
distance, 205 yards, to the dead antelope. He was a fine
fat beast, with horns 22 inches between the tips. After

DEAD HARTEBEEST ON THE SAYLAH BUN.

this we went after another herd, leaving two camel-men to
skin the hartebeest and load the camel with his head, skin,
and the best of his meat.

As we walked along, I suddenly spied an oryx lying in
the grass, about 200 yards away from a little bush. If I
could only get to that bush, I should have a lovely quiet
shot. Bending down, I ran towards it; but no, the wily
old oryx saw me, and was up in a moment. But so curious
was he, that I gained the shelter of the bush whilst he

advanced to have a better look at me. Aiming for his shoulder as he stood nearly broadside on, I fired ; but the bullet went thud much too far back, and he galloped off like the wind. I shouted to my syce to mount the pony and give chase ; but although he followed it for upwards of two miles, he never got within revolver-shot of it. Some hunters say that this antelope can be ridden down by an average horse. This I cannot believe after seeing this wounded animal outstride and easily leave behind my pony, which was by no means a slow mover.

After this I got within range of another hartebeest, and knocked him down, where he lay struggling; but just as my shikari was racing up to give him the *hallal*, the antelope regained his feet, and galloped off as if he had not been touched, leaving me with an unloaded rifle 300 yards behind. As the pony had not yet returned from following the oryx, we eventually lost him altogether. He joined another large herd of over 200, which took him clean away.

I shall ever remember that day upon the Saylah bun (Saylah plain), when perhaps I saw more big game in a few hours than I have ever seen in the whole of my other shooting days put together. Coming home, we saw herd upon herd of oryx, in several of which there could not have been less than 100 antelopes. I shot another hartebeest, and the camel having been laden to overflowing, we wended our way back to camp, my shikaris, gunbearers, and syce singing all the way.

On nearing camp I was received with shouts of approval by my men when they saw the quantity of venison I had brought them, and dancing, eating, and singing was kept up till the early hours of the following morning. (My camp was pitched at a place called Larndare.)

We made an extra long march next day through thick bush again, and very dismal work it was. One could not see more than 80 yards in front, and there was very little game to be seen except gerenook, which, by-the-by, never follow in thick bush, after they have once seen you, unless you have absolutely nothing else to do. You *may* get a very difficult shot after following them for miles ; as a rule, they are the most aggravating animals I have had as yet to deal with. After trotting away for a couple of hundred yards, they will stop and feed, as if to tempt you to still follow them. Then, just as you get within range, off they bound again.

We killed a small black snake, which the men declared was very deadly ; and after firing three shots out of my choke-bore gun with ' B B ' shot, I at length brought to a standstill a grand specimen of big bustard, which we skinned on the spot. My ' bony,' as my shikari calls my piece of horse-flesh, was now troubled with a horrid species of tick, which burrowed its head deep into the flesh at the roots of the hairs of his mane, face, ears, and tail. Some of these creatures swell out to the size of a large hazel-nut, and look like miniature inflated bull's bladders. The result of using Keating's Powder upon the pony was that the pests left him and settled upon me, in spite of the constant use of carbolic soap.

At 4.15 p.m. we camped near a village, and heard that a lioness and her cub were constantly chasing the sheep, and that there were also some leopards about. At this place, called Abriordi Garodi (the Graves of the Old Men), Said Hirsi, the headman of the tribe of Summathar Abdulla, came to call, and presented me with some fresh goat's milk and two fat sheep. I gave him some *tobes* in return. We could not now proceed further south-east owing to the scarcity of water. I sent out three men with camels to look for the precious fluid, but they returned saying all the water-holes were dried up. So I was obliged to buy two days' water-supply from the village at an exorbitant price, and blew my headman up for his bad management in not taking enough water, and allowing us to run short.

Whenever I killed an animal my shikari never thought of giving *me* any praise. He would say :

' You have good bullet—best bullet I see !'

My cartridges for the ·450 Express were 3¼ inch solid
drawn brass with a solid bullet, with gun-metal plug
weighing 270 grains, having a black powder charge of
120 grains behind it. Before I left the village the headman again appeared, and asked to be given a *chit* (a piece
of paper) signed by me, and setting forth how kind and
good he had been to me, and what handsome presents he
had given me. I drew it as mild as I could, considering he
had received from me thrice the value of his trumpery
presents, and had kept me on a wild-goose chase after a
lioness, the tracks of which we certainly found, but which
were at least three days old. But their game was to keep
us, in order that we might go on buying water.

On leaving, they confessed that the whole village had
turned out three days before, and driven the lioness, which
had killed a camel, right out of the country, and that she
had not since reappeared. We found, however, the fresh
tracks of a leopard, and spent the whole of a hot afternoon
looking for him, with no result. My liver was now giving
me a great deal of trouble, probably owing to the uninter-
rupted meat diet, no vegetables being procurable in the
country. Just as we had bought some more water and
were about to start from this extremely dull place, which
was devoid of all game, down came the rain in torrents,
wetting all the camels' mats through and through, and
preventing our marching. The sun at length appearing,
and the camel-mats being dried, we set off, only to halt
again after going eight miles, on the news of another lion.
We made an extra-strong zareba, tied up a donkey outside
at night, and awaited results; but not the ghost of a lion
did we see, probably owing to the noise my men made after
supper, shouting 'Tablo libah tablo!' (Lion, lion, come and
be killed !).

CHAPTER III.

We sight a large lion—Sitting up at night for lions—Lost in the jungle—
Lost again—Oryx antelope—Fight in camp—Tracks of lions—
Reports of leopards—Night adventure with a leopard.

NEXT morning the ground was covered with a heavy
dew. We marched at 5.30 till we reached a spot where
thirteen lions were reported to be about the neighbourhood,
and two had been seen the day before. Since leaving
Hargaisa six days ago, twenty-one lions had been reported,
yet not one had we seen. In the afternoon I wounded an
'owl' gazelle in the shoulder, and as we were within a mile
of the camp, I sent for the pony and galloped after the
gazelle till I brought him to bay. When at bay, he butted
at the pony's legs in very game fashion, poor brute! and it
was all I could do to keep in the saddle. At length I shot
him through the neck with my revolver. Unfortunately,
in the scuffle one of his horns got broken, otherwise he
would have made a very handsome trophy. I reached
camp just as a terrific thunderstorm burst upon us.

Another wet night was followed luckily by a fine day.
I went out and soon caught a glimpse of a bull koodoo
retreating before us. After following its spoor, which was
easily seen in the wet ground, we came across the tracks
of three lions going in the opposite direction. As they
were fresh, we followed the track, leading us into thick,
low tree jungle, with next to no undergrowth. After
following for upwards of three miles, the tracks showed
that the lions had separated, and that two (evidently a
female and half-grown cub) had gone one way, whilst the

3

other, a large male, had parted from them. We followed
the big one, of course. The sun was now right above us,
and the heat in consequence intense. The jungle was as
still as death. I could only hear the tramp, tramp of the
pony as he was led some yards in our rear. We crept
along, peering into every bush, when, from the base of an
ant-hill, up jumped an enormous lion with an angry ' whuff.'
But before I could get my rifle to my shoulder he had disappeared at a quick ambling trot among the thick bushes.
After following for a short time, his spoor was met by and
crossed by that of two other lions. We followed the undisturbed ones now until my shikaris voted that we should
return to camp, and quietly come back and tie up a donkey,
building a small zareba there in which to sleep at night.
I suspected, however, that the thickness of the bush and
the fact that we possessed but one pony frightened them,
and that they wished to beat a retreat out of sheer funk.
I argued with them for some time. I tried to persuade
them that, as we had at length found lions, we had better
stick to the spoor and not leave it till night, when they
would in all probability be miles away.

However, eventually I had to give in to them, much
against my will, and returned to camp feeling very sullen
at the thought of having a couple of cowardly shikaris with
me. I spent the afternoon catching butterflies, and in the
evening I went down to the little zareba I had ordered to
be built in the middle of the lion tracks. Such a snug
little place they had made, and so like the surrounding
thorn-bushes, that I did not observe it until I was within a
few feet of it. One of my men who had been engaged
building it now produced a young dik-dik which he had
caught alive in the grass. We tried to rear this pretty
little antelope on milk, but it would not touch it, and as it
was evidently dying, I put it out of its misery.

My two shikaris and I took turns to watch the donkey
tied up as a bait for a lion outside the zareba. We watched
it through a little porthole made on purpose. It was my

turn to watch, when I noticed the donkey suddenly prick up his ears and stare away into the darkness. There was not a sound to be heard in the jungle, save the everlasting chirp of crickets, and the hum of some large beetles as they flew through the air from bush to bush. The donkey stood rigid, but although I strained my eyes through the port-hole, I could see nothing. Suddenly a large gray phantom appeared before my eyes some 20 yards from the donkey. I was aware that a lion was watching the ass intently.

I waited and waited, but the gray image did not move. At last I thought I must act, so, pushing the rifle out of the porthole, I stared down the barrel, but, alas! I saw nothing. The large gray mass had disappeared. The donkey put down his ears, nodded his head, and soon afterwards lay down. Nothing else transpired, and having been thoroughly well bitten by mosquitoes, I awoke to find it very cold, and the ground covered with dew. It was about 5 a.m. when we made our way out of the tiny zareba, and, on walking round, we found that a large lion had come within 20 yards of the donkey, but, owing in all probability to the moonlight night, he had either noticed something unusual about the zareba or had got our wind. At any rate, he had not had the courage to make his deadly spring, for he must have seen the donkey.

At seven o'clock some of my men arrived to see what had transpired during the night. They were accompanied by the guide who had directed us to this haunt of lions, He was mounted on his charger. We then determined to track the lion, so ten of us started with two ponies. We tracked that lion's spoor from seven till eleven over miles of country, but not a 'blence' of him rewarded our exertions. The natives frequently sat down and consulted with the fates by counting off beads on a string, and the fates kept on saying we should kill something; but they were not good enough to vouchsafe what that something would be. At length we lost the spoor altogether, and after a long council of war we decided to return, as we were now very far from water. My head-shikari told me to accompany our mounted guide, as he would take me home faster than they could walk.

So we trotted off together. When we had been going half an hour, we came across fresh tracks of another huge lion, but, as I had left my rifle behind, we were obliged to proceed. In another hour we cut the tracks of three lions, and I began to wish for my rifle. In an hour and a half I began to suspect that my guide had completely lost his way in the dense jungle, and I was wishing I had brought my water-bottle and revolver with me, expecting to be obliged to spend a night of it in the thick jungle.

We kept turning and changing our course, and the guide seemed to be completely at sea, and, to make matters worse, he could neither speak nor understand a word of English. We at length dismounted and rested our horses for a while. On again we went through the maze of thorn-bushes, and I began to cough, for I felt very thirsty. At last, just as we were trying to find our way out of some extra thick bushes, we heard a shot fired a long way to our right. After cantering in the direction of the joyful sound for a few minutes, another shot was fired, and after following the direction of the sound for another hour or so, we at length came in sight of some of my camels, and a few minutes' gallop brought me in sight of my tent and zareba. I was tired out, but not too tired to eat, as I was very hungry, not having tasted food for over twenty-four hours, my last feed having been at 3 p.m. the day before. I also put away a few gallons of water. On my return to camp I found that my two shikaris had arrived before me, and, finding I had not returned, had fired the signal-shots I had heard. Two of my men, one of whom was carrying my big elephant rifle, had not returned, and were for the present lost. However, they eventually turned up a few hours later.

After a good meal, I set out once more for the little zareba, whither we had despatched one of my sick camels as a bait for the lions. This poor brute had hardly touched food since leaving Hargaisa twelve days ago. Having been much too early the night before, I made a later start, but what did we do but lose our way for the second time that day ! In two hours we had not reached the zareba we reached the night before in one hour. The sun was fast sinking. In another quarter of an hour it would be dark. With walking so fast after a heavy meal, I was now attacked with violent indigestion, and was obliged to sit down in agony.

'What we do now ?' asked my shikari.

'Go to the devil and leave me alone,' I thought to myself, but said nothing.

At length I suggested they should build a zareba where we were and sleep the night there, tethering up the donkey which had brought my bedding.

'How we build zareba without axe ?' he answered.

I produced my tiny penknife, the only cutting implement amongst us. My shikari grinned. By this time it was pitch dark, and we were utterly lost in dense thorn-jungle in a country infested by lions. But at that moment I felt so bad that I should have been quite happy if a big cat had pounced upon me and finished me off quickly. At last, feeling better, I got up, and after wandering aimlessly along for another half-hour, we luckily came upon our track of the night before. This we followed with great difficulty and very slowly until we eventually reached the little zareba, where, having tethered up our donkey on one side and our camel on the other, we blocked ourselves in with thorn-bushes, and watched in turn throughout the night. But the clouds clearing off unveiled the full moon, which, although no doubt a very beautiful object, was that night detestable to me, as it destroyed our chance of killing a lion. The reader will probably say : 'Serves you right for using such a cruel method for killing game, by baiting with living animals.' But it must be remembered that it is the only way of getting this most magnificent of beasts in thick thorn jungle, where when tracked in the daytime

he can invariably hear you coming, and when he jumps up
you can never get your shot in before he disappears from
view.   At the sound of your footsteps he will go slinking
off, and you may be only 20 yards from him, but you may
never see him.   So that in very thick bush there is only
one course open to you—to build a zareba and bait with ·a
donkey, and try to kill the lion as he drinks the animal's
blood.   It is all over very quickly for the baited animal.
The lion springs (or, rather, he doesn't in my case) upon the
animal, and with one bite through the neck kills it instantly,
before it is aware of what is going on.   The three methods
of hunting the lion in Somaliland, then, are : Tracking him
to his lair ; riding him to bay in the open ; baiting for him
at night.

At 5.30 next morning the so-called ' guide ' and some of
my men turned up to let us out of our miniature castle of
thorn-bushes, looking very crestfallen when they beheld
the donkey and the camel both alive.   I sent home the latter
animals with my bedding, and, taking the ponies, went forth
to view the nakedness of the land.   And very naked we
found it, as far as game was concerned, for several miles.
At length my syce, climbing a tree, found a herd of five
oryx, which we commenced to stalk.   I don't know how it
is, but antelopes seem to be always on the move, morning,
noon and night.   Now, these animals were walking straight
for a small bush, and would pass us broadside at 100 yards.
Good !   We crawled for that bush as hard as we could go,
but we found they had turned round and were walking in
exactly the opposite direction to that which they were
taking a second ago.   But antelopes are not Scotch red-
deer, the pursuit of which is mere child's play to the
pursuit of the former, for I have tried them both.   Antelope will lead you on and on, and then when perchance you
do get a shot, they will stand with their heads and necks
covered in branches and trees, and probably you see nothing
but haunches.

I thought that I had now lost all nervousness in stalking

antelopes, but that day I sat down and deliberately pulled the trigger, to find I had forgotten to cock my rifle. Ready at last, I sat down and aimed through a lot of thorn-bushes at a place where I expected the shoulder would be. Bang, bang! Off they went as usual, my shikari wringing his hands and swearing in Somali. But not so fast! I was certain I had hit with the first barrel. And on following up, there sure enough I found the blood-trail. I must have hit him high up on the shoulder. The ponies were off at a gallop, and soon I heard a shout, but on running up they were off again. We followed the pony-tracks for upwards of two miles, and then sat down for a rest, when I heard a shot fired very far to our west. I sent my head-shikari on after the ponies and returned home.

In the afternoon I went out bird-collecting, and about 5 p.m. my syce and Jama Mehemet, my guide, galloped up singing, so I knew they had got my oryx. A few minutes after they entered the camp bearing the skin and head of the oryx and the skull of a gerenook they had picked up. My syce had been obliged to fire five shots from my revolver at the antelope, and when the poor brute was done he dismounted and lassoed it with the pony's reins, bringing it to earth. Unfortunately, as very frequently happens, one of her horns got badly split during the scuffle.

Jama Mehemet, my guide, amused me on his return by producing a little coffee-pot which he invariably carried, and pouring the contents (water) first upon his feet and then down his throat. After this he placed the sacred coffee-pot before him and began his devotions, first of all standing before it with hands clasped, then kneeling, and lastly placing his forehead on the ground before it. I asked him through my interpreter how much he wanted for his pony, which could gallop well but was very thin. He replied :

' Give me one rifle and fifty rounds of cartridge and take the " boney." '

I replied that it was against the rules to let a native have a rifle.

'I not let Political Resident know you give me,' he said.

But I knew how fast news spreads in Somaliland, and how it would soon reach the coast that this man was possessed of such a wonderful *bundook*. So, as he would take nothing else, I was obliged to let the pony go.

That night I tied up a donkey as bait for a lion, but did not sleep over it. We were encamped at a place called Lanlibi (the Village of Male Trees).

Early next morning I got up and went to look at the donkey; there sure enough he stood where we had left him, alive and well! After sending him home, I got a ridiculously easy shot at a young oryx with a poor head, and made a disgraceful miss. He had been sighted from the top of a tree by my head-shikari. We crept quite close in the thick bushes, and I got a broadside chance.

After this we sighted a herd of upwards of fifty oryx, some of them having remarkably fine heads. Where they were feeding it was very ' oppen ' country, and ·it was impossible to approach them, so we showed ourselves to move them, and then followed for at least a couple of hours, when they very kindly led us straight back to camp, and all passed within 60 yards of my tent, taking no notice of it whatever.

In the afternoon I bought a chestnut pony, saddle and bridle for 100 rupees after a great deal of bargaining, and at length possessed an animal which could at any time stop a lion in ' oppen ' country. It then commenced to pour with rain, just as I was going out hunting again, so I had to content myself with listening to the singing and chattering of twenty-three idle men for several hours. When I say twenty-three I forget the caravan which had joined us. In all we were thirty-one souls (if black men have souls), twenty-eight camels, two donkeys, three ponies, and a flock of sheep. The natives hated the rain, and dreaded

the idea of going to the Webbi Shebeyli (Leopard River)
during the rainy season.

Complaints were now made that the ghee was all bad,
but knowing that that was only said to persuade me to buy
more, I told my headman that that was his look-out, as he
should have tasted it before he bought such a quantity. I
liked to see the camels driven into the zareba every night ;
the sight was picturesque in the extreme. And when they
all lay down surrounded by the camp-fires, which shed a

HERDING UP THE CAMELS FOR AN ONWARD MARCH.

bright yellow glow upon them, and the little crowds of
natives clustered round each fire, clad in their white *tobes*, the
effect was very striking, and made me wish I had brought
my paint-box with me, although I could have done but poor
justice to such a scene.

That night's proceedings were enlivened by a fight
between the cook's boy and a boy from the other caravan,
which ended with many boxes on their ears and kicks on
their behinds.

Next day I moved my camp two miles eastwards, passing a zareba filled with camels belonging to people of Hargaisa. The grass here was good. The natives gave me a *harn* full of excellent camel's milk, warm and covered with froth. In the morning I saw a lot of owl and oryx, all very wild, and I refused to shoot at 300 yards. This made my shikari angry, for he remarked :

' Every officer shoot dar lion, dar owl, dar aliphint all same distance.'

To which I replied :

' But in the first place I am *not* an officer—I am a humble civilian only ; and in the second place I don't believe a word you say.'

And so we went on quarrelling the whole day. I got perfectly sick of hearing of the deeds of daring, and above all the extravagances, of ' other officers,' and could easily see that these men had been utterly spoilt by ' other officers ' giving them exactly what they asked for.

The wages in Somaliland are far too high, a camelman receiving 15 rupees a month, and three times as much food as any native *posho* in East Africa. However, I must add that one or two civilians have done more to spoil the Somalis and ruin shooting-parties than all the garrison of Aden put together for the last ten years.

The country now was more open, and the game being so wild, the result was long shots and plenty of misses. When I got back to camp there was a row going on. A man turned up, and said :

' Give me back my boney ; my brozer sold him, and he belong me.'

To which I answered :

' Off you go and quarrel with your "brozer"; don't quarrel with me. I've bought the boney, I've paid for the boney, and I mean to stick to the boney.'

He went away, and brought half a village with him, all armed with spears. I blew my whistle, and instantly every man put on his cartridge-belt, seized his rifle, and stood in line waiting for my orders. Seeing this, down went all the villagers' spears, and the 'brozer' came forward unarmed to speak with me. Eventually I made both 'brozers' shake hands and swear eternal friendship, giving them to understand that if they ever brought out their puny little army near me again I would blow up their whole village with soda-water, which seemed to impress them greatly, for they went and fetched me two fat sheep as a peace-offering.

Next day I went to see how the sick camel was getting on, which we had tethered up where it could feed and be fed upon by lions. There he was safe, but by no means sound, for he was so shaky he could hardly stand. I wanted to shoot the poor brute, but my men said that he would recover; so I left him, although I thought another two days would see him dead. I left one man to change his position, in order that he might get better food, and went away. Shortly afterwards this man was to be seen tracking us, and when he reached us in breathless haste, and with his eyes staring out of his head (or, rather, his eye, for he had but one), he related between great gasps that he had heard three or four lions roar quite close to him and the camel we had just left. To the right-about we went, sending off a man for my big rifle and another pony.

When we again reached the camel, we found upwards of ten men had already arrived with the rifle, having heard the lions roaring from camp. When the other pony arrived, we all walked in line seeking for the lion's spoor, but although we spent the whole morning scouring the country for miles, we were rewarded with nothing more than the sight of old tracks of two lions. The roar of a lion often sounds a great deal closer than it really is, and in all probability these lions roared several miles off us. Coming home, I all but stepped on a snake, which I afterwards killed. The men picked from a thorn-bush some light-coloured gum, and gave me to eat. It had a very pleasant flavour.

In the afternoon I hit an ' owl ' gazelle right behind the shoulder, and he lay down. In the twinkling of an eye a jackal appeared, and, coming up behind the antelope, jumped high upon its back. The dying antelope was up in a second, and, shaking off the plucky little jackal, kept him off with its horns as they both ran round and round, the jackal always trying to jump up behind. At first I did not know which to fire at, but wishing to end the poor wounded beast's misery, I put another bullet behind his shoulder within an inch of the first ; but he still stood, demonstrating what marvellous tenacity of life gazelle possess. I then dragged him to the ground by his horns, and finished him with my hunting knife. This was no easy task, as with the frantic kicks of his hind-legs he went nigh ripping me up. Meanwhile, the jackal was squatting in the bushes, no doubt watching us intently, and no sooner had we ripped off the skin, taken the best of the meat, and turned our backs, than out he came, and began a hurried meal on the remains. After this we unsuccessfully stalked oryx, when my shikari coolly observed, ' Now we go home.'

Next day, through being hurried by my shikari, I missed a ridiculously easy shot at an oryx. He kept repeating afterwards, ' Forty yards—forty yards !' I didn't say anything, but I *thought* a lot. We then sighted a fine herd of oryx, which we stalked, my shikari again wanting me to fire at long range ; but I seized the rifle from him, beckoned to him to sit down, and crept another 50 yards nearer to them without being observed. Sitting down, I took a nice quiet shot all to myself. I hit the animal I aimed at, however, too far back, and after tracking him into thick bush, he jumped up again and was out of sight before I could fire. We followed the blood-spoor for miles, until at length, after taking a drink from my water-bottle, I returned home with my pony and syce dead-beat, having had quite enough of it under the roasting sun, leaving my shikari to keep on following the oryx. It was several hours before we reached camp, when my headman greeted me with the pleasing intelligence that my sick camel had died during the night. He shortly after remarked, ' Sare, I want to ask you queshun.' But instead of asking me a question, he complained that he had just bought three sheep at the exorbitant price of 6 rupees each, as we were short of meat for the men. I blew him up, as usual, and told him I suspected he had paid but 3 rupees each, and had pocketed the remaining 3 rupees ; but he only-threw up his hands in amazement, and replied, ' Sare, I no swindler !' which was one of the biggest lies he ever uttered.

I scratched myself fearfully that day in the thick thorn-bushes, and two little bits of thorn refused to come out of my nose, giving me not a little pain ; added to which, whilst skinning a large kind of centipede, the short hairs came off over the tips of my fingers, causing a very annoying rash. In the afternoon I went to see if there were any tracks of lions round the dead camel, and found dozens of vultures devouring it, and the fresh tracks of a leopard, so I went back to camp, and ordered out half a dozen men to build a zareba close to it. Just as the sun set my shikari walked in with the head and skin of my wounded oryx, so the day did not turn out to be blank, after all. I was too tired to go to sleep by the dead camel, which was some distance from the camp, so sent two men to watch over it. In the morning they returned, and reported eighteen *shebelles* (leopards). I sent to the village, and bought three kids to tie up for them.

We had now been loafing about this part of the country for eight days, and had seen nothing but gerenook, oryx, and ' owl,' ' owl,' oryx, and gerenook, day after day. We had had some bait out every night, but the lions appeared to be venison-feeders here entirely. I determined to leave the place on the morrow in disgust. On examining my old pony's back, I found it in such a swollen state that I determined to lance it ; so, having hobbled and thrown him, I successfully performed the operation, getting rid of a

great deal of white matter, and anointing the wound with
carbolic oil.

My syce and gunbearer, on returning from the village,
reported that on the way back they had encountered two
lions, which calmly walked across their track, looking at
them out of the corner of their eyes.

' What did you do ?' I asked.

' Oh, we got up trees,' they answered.

I wished lions would walk up and have a look at me.
That night I watched over the dead camel, which was now
beginning to ' hum ' a good deal. About one in the
morning I was touched on the shoulder by my shikari,
and when I looked through the peephole I beheld two fine
leopards walk quickly past at about 50 yards. But the
hole had been constructed to face a kid we had tied up
outside, and the camel upon which the leopards were about
to feed, by some bad management, could not be seen. It
was most tantalizing. Here was I boxed up in a zareba
within 40 yards of the leopards, and could not see them.
Crunch, crunch, crunch, went the ribs of the camel in their
hungry jaws till I could stand it no longer. I got up and
told my shikari I must go out.

' No bleck man go outside zareba night-time,' said he.

' Well, white man must,' I replied, as I tried to push
back the thorn-bush which barricaded us in.

After a great deal of noise we at length succeeded in
making an opening large enough for me to crawl through
on hands and knees. When I crept round the corner of
the zareba I discovered that the noise had driven the
leopards away from the carcase, as I had expected, but I
could just distinguish a light figure, like a huge dog, with
flaming eyes in the moonlight. I raised my rifle, but could
then see nothing down the barrel. I must get nearer, I
thought. It was a bit risky, but I was excited now to
obtain that beautiful skin. I began to crawl towards him.
On sighting me, he turned from broadside on to face me,
and I could now only see two glaring eyes in a dark mass

before me. In another second I was quite close to him. He didn't move a muscle, but commenced a low gurgling growl. Now, I thought, was the time to act, before he charged me. I raised my rifle, but his curiosity was so great at seeing such an uncommon object crawling along the ground towards him that he never moved. At that second a great flash of flame flew out, and amid the shrieking of the birds as they flew up, terrified by the report of my rifle, I heard a low growl of rage. Looking under the smoke, I could see nothing in the darkness. I then quickly entered the old zareba of the night before, which overlooked the dead camel, and could then hear the leopard's low moaning growl in the bushes close at hand. This went on for a couple of hours or so until morning began to break, and we heard the men coming to let us out of our prison. We shouted out to warn them not to approach the bushes, so they hurriedly came round to our zareba, and waited with us until it was fairly light. I then posted two men with rifles to watch, and squatted myself behind the dead camel, telling the men to go round and make a noise to drive out the leopard. They shouted, yelled, threw stones and burning sticks, to no purpose; the leopard would not come out.

'Fire the bush,' they said.

But I thought the animal must be dead inside, and feared to spoil his skin. Who would crawl in and have a look ? Not one of my men volunteered.

'Well, I suppose I must do it myself,' I said.

To tell the truth, I didn't like it at all, but one does things in a case like this which one would never dream of doing in one's quiet moments. I felt like Bill in 'Alice in Wonderland,' when he had to go down the chimney. Into the thick bushes I stooped and crawled, following the tracks in the sand, when, on reaching the thickest part, I discovered the leopard all doubled up lying in some grass. I cocked my rifle, and prodded his tail with the muzzle of it, ready to fire in an instant; but he lay dead and stiff.

So, catching hold of his fore-leg, I yelled, ' Look out, he's coming !' as I dragged him at a run out into the open. You should have seen those niggers run on hearing me ! When I got out of the bushes, there was not one to be seen nearer than 50 yards. However, they soon ran up on seeing the dead leopard, and very sheepish they all looked. He was very prettily marked, and his skin lies by me as I write.

CHAPTER IV.

Native *tomasho*—Sick list—Three lions seen—A crowd of natives—I shoot
a leopard—Curious roots—Camels.

I ORDERED a march to a place called Segooden, whilst I
went to track the two lions seen by my men the day before.
We tracked those lions from 6 a.m. till 2.30 p.m., and must
have covered over twenty miles when we overtook the
caravan at Segooden. We found that the two lions had
killed and half eaten a female gerenook, and had then made
a very long march. We finally lost their tracks in long
grass. At Segooden we found water in a rock in plenty.

After having breakfast and filling the water *harns*, we
started off again. I now discovered that my best pony
was contracting a bad sore back, so that I now possessed
two ponies and one donkey which were utterly useless for
the present, and should have to foot it for at least a week.
Marching through the thick thorn-bush, we found the first
tracks I had as yet seen of a huge rhinoceros. We pitched
camp at 5 p.m., after I had been on my legs nearly the
whole day from 4.30 in the morning, and hearing a
shebelle (leopard) outside, we tied up a kid. I then
discovered one of my men groaning in agony, and on
making inquiries, discovered he had sat upon a large
scorpion, and had been stung in two places. I applied
strong ammonia, and heard no more groans during the
night. I slept, for I was tired out with the long tramp in
the sun.

Next morning I tramped on, seeing the tracks of another
rhinoceros. Whilst on the march I saw two foxes run to

4

earth, and as I was prodding a spear down, one of them bolted. I then took off my coat, and set my shikari to work poking away with the spear, whilst I kept watch at the bolt-hole, holding my coat in my hands. After poking and digging for about five minutes, number two fox bolted, whereupon I grabbed him, luckily, by the scruff of his neck. He bit out right and left, and finally caught my coat in his sharp teeth, and refused to let go. As he was an old one, and would have died in confinement, I despatched him with a blow on the head with a spear. He possessed a very fine skin, far darker than the European fox. The natives called him 'guda dowwow' (the beast that lives under the big trees).

At length we reached a place called Owari, where we found a large lake, quite a novelty to me. Around it waddled some Egyptian geese, which appeared to take no notice of us whatever. I was glad of a rest, as marching in deep sand is very tiring work, one's foot slipping back 2 or 3 inches at every step.

Next morning I wandered about from 6 to 10 a.m. without seeing anything but gerenook and dik-dik. The headman of the place came and said 'salaam' to me and presented me with two sheep and two *harns* of camel's milk. The milk is excellent if the camel is milked into one's own tin vessels, but the native *harns* make it taste badly.

In the afternoon I shot birds round the lake and skinned them in the evening.

Next day we marched from the lake for two hours until we came to several large villages full of people, and as there was no chance of finding game, I went back to camp early for breakfast.

In the afternoon, as I was writing, I beheld several men on horseback approaching fully armed, followed by upwards of 400 men, women and children. I blew my whistle, but my headman said they were coming as friends. The three headmen of the villages now advanced up to my tent, where they saluted me, shouting, ' Mot mot mot io mot.' One of them chanted a long speech, the drift of which was interpreted to me by my headman as follows ;

' O you white man whose cheeks and hands, and especially your nose, are as red as the sand which lieth in Abriordi Garodi, we people of Owari say salaam to you. Why you come here if you do not wish to steal our sheep and camels and possess yourself of our wives, we know not. May you be as strong as the lion you say you come to hunt, and when you go home may you smite your enemies in the hinder part. May your camels, your goats, and your sheep bring forth thousands, and may you have wives and children by the score. We observe that you are a wealthy man, seeing that you possess such a multitude of camels here. We expect that you will give us a very handsome present, considering how kind we are in coming to salute you.'

After this I was requested to make a speech suitable to the auspicious occasion. I said :

' O ye Sultans, chiefs, headmen, people and whatnots, I thank you for your kind words. May no man cast his spear at you when you are not looking. May the Abyssinians refrain from taxing and looting you.' (' Hear, hear !') ' May your ponies and camels be free from sore backs, and may you eat so much fat that you can barely stand all the days of your life !' (Roars of applause and shouts of ' Give us some more !')

After the speeches the horsemen treated me to a *tomasho*, or native display of horsemanship. Two lines of men and children formed a racecourse, the women standing apart giggling under the trees. The riders gave a display of spear-throwing at full gallop, jumping in and out of the saddle at full gallop, bareback-riding and riding with face to tail. But what pleased them most was to gallop past at full speed and then bring the ponies to a standstill in a second, pulling the poor brutes on to their haunches with a very cruel bit.

Some of my men then performed, one of them being extremely clever, riding 'bareback' and turning somer-saults on the pony's back and upon the ground, and then regaining his seat in the saddle at full gallop. The dis-play was not brought to a close without accident. One of my men got kicked by a pony, and then picked a quarrel with the tribesmen, saying their horse was trying to kill him. Daggers were drawn, but after kicking them both vigorously I at length restored order.

Then one pony with a very hard mouth bolted and rushed headlong into a very thick thorn-bush, cutting its face and mouth in a shocking manner and severely mauling the rider.

I took some snapshots with my camera of the riders, but in order to get near the women I was obliged to stalk them. They of course wanted to know what was inside 'that box.' I answered them that it was a counting machine to tell me how many people were there. The display lasted upwards of two hours, at the end of which time I was very tired of sitting in the dust kicked up by the horses, added to which I received a nasty blow across my face from the whip of one of the riders as he galloped past.

After the performance, there was a long consultation as to what we should give them. My headman wished to give them nothing, as they had given us no present, that being the custom of the country. On the other hand, my shikari, who was of the same tribe as the villagers, of course wanted to give them far too much. However, after a great deal of argument, in which my man who had been kicked by the pony joined in lustily, shouting 'Give 'em bullets in their stomachs!' I finally said I would give them four *tobes* of *merikani* cloth if they gave me one sheep, which they accordingly did. The squabbling amongst the fifteen or twenty headmen present, the brandishing of spears, and the arguing as to who should have those four *tobes*, will not soon be forgotten, and it was only the darkness that finally cleared them off.

We were now in Ogaden, having just passed out of Abriordi Garodi and the red sand district. I determined to go west to the hills, as there did not appear to be any good game in this country.

We marched from five next morning until ten, when we pitched for the mid-day rest near a large and old tree covered with spear-cuts, which I was told denoted the number of camels possessed by each passing caravan, though why they should want to give their enemies so much information gratis I could not understand.

On restarting, I saw no game but gerenook. Shortly after I killed a snake. We were now *en route* for Bolarli, the river Faf, Sassabanah, and the Boorgha country, where elephant and rhinoceros were reported in numbers. On the march I discovered that one of the men was missing, and was told that he had a sore leg, and could not keep up with the caravan. I sent a pony and two armed men back to find and fetch him. About 4.30 he arrived—a man with a sore leg riding upon a pony with a sore back. The list now in hospital and utterly useless for work comprised two ponies with sore backs, two camels with ditto (one of which I had to lance, having first thrown him with great difficulty), one man with a sore leg, and one donkey dead-lame.

About four that afternoon we came to the edge of a deep gorge, or nullah, with steep rocky sides, along which we had to march until we came to a pass. This gorge, which was thickly covered with trees for miles, had a dried-up river-bed running through it. In the afternoon a cool strong breeze began to blow, rendering marching less trying. *En route* we saw some koodoo and numbers of gerenook, which try one's patience so in thick bush. The ground became more open, and the country generally appeared to be altering. At night there was a thunderstorm, with a lot of rain.

Early next morning we were overtaken by two horsemen from Owari, who informed us that one of their ponies had been killed by three lions during the thunderstorm, and wished us to go back again and try for them. They reported that the lions had eaten only the buttocks of the pony, and that they had not moved the pony. After making them swear that what they said was true, I determined to make Owari if possible that night, build a zareba by the dead pony, and await the result. I judged that we had a march before us of twenty-four miles. I packed up three camels with bedding, water, etc., and sent off two men with our informants post-haste to build a zareba, whilst I and my shikaris started to tramp back. We did that twenty-four miles under the blazing sun in six hours and three-quarters, including a short rest and drink of camel's milk at a '*woolidye*' halfway. Two hours after the three camels arrived, and after a very hurried meal I went down to the zareba by the dead pony, where I was to spend a watchful night. The instant I saw the pony, or, rather, what remained of it, I said to myself, ' The lions will never come back to it.' In the first place, there was nothing but skin and bone left of it. All the soft juicy parts were gone, and there remained but the neck, the hide, the meat on the ribs, and a little on the legs. In the second place, it had been moved by the natives from the place where it had been pounced upon and killed, though not very far. The result was as I anticipated. Although we heard the three lions roaring about a mile off, not one came near us. The night was rendered lively for us by having to keep up a continual shower of dirt over the zareba to drive off the hyænas, which persisted in crunching up the pony's ribs.

About five next morning we determined to track the lions which had been roaring the night before, and after a very long delay looking for a good fresh spoor to follow, we at length found what we wanted. The spoor was that of two lions, which were soon joined by a third, and led us, of course, into fearfully thick bush, where our four ponies (two belonging to our guide) were utterly useless. My shikari was in a very bad temper, and after going for some

way finally declared we should never come up with them.
When he exclaimed, as he generally did on occasions when
the scent was becoming very warm, ' Now we go home,' I
packed him off home, and, seizing his rifle, went on following the spoor, determined to catch a glimpse, at least, of the
lions.

The bush got denser and denser. The thorns scratched
one horribly. From walking we got to stooping, and from
stooping to crawling under it. The spoor now separated,
and finally got lost. We walked up and down trying to
find it, and I had just gone back to examine the last track
we had seen, when I heard a loud crashing sound, accompanied by an angry ' whuff.' Looking up, I beheld two
lions and a lioness bound out of a thicket of grass and bush
and amble along right through the middle of the men, who
threw down their rifles and decamped in every direction.
The lions had been entirely surrounded by us. I put up
my rifle, and was just about to pull on the biggest lion,
when a man ran right across me, and I just refrained from
firing in time. When he was past, the lion had disappeared among the bushes. I crawled through an opening
on hands and knees, and again caught sight of two lions
going fast to the right of me, and another to the left.
When through, I dashed across a bit of open ground after
them with all my might, but they had entirely vanished.
We followed the spoor of the two (the third left them) for
several miles, but never saw them again, and as it was
getting late, and the spoor again entered the thick jungle,
I was reluctantly compelled to leave them. I spent another
long sleepless night in the zareba by our friend, the rotting
pony (I seem to smell him now !), but not a bark of a lion
did my ears catch.

Next morning we loaded up, and marched towards the
main caravan again. We camped for the night at a place
called Uruthsami. Sitting under the grateful shade, I
watched my followers at work, and a busy scene it was.
The camels all knelt down, and in a twinkling every load

was upon the ground, and the hungry beasts turned off to feed. Some of the men were hacking down the surrounding thorn-bushes to form our nightly zareba, a stout fence of thorns to keep the camels, goats, and sheep in, and the lions, leopards, and hyænas out. They sang or chanted as the axes fell, whilst some natives who had come out of curiosity helped to pull away the fallen boughs with long wooden crooks, called *hangols*, and began to build the zareba. My tent was up in a minute, a fire lighted close at hand, by the side of which squatted the cook, a black, curly-haired boy with an intelligent face. A savoury smell which reached my nostrils foretold my supper of antelope soup. My bath stood ready before my tent door, and I got up to have a welcome wash, when, on looking up, I perceived the whole village pouring down upon me. Men, children, and women followed each other in a huge procession. The zareba was finished, and I walked through the opening, my men closing the door (or, rather, filling up the gap in the fence) behind me, as a gentle hint to the crowd to keep outside. The villagers seemed greatly disappointed, and soon shouts arose.

' What do they say ?' I asked.

' They hef news, sahib,' answered my shikari.

I allowed the headmen of the village to enter the zareba. They came forward and took my hand, bending their heads as they did so. I begged them to be seated. They squatted down in a semicircle in front of me, and I seated myself on a camp-stool. Through an interpreter I made out that their villages had for months been infested with leopards, which had carried off sheep, goats, and even babies, in spite of every precaution and the most impenetrable of zarebas. They hailed the white man with great delight, as he would surely rid them of these pests. I assured them I would do my best that very night. They all then stood up and walked away, with the exception of one gray-headed old man, who, pointing to the crowd of women outside the zareba, said :

' My wife, my mother-in-law, my daughters—they never see white man ; they not believe him all white, but only face and hands ; they call me liar when I say all white. Show them, I beseech you, that I am no liar ; bare yourself' —here twitching at my clothes—' of this, and show them.'

I answered as politely as I could that it was not the custom to appear naked in public, and, bidding him good-evening, walked into my tent. It was some time before the old chap could be persuaded to clear out of the zareba. How I enjoyed my bath after the hot tramp in the sun ! On getting out and turning round, I perceived in the distance a crowd of women and children, hiding behind thorn-bushes, gazing intently upon me. So they were not disappointed, after all.

Supper was soon afterwards served, and a very tempting one it was—antelope soup, hashed antelope, and roast guinea-fowl, washed down with whisky-and-water full of red sand. By this time the crowd, getting bolder, had again approached my zareba, and, peeping over the fence, watched me feeding with huge grins upon their ugly faces. I began to get quite nervous, and could scarcely find the way to my mouth, even prodding myself in the lips with my fork, which caused roars of laughter. They utterly refused to go away, in spite of the frequent cries of ' Scutter !' (Go away !), and great brandishing of spears and rifles.

After supper I went outside to superintend the tying-up of a goat as bait for a leopard about a yard from the thorn-fence. Upon my appearance outside, an enormous crowd collected round me, the more courageous stretching out their hands to feel my clothes. I noticed one poor thin deformed man amongst them who appeared to be very badly used and pushed about by his fellow-villagers. I asked who he was, and why he looked so thin and miserable, but they all answered :

' Never mind him : he is a madman—he is nobody ; take no notice of him.'

But I could not help taking notice of him; his poor thin
face haunted me. I went back into the zareba and ordered
out some antelope meat, for we had more than we could
eat ourselves, and distributed it among the villagers, giving
the poor lunatic the largest share. They took the meat
some distance away, and then began such a row, such a
babel of angry voices, such a brandishing of spears and
daggers, as I had never heard or seen before. They hacked
at one another's portion with knives, and every now and
then a frantic yell would go up, as some poor unfortunate
man received a knife across his knuckles as he strove to
hold what had been given him. At length I could stand
the din no longer, and gave them to understand that, unless
they cleared off to their own village hard by, I would take
all the meat back again by force. This silenced them, and
they all bustled off to continue their wrangling within their
own zarebas.

It was now getting quite dark, so, having brought out a
camp-chair, I sat in it, enveloped in a rug (for the nights
were very chilly), opposite the kid tethered outside. A
small peephole had, as usual, been made in the fence
through which I was to keep watch, little thinking after
the noise of the evening that any leopards would come that
night. It was quite dark except within the zareba, where
the glow of the camp-fires presented a curiously weird
scene. There in the centre lay the camels, complacently
chewing the cud, their eyes every now and then flashing
out like brilliant sparks in the firelight. Huddled together
in small groups round the fires squatted my tired-out men,
their blankets wrapped closely around them, and talking
in undertones. In the distance could be heard the singing
of the villagers as they danced to the doleful sound of
drumming tom-toms.

Presently I dozed off in my chair. How long I slept I
know not, but something made me start up and open my
eyes. I peered through the loophole into the darkness.
There stood the white kid tethered to the stake. All was

quiet save an occasional snore or a groan from a fever-stricken man, as he restlessly tossed to and fro on his camel-mat. The drumming in the village had ceased. I again peered out into the darkness. The kid suddenly stood rigid, and stared away from the zareba with ears cocked. I stared and stared, but could see nothing. I rubbed my eyes. What was that? I seemed now to make out a gray shadowy form with head bent low, gazing intently upon the goat. Should I fire now, I thought, or wait till he charged the goat? Cautiously I pushed my rifle through the loop-hole, and slowly raised it to my shoulder, peering down the barrels. I saw nothing. I pinched myself to see if I was dreaming. No, it must have been imagination. The kid lay down. A shudder passed through me, and I wrapped my rug more tightly round me as I lay back again in my chair. I had hardly dozed off again when I awoke. I swear I heard a growl. Again I peered into the darkness. The kid was up and staring intently in every direction, and beyond stood the same gray phantom. It was getting lighter. It would be now or never. The shadow slowly crawled towards the now terrified goat. Out of the loop-hole went my rifle, as my heart beat hard against my ribs with excitement. Yes, I could see his spots now. He was within 15 yards of me with his head carried low. I took a hurried aim, and—bang!—every camel was upon its feet; the sleeping men started up and hurried towards me. I stared through the smoke, and beheld the goat still standing as if petrified, and just beyond it a gray heaving mass.

'Well done, sare!' shouts my headman; 'your bullets is good—your bullets is good!'

I told him to make a way through the barrier, and fetch in the leopard. I got the usual answer.

'No bleck men go outside zareba night-time,' he replied, with a huge grin.

I broke down the zareba, and ran out to examine my prize. There within 15 yards of me he lay, his dark spots showing up clearly in the now fast-approaching dawn. That morning the whole village turned out to see the dead leopard, and I left them a priceless curio in the shape of an empty whisky-bottle as a souvenir.

Early in the afternoon we set off again. We soon reached the edge of a precipice, 400 or more feet high, from the top of which we got a magnificent view of the sea of trees below, and the hills near the river Farfan, backed by the mountains of the Boorgha Country, looking west. Then we descended a steep kind of staircase when we reached the bottom of the ridge of hill. During the night there was heavy rain.

In the morning we traversed open bush, where I shot at, and unfortunately missed, a lesser koodoo (*Strepsiceros imberbis*), the first we had seen.

We then came to what looked exactly like a wheat-field, when the green is just beginning to show up out of the brown earth. Through this imitation wheat-field we trudged, and as it was ankle-deep in soft soil and mud after the recent rains, the walking was terribly tiring work. Presently the grass disappeared, but the brown mud con-tinued, until about 9 a.m. we reached the Webbi Bolarli, in the middle of which sandy water-course we found a tiny stream of real running water.

Close to the river-bed were the most luxuriant and brilliant green grass, and high trees covered with birds' nests. By the banks of this river bird and insect life swarmed. At the bottom of two wells by the side of the river could be seen some water-tortoises with flat shells.

All along our route during the morning we had seen gigantic land-tortoises slowly wending their way to the rich grass by the river-bed. The birds here were ridiculously tame. Weaver birds in plenty, including the pretty white-headed weaver (*D. leucocephala*), and the superb glossy starling (*L. superbus*). The curious yellow-billed hornbill sat in the trees above me and croaked aloud. The pretty little gray plovers ran before me in the grass, and with a shrill scream flew off a few yards on my near approach. Doves of many kinds were to be seen drinking the water as it trickled along the sandy river-bed.

I had my breakfast under a huge tree, from the branches of which dropped little green fruit the size of cherries, and called by the natives 'good,' and which tasted like dates. By-the-by, the dates I bought for the men tasted excellent,

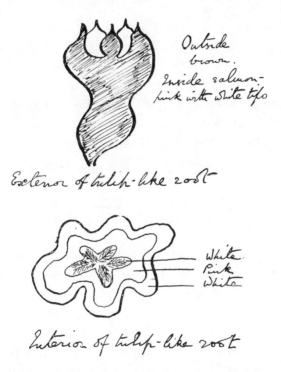

Outside brown.
Inside salmon-pink with white tips

Exterior of tulip-like root

White
Pink
White

Interior of tulip-like root

although they did not look nice, being squashed into large bricks. The natives dug their dirty fingers into the mass and abstracted a handful of what looked like mud, which they ate like a piece of cake.

Under this tree there crawled in myriads an insect which bit one's naked legs horribly. I called them gingerbread insects. They were round, and had the exact appearance of little gingerbread nuts. Under the tree were also to be found some very curious roots, shaped and coloured like a huge tulip, the colouring of pink and white inside being most delicate and pretty.

As I sat having my breakfast, two wild-geese passed over my head. I watched the men unloading the camels for the mid-day rest as they sang what sounded like ' Alima tadema alima 'tay, alima kedgeree alima ka.' I asked what they were talking about, and was told it meant : ' Now, camel dear, if you will be good and keep still we will unload you as fast as we can !'

The afternoon I spent at Bolarli was the hottest I had experienced since leaving Berbera thirty-four days before. The perspiration poured out of me the whole day.

I noticed thorn-trees, as I was tramping through the sand, with trunks of a brilliant greenish-yellow. They looked as if they had all been richly coated with Aspinall's

enamel. This thorn-tree bore a thorn which beat the record in length of any I ever saw. Above is a specimen reduced to half its actual size.

I went out hunting in the evening, and saw some oryx which must have heard us coming over some stony ground. I also saw a perfectly black ground squirrel, and wished I had my gun with me, as I had never seen one like it before. Dik-dik antelope were very plentiful here.

At 4.45 we pitched for the night close to the rocky Farfan hills, which were thinly covered with bush. My men now held family prayer three times a day, and a very impressive sight it was to see them all stand up in a long line and touch their ears as a hint to Allah to listen to what they were going to say. But I got tired of the sight as I got to know the characters of the men better, and when I knew they were such hypocrites, it made me want to kick them when I saw them flop down on their knees every other five minutes.

One of my camels now showed signs of caving in. The camel, one of the most useful animals in the world, is born in Somaliland about the end of May, the period of gestation being one year. The best animals are selected to be mothers. These are often very fine beasts, having enormous humps, and have never carried a load. The udder is nearly as large as that of a small cow, and has four teats. The Somali camel will not carry much more than 275 pounds. It can be easily seen when a camel is overladen, as he will refuse to rise. Never take a camel with a sore back, or one that flinches when his back is touched, showing that he has lately had a sore back. Also look for sores at the root of his tail. Both these sores are caused by careless loading. Watch him kneel. If he flops down all on one side, and does not kneel with his fore and hind legs together, don't have him : he has some internal ailment. When sick, dose your camel with soup at night, and keep him separate from the others. A camel will often eat some poisonous food, after which he will refuse to eat, grow to a mere skeleton, and finally die. I have heard of no cure in this case. The age of a camel is judged by his teeth. He has no incisor teeth until the end of the third year ; after this two appear. When five he has four ; when six years old he has six ; at eight he has canines and molars. A camel will eat any green vegetation, but you will tell by his hump if he is well fed, and not overworked—it will be full and big. The stomach of the camel is a sort of store-chest, holding water and food ; the former will amount to 15 pints, on the average, on examination when dead. This is not to be forgotten when dying of thirst, for the water is wholesome, though of a turbid green colour. A Somali camel will go fifteen, twenty, or even twenty-five days without water when working, and when he drinks, which should be once in seven days—not more—he takes in 5 gallons. Carbolic oil is a good thing for sore backs of camels and ponies, or burned leather reduced to a powder. My camels had different marks upon their necks, branded upon them by the different tribes as a mark of distinction. Here are a few of them :

/// o/o ᏕᏒᏒ ☐☐ Ǝ·)

CHAPTER V.

Gazelle shooting—Headman's excuses for not marching—Troublesome followers—More grievances—Glimpse of a lioness—Camel killed by a lion.

A SHORT march brought us to Sassabanah, situated amongst hills, and my camp was pitched under some big trees close by the dried-up Webbi Farfan. On the hillside opposite, looking up north-west, was an old and gigantic zareba encircling several hundred yards, and used for the herding in of cattle for safety at night. Here six months before the Abyssinians stored the cattle they had looted from the Somalis. Whilst having breakfast, the vast plain

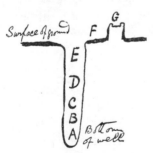

SECTION OF WELL.

below this hill became covered with camels which had come to drink from the salt-water wells situated near the river. My headman estimated that during the day 25,000 camels drank at those wells. An extremely pretty sight it was to see this vast number in little bands of forty or fifty, like the different companies of a huge army, marching across the plain. The wells were very deep, and the water was

5

got out of them by men with conical wooden buckets in the following way : A stark-naked man (A) descends to the bottom of the well, which is 4 or 5 feet wide by 20 or 30 feet deep, by means of foot-holes dug in the sides of the well. He then fills his wooden conical water-bucket, and throws it upwards to another naked man (B), who stands above him in the well with legs stretched out, standing with one foot in a hole on one side of the well, the other foot in another on the opposite side. As A throws a full bucket up to B, he receives at the same moment an empty one from B to fill. B throws up the full one he has received to C, receiving an empty one, and so on to the sixth man (F), who empties the full buckets he receives into the drinking-trough of mud (G), and returns them empty to E to be again passed down to be refilled by A. As fast as the water is in this ingenious and expeditious manner poured into the trough, it is drunk by the thirsty camels, which are driven up in relays of five or six at a time. The men as they work sing the whole time. When tired of watching this interesting sight, I repaired back to my big tree, where I found some ants busily engaged in carting all my date-stones to their hole. Here is a life-size portrait of one of these gentlemen :

I have seen one of these insects lift a date-stone bodily off the ground with his nippers (A) to get it over a small stick or stone. And to see two of them pick up a stone and carry it together, one grasping one end and going backwards, and the second taking the other end and following, is a truly ludicrous sight.

Soon after leaving Sassabanah we crossed the river Farfan and wended our way westward, passing miles of camels which had come to the wells for their monthly drink. (N.B.—Camels which do no work, and have good green grass to feed upon, are watered once a month only.) Several of my men were now laid up with acute stomach-ache from drinking this bitter water.

After turning round a small rocky hill, we crossed a large plain thinly covered with bush. Here we found several herds of 'owl,' which, however, were very wild, and after two unsuccessful stalks we found a single beast, which allowed me to empty both barrels at him, reload and fire another, before he bounded off, when I fired the fourth shot at him galloping and struck him in the shoulder, bowling him literally head over heels stone-dead like a rabbit. On running hard up to him, I put my foot in a hole and came heavily to the ground, choking up both barrels of my rifle with sand, cutting my right thumb, and severely spraining my left thumb. When I reached the antelope, which was a good 170 yards off, there was more blood apparent on me than on him. After another unsuccessful stalk, we slowly walked up to a large herd, and as we wanted meat badly and could not get any nearer than 250 yards, I sat down slowly and took aim at the nearest buck. I struck him in what my shikari always termed the ' billy,' and off he went with his head hung low, followed quickly by me, my shikari roaring after me that he was not touched. I shouted to my syce, who galloped up, and, soon outstriding the antelope, brought him back to me after a fine chase. Hiding behind a bush, I fired at him when within about 15 yards of me, missing him clean. I broke his hind-leg with the second barrel, when he made off at an astounding pace, and when he joined another large herd of antelopes I quite gave him up for lost. But so good were my syce's eyes that he followed that beast till he had separated it from the herd and brought it to bay, when he dismounted and shouted, having forgotten, as usual, to take out my revolver. We arrived

at last, and running up discovered the poor beast crouching under a thorn-bush dead-beat. I caught hold of his
hind-legs, but was promptly sent flying backwards by a
gigantic kick. At last my shikari collared him by the
horns and cut his throat, after first having received a
nasty gash in the side from his fore-foot. Having loaded
the pony and men with the meat, we set off once more to
rejoin the caravan, when a terrific thunderstorm burst upon
us, wetting us to the skin, and after losing our way we at
length heard a signal-shot fired far to the west of us. We
reached camp in a half-drowned condition. The excuse
made by my lazy headman next day for not marching was
that the camel-mats were not dry.

As my shikari was still suffering, like myself, from sore
legs, produced by my saddle, which not only wounded
horses but men, my second shikari and one gunbearer
started with me to reconnoitre the plain. On the way we
were obliged to ford a small river, swollen by the rain of
the night before On reaching the plain, I soon found a
herd of ' owl '; but walk, walk, walk, they would not stand
still. I crawled to a bush to cut them off, hoping they
would stand for a moment ; however, they refused : so,
putting up the 200 yards sight, I aimed well forward on
the leading one's shoulder and pressed the trigger, when he
fell forward stone-dead, the bullet entering his shoulder
and breaking to pieces inside. This animal had a beautiful
head, the horns measuring 17¾ inches round the curve,
circumference at base 6 inches. The skin, however, was
infested with a huge bot-like grub, very fat and cylindrical,
of a dirty olive-brown, and about half an inch long. This
grub burrowed between the poor animal's skin and its flesh.
I squeezed several out of small holes made by them in the
skin, by pressure of the finger and thumb.

Coming home with the head, skin, and as much of the
meat as we could carry, we found the spoor of an ostrich,
which had crossed our track of four hours ago. When I
got home that scoundrel of a headman of mine wanted to

delay us another night, by saying that the men had no
water, and that the river-water was too thick to use, which
of course was all nonsense, as a little alum would soon set
all right ; but I had also seen a pool of still water, which I
offered to show them. However, seeing I was bent on
proceeding, they set off for the water without me.

The men were now becoming very troublesome, and the
excuses put forward by my headman for not marching were
always very lame. First of all it was, 'Two men got
stomach-ache, they no march'; then it was, ' No water ' or
' Too much water.' Next, 'Lart (lot) camels seek (sick),'
yet he would always add : 'I shall tek you straight
Boorgha country, no stop.' It was only by being firm
that I could make them do what I wished ; yet I hated to
see them loading up the camels grumbling, growling, and
swearing at each other, and probably at me, and kicking
the poor animals as if they had been the cause of it.

My headman came and said, as a last resource :

' If rain come, how we cross river upstairs (up the
hill) ?'

I answered : ' If rain comes we will camp on this side of
the river.'

At length back came the camels I had sent for the water
I had spoken about, and accordingly off we started up a
steep and rocky mountain pass and down on the other side.
When my shikaris and I had reached the bottom, we waited
for the camels, and presently they appeared, headed by one
of the biggest villains I have ever met, namely, my headman, who with a broad grin on his face walked up and said,
in his most jovial manner, ' Sick camel dead !' and then
stood and grinned another horrid smile, as if he had con-
veyed the most pleasing intelligence.

I was certain he was lying and had sold my camel to
natives, who appear everywhere like vultures, and swoop
down upon a caravan like magic. How they know of one's
approach I can't conceive, unless they have sentries continually on the watch. (My boy a few days afterwards

told me that my headman had sold my camel as I suspected.) Well might he grin, for now he had another camel less to load and lead. I could have shot him as he leered at me with his wicked eyes.

We pitched camp at the foot of the hills, at a place called Darrah Sor, and had hardly commenced building a zareba, when I sighted four or five 'owl' close to camp. Seizing my rifle, I made good use of a little dried-up river-bed and came close up to them. I made the most of it by firing three shots and laying low three antelopes in the same number of minutes. The yells and singing of the Somalis on beholding three animals on the ground at once can better be imagined than described. Twenty minutes after, having photographed the trio in front of my tent, I was eating their venison in the setting sun. Such is life and death. As usual, after sunset the lightning flashed, the thunder rolled, the wind blew, and down came the rain again, as rain it only can in Somaliland. This would be another excuse for not marching on the morrow, I knew. The rain ceased in a couple of hours, and the men made night hideous by singing and dancing until a late hour. As I expected, next morning up came my headman with :

'No march, camel-mats too wet.'

However, on examination I found nearly all perfectly dry, as it had not rained again during the night. So I ordered 'Quick march!' On the way we found two gerenook, one of which I struck in the shoulder as he faced me, whereupon he took downhill, the worst thing possible for himself when hit in that place, as the blood all ran into his gullet and choked him. Owing to the thick bush, he was very difficult to find, but after a long hunt we discovered him under a bush, and after stalking him I seized him by the horns whilst my shikari finished him. He possessed a most graceful head and neck. This beautiful antelope is longer in the neck and leg than the owl, and is of a pretty reddish-brown colour. The tips of the horns bend forward. The gerenook is much more difficult, in my experience, to obtain than the 'owl,' owing probably to its frequenting thick bush, whereas the 'owl' likes the open plains. The result is that one gets closer, perhaps, to gerenook owing to the thick cover, but the shots at him are hurried, as he is almost always either partly covered by bush, so that one cannot see him distinctly, or he is trotting off, giving snap-shots only. The 'owl,' on the contrary, although in the open, and often a long way off, offers a better chance, as one can generally see him well and take plenty of time with a long, steady aim, sitting down, as he walks slowly or stands broadside on, staring at you, at 200 yards.

We pitched camp at 9.15 a.m., when two of my men picked a quarrel with the headman, saying that he had not given them their proper rations, and threatening to shoot the 'old full' (fool). They both came and stated their grievances ; the headman came next with an entirely dif-ferent story, followed by the whole gang, who quarrelled, jabbered and gesticulated till I wished them all at the devil. I have taken shikaris and followers in Egypt, Ceylon, India, the Malay Peninsula, China and Japan, but never have I come across such detestable people as the Somalis. Verily they beat all other black people for cowardice, treachery, deceit and cunning. At length I settled their disputes, and they left me in quiet, if not in peace of mind, to go and jabber on among themselves. In case of a murder, I was debating within myself whether I should shoot the murderer and save a lot of trouble, or should I be expected to send him bound 300 miles back to the coast under an escort, when he would probably escape or bribe his captors to set him free. All the afternoon we marched through uninteresting thorn-jungle, seeing a few gerenook, and pitched camp for the night at 5.15 p.m.

Next morning I was off at 4.30. Oh, how tired I was getting out of the inevitable thick bush, where you can see barely 100 yards before you, and where your face, hands and clothes get so torn by the thorn bushes !

My headman came up with another grievance. He said
that one of the camels had fallen down and broken four
harns (native water-vessels), so that they now leaked badly,
and that I should have to buy more when I reached Sucut,
a village to our west. I knew I should have to examine all
those *harns* myself before I could believe a word of it.

The forests here swarmed with a very pretty parrot
marked with green and orange, and another bird gorgeously
clothed in blue, with a brilliant yellow breast. I caught some
purple butterflies as they fed upon the putrid meat upon
my antelope skulls, and thought of the Purple Emperor
at home, which can be caught in the same manner. A long
dreary march brought us to a lonely spot called Sheelo,
where we encamped for the night, and where we discovered
one of the men was missing. I sent off half a dozen men
to look for him, and fired signal shots at intervals.

In about an hour shouts for water were heard, and shortly
after sending it out the lost one was brought in saying he
was ' seek ' (sick). When anything ails a Somali, he sits
down, determined to die, and has to be watched, kicked up,
and set going again. He utterly refused to say where he
felt it most. His temperature was very high, and at length
he owned up that he felt ' now hart, now cold,' so I settled
him with quinine. Next day, after marching for two hours
and a half through dense bush, we went up a little rising
ground, from the top of which we could see the mountains
of the Boorgha country, about two days' march to the west
of us, and a huge sea of trees in every other direction.

Skirting northwards round this rise in the ground, we
encamped near the walls of Sucut for the day, to get news
and try to obtain a guide for the Boorgha country. Here
I bought a camel with a broken leg for six *tobes* of *merikani*
cloth, for the men to eat, to encourage them to march a bit
faster. The number of camels which passed our camp at
night, on the way to their zareba, was amazing, the wealth
of the Somalis here being very great. Next morning I
found the thorn zareba festooned with camel-meat, whilst

a lot more was simmering in the large round cooking-pots, out of which each man fished for his share, like the priests before the tabernacle in Exodus. Indeed, my caravan often reminded me of the story of the Children of Israel wandering round Mount Sinai, especially when they grumbled and murmured on my making them wander in the waste Boorgha country, devoid of villages, instead of staying in Abriordi Garodi, rich in flocks and herds, and a land flowing with milk and sheep's fat.

Many of the expressions, sentences, and speeches of the natives remind me also of those in the Bible. The man with a bad leg came to me with a grievance. He said :

‘ Another tribe loot me one year since ; he taketh from me one camel, and sought also to take my life. I cometh here and findeth my camel—my long-lost camel. Verily it is mine camel, for I knoweth my mark that I maketh on his ham.’

He drawled on like this for several minutes, the drift of it being that he had now taken back his lost property from the village by force, and he requested my aid to help him to keep it until we again reached Berbera. As all the rest said it was a *bonâ-fide* case, I at length consented. I told him I had enough trouble of my own without entering into other people's, but that if he swore that the camel really belonged to him, I would allow him to let it join my herd on condition that it carried its share of my loads, and that, in case of being attacked for the possession of it, I should shoot it at once and throw the carcase to the hyænas. Not a man should have an ounce of its fat. I suspected all the time it was a put-up job, yet the natives in the villages all seemed very friendly. Just before we started, one of my men ran an oryx horn, which is often very sharp at the tip, about 2 inches into his leg. I bandaged him up, and he had to be carried on a camel.

We took a guide and started. We had not been marching more than one hour when our so-called guide evidently got out of his latitude, and, after wandering about for another

hour, he blandly confessed that ''E dunno whar 'e are !' At
length we met some natives, who directed us to a village,
near which we encamped for the night. On the way we
saw a number of zebra tracks for the first time. Next
day we passed several large villages, with thousands of
camels. I dismissed my guide here, and took another man.
A very grand sheikh appeared to expostulate with my man
for having taken away his camel. He followed us all the
morning. My shikari told me that my man, the supposed
rightful owner of the camel, although now a fairly old man,
was once upon a time a bit of a blood. He was a very
strong fighting-man, and had in his time killed eighteen
men, of which accomplishment he seemed vastly proud ;
but to look at him now, you would have thought him
incapable of killing a flea, much less a man. The skinny,
scraggy, wizened old reprobate !

Two of my men had now a chronic sore throat with
continual shouting. In fact, they *cannot* speak quietly, or
you could not hear a word they said, so they are obliged to
shout. Confound their noise !

About 3 p.m. we found the fresh tracks of a lioness,
dragging something along the ground. We followed, and
for the second time whilst out tracking lions, my head-
shikari said he was taken violently ill, so I left him in
disgust, as I knew he was shamming, and he had to find
his way back to camp alone I followed the spoor with a
few men, when, on entering some very thick bush, we saw
some vultures hovering above us, and a minute after we
discovered the remains of a baby camel. The lioness
had evidently heard us and made off. I ordered a small
zareba to be built 2 or 3 feet off the dead camel, hoping
the lioness would come back during the night, and rejoined
the caravan, which had just now unloaded for the night.
I found that my man-killing follower had at length made
peace with the villager from whom he had taken his camel,
by presenting him with his wife, who happened to be in a
neighbouring village at that time. The wife turned up,

and seemed highly pleased with the bargain. She had now got a younger if not a prettier husband; and the thought of an *amour* with a stranger is always dear to the heart of the female black. My head-skikari now appeared to be really ill; but the men said he was all right, but had eaten too much. I made him violently sick with an emetic, and told him to go to sleep. This man had gorged himself with three different foods during the day—camel's milk, meat, and dates. He would have been all right if he had stuffed himself with one only, but mixing them had made him ill. Somalis have very delicate stomachs. Don't hit a Somali hard below the belt. He will lie down and die in a very short time.

After supper I adjourned to the small zareba, where I found to my horror that the remains of the camel which I had tied with a cord to a tree had vanished. It had been taken by the lioness directly our backs were turned. On listening, I could hear crunch, crunch going on in a thick bush close by. I went round the belt of bush, and wanted the men to rush her through to me, but not a man would enter, although they were all armed with rifles. I had to go in by myself. It was ticklish work, and it was getting very dark, but I crept into the thick bushes and grass with my rifle at full-cock. I had not gone more than five or six yards when I heard an angry snarling cough, followed by a great rustling of grass as the great brute charged out on the other side. I just caught a glimpse of her hind-quarters with her tail held up on high as stiff as a poker. My disappointment was very great. It was so hard to be so close to lions and never to get a shot. I felt I was always alone, and never properly helped or backed up by my followers.

It was now dark, so I slowly wended my way back to the little zareba with a heavy heart, dragging what little now remained of the dead baby camel. I sent for one of the donkeys, and tied him up in the moonlight—bad luck to the latter! The donkey kept up a lively conversation most of the night with his brother in the main camp, close at hand. I sat in a chair, peering out into the darkness the whole night, with my rifle ready through the port-hole. I heard a lion roar to the south of us, and soon after the donkey lay down. Suddenly I started, as I saw a gray form appear, but it was only a hyæna. He approached the donkey, and the latter jumped up and turned round to kick. The hyæna bolted. After this the donkey became restless, and I was sure there was a lion about, for he cocked his ears and stamped his feet incessantly, keeping his mouth shut for the rest of the night.

Next morning some of my men arrived to let us out of the zareba, with the intelligence that a lion had killed a young camel; so after a cup of coffee I walked down to where it was reported, but on inquiry found it was all a lie. One of the villagers, however, volunteered to show us ostriches—a cock and a sitting hen with four eggs. So off we started, to again meet with disappointment, for after a long tramp we found the nest, certainly, but the mother bird, having been disturbed the day before, had broken all the 'hegses' and decamped. After collecting a few mangy black and white feathers I returned to camp.

We then marched to a place called Gobtelleli, where there was a well of filthy water full of tortoises. Around here there were countless tracks of zebra; but although we spent the whole afternoon looking for them we saw none. Next morning we found that lions had been walking all round our zareba during the night, but the ground was too rocky to follow them. Some men now came in saying a lion had killed a camel at a zareba three miles off. Before ordering the camp to be pitched, I determined to see the spoor myself, knowing full well that all Somalis are champion liars. We found that zareba after a long hunt, and for a wonder I found that the news was true. But of course they had cut up and taken away the dead camel, leaving only the entrails, in the midst of which sat a little girl toying with them. The lion had jumped right over the zareba; the 'pugs' where it had taken off, and where it had landed inside, were plainly visible. It had killed the camel, and had then been driven off with stones. In another zareba close by was a second dead camel, which had died in giving birth to a young one, which lay beside its mother with its throat cut for some unearthly reason. Surely they could have found a foster-mother for it out of the thousands round about. But the Somalis are very superstitious, and probably considered the baby guilty of murder. I ordered two little zarebas with two port-holes in each to be built. The caravan then came up and pitched close by, when, as usual, a large crowd of natives surrounded my zareba, and one boy with more cheek than the rest came and sat within two or three feet of me, and after staring at me for the space of half an hour, as I was writing, began to feel and touch everything within reach.

CHAPTER VI.

Tracking a rhinoceros—Zebra seen—I shoot an 'owl' for the pot—Grévy's
zebra—Curious moon effect—I shoot a spotted hyæna—Abundance of
game—Exciting ride after a leopard—Attack of fever.

MY headman now said that we must send back to the
coast for more food, as we should run short in a month's
time. So I reluctantly sent three camels and three men
back with orders to return as soon as possible, and to take
news as to where they should find us. I sent back all my
skins and skulls to the care of a merchant in Berbera, as
the latter were sure to get broken sooner or later on this
uneven ground covered with stone. I parted with them,
however, with a good deal of misgiving, wondering if I
should ever see them and the camels again.

Nothing came near the dead camels, and next morning
natives reported that the lions had moved to the next
village, and had killed a camel; and later on in the day
other natives appeared like vultures out of space, and
reported that a lion had jumped over their zareba and
carried off a big girl of nineteen. On the natives setting
out in pursuit, the lion had let drop the lower half of the
girl, which the natives had found, and made good his escape
with the other half. After a cup of coffee I started off
at 5.30 a.m. south-west. When we had gone about
300 yards we came upon a large grayish snake with white
belly (the African cobra). He required a great deal of
killing. He raised himself bolt upright in a small bush,
puffed out his neck, and ejected a copious white fluid at us.
Shortly afterwards we came upon the fresh tracks of a

' rhino ' of the night before, and sending back for my big
rifle, I commenced to track. We had not proceeded far,
when there was a dash made by something on our right,
and out of the thick cover strode a large cock ostrich in
splendid plumage. If I had had my rifle in my hands I
should have got a snap-shot at him at very close quarters :
as it was, although we raced after him, he disappeared
entirely among the bushes. On returning to the spot where
we had started him, I found a nest with eight beautiful
eggs (the cock bird sits on the nest in turns with the hen
ostrich). It is not strictly speaking a nest, but a hole
scraped in the sand, a place where the sand is deep being
selected, and on it the eggs are laid and covered with sand,
not, as some people think, to hatch them, but to keep them
out of sight of the hungry vultures. My shikari, on seeing
them, held up his hands and exclaimed :

' Greaty Scot ! ostrich hab eight little boys !'

Hoping that the male would come back, and fearing lest
the vultures should swoop down upon and break the eggs,
we covered them over with grass and sand, and continued
tracking the rhinoceros. The track led us on for miles
and miles through thin bush (where we saw a second
ostrich), across plains and over rocky ground, where tracking was extremely difficult, until we reached the edge of a
long gorge, or nullah ; then we knew he was making for the
water, and at length he walked down a small precipice, where
you would have fancied no animal of his build could possibly
have descended. At the bottom of the rocky nullah were
several pools of water, and at each we found our friend's
tracks, but at length we lost his spoor among the hopeless
mass of boulders, and as I had been following him for five
hours, I was glad to retrace my steps homewards.

Walking up the steep sides of the nullah with great
difficulty, we started a fine bull koodoo, but the bush was
too thick to offer the chance of a shot. At last we reached
the top of the gorge, and wended our way, pouring from
head to foot with perspiration. We saw the tracks of two

more 'rhino,' two days old. As I walked along I became
aware of the presence of the first wild zebra I had ever set
eyes on. He was close to me behind some trees, quietly
walking along alone. My head-shikari was carrying my
rifle some way in front of me, as I could not keep pace with
him, being very tired after my long tramp after the 'rhino.'
I was obliged to whistle to stop him, as I dared not move,
but before I had the sight properly on him he had seen us,
and with a twist of his tail bounded off, when I missed him
as I shot through the trees. The shot startled eight or
ten oryx, some having very fine heads, which went over a
small hill out of our sight.

After breakfast I started out again to try and get a
shot at our friend the ostrich of the morning. When we
reached the spot, as I expected, up flapped a dozen infernal
vultures, and on examination of the nest we found that
they had already broken and eaten one of the eggs,
although covered deep in grass and sand! This demonstrates the enormous power of a vulture's beak, as the shell
of an ostrich egg is extremely hard and thick. Knowing
that it would be now useless to hope to save them from the
greedy birds, I became greedy myself, and sent the remaining beauties to camp. After this we saw plenty of game,
gerenook, a couple of oryx which would not allow us to
approach them, and dozens of dik-dik antelope.

I returned to camp after a disappointing day, considering
the game we had seen. I was far too tired to sit in a
zareba over a now putrid camel and spend a watchful
night, so I sent my shikaris instead, and spent my evening
'blowing' my ostrich eggs and skinning a snake. One of
my men complained of fever and looked very sick. During
the day I had seen jackal, dik-dik, ostrich, bustard, gerenook, koodoo, oryx and zebra, besides countless game birds.

Next day, June 4, I marched away west of the villages,
and camped again at 8.30 a.m. My guide, Mr. Nur Korfdrop, or some name sounding very like it, who until
now carried a beautiful sword given him by Abyssinians,

requested to be allowed to carry a rifle, as he asserted that
we might now encounter Gallas at any moment, that they
were hostile, and that their young men were not allowed to
marry until they had killed a man, so that the youngsters
were always very eager to get 'first blood' out of any
stranger they might meet. The Gallas have a nasty habit
of stalking one, and in the event of a kill they cut off a
piece of one's flesh and present it to the fair damsel, as
a proof that they have killed a man!

Tsetse fly was reported to infest the country a little
further on. My headman assured me that, as a preventive
against the poison of this dreadful little pest, sheep's fat
should be rubbed over the horses and especially poured
into the ears. I let him do this, as he seemed so confident
about it, but remarked that it attracted other kinds of flies
by the dozen. Being an old Etonian, I celebrated the
Fourth of June with a bottle of champagne!

The mornings were now overclouded, and there was
always a gentle wind, consequently it was comparatively
cool and pleasant. During the night I heard zebra neighing
close to camp; but, although we hunted everywhere next
morning, we could not find them. We saw three ostriches,
which bounded away among the bushes before I could shoot.
These magnificent birds appeared to be fairly plentiful about
here. We next sighted some oryx, and shortly after a
koodoo, but had no luck with them. Wanting meat, and
seeing three 'owl' close to me on the right, I sat down and
let drive at the biggest, breaking both his fore-legs, when
he rushed along at an amazing pace for an animal so dis-
abled, ploughing up the dust as he dashed headlong through
the sand into the high grass. We found it very difficult
to get hold of his horns, and when this was at length
accomplished, the kicks from his hind-legs were so violent
that we had to let him go. He jumped up and bolted
again. I threw down my rifle, and, fairly racing after him,
tackled him by the hind-legs as I threw myself upon him
in true Rugby football style. My shikari then ran up and

finished him with the knife. He was a splendid fat animal (huge grins on the faces of the Somalis), and had a magnificent head, the finest I had as yet obtained. Having loaded men and pony with the meat, we again set off homewards, the vultures pouncing down upon the gory carcase before we had advanced half a dozen yards. They appeared, as it were, out of space. I had noticed none in the sky during the skinning operation. We had not proceeded far, when four or five gerenook made their appearance. I fired, and heard the bullet go 'thud' against the male, but he made off with the others; we followed, but owing to the long grass we could make out no track. We had gone some distance, when we heard a shout from the syce who was leading the pony behind us, and, going back, we found the gerenook lying dead at his feet, the bullet having gone through his middle. The Somalis would not take any of its meat, the Mohammedan religion not allowing them to eat of the meat of an animal found dead. We ripped off the skin in double-quick time, my shikari talking all the time after this manner :

'We no mind work if we get good game; if you get good game, all same aliphint, rhino, lion, then you give me plenty backsheesh. When Lord How-is-he and Prince What's-his-name killed aliphint, they gives me 50 rupees; you do all same!'

We had to remain here for three days, as the men we had sent to buy sheep with cloth did not return from their spree. Two of the men had fever badly here, and I was troubled with large white spots all over my body, which itched dreadfully : it was not prickly heat, nor was it caused by mosquitoes, for luckily there were none of these pests here.

When the Somalis wish to cook a large quantity of meat, they dig out a trench in the sand, about 4 feet long, with their spears. They place across the trench a network or grid of stout sticks, upon which they place the chunks of meat ; they then light a fire of dry sticks at the bottom of the trench, and keep turning the meat until properly cooked. Cooked in this manner, the meat is most tooth-some.

Next day I went over a lot of ground, and saw a couple of koodoo hinds and an animal I had never seen before. As the Somalis said it had never been shot by a white man, I was most anxious to procure a skin. It possessed a beautiful glossy black coat, was the same size and shape as a collie dog, and had a perfectly white tip to its tail or brush. There were two of these pretty creatures together, and on sighting us they barked at us like little dogs, and then scurried off without allowing me time to shoot. When out of sight they kept up a curious noise, very similar to that made by a large bird which is common in Somaliland. We followed this sound, and caught another glimpse of them, when I fired ; but 'What's hit is history, and what's missed is mystery !'

We came next upon the fresh spoor of zebra, and on looking about, I found a pool of water, where they evidently drank daily. Round the water-hole were the spoors of rhinoceros, lion, koodoo, and hyæna. My guide, who had gone exploring, came back at night, saying he had *seen* zebra in hundreds, and tracks of rhino further south. So next morning we marched at 4.30 to wells about twelve miles south. After walking for two hours without seeing anything, I began to think that Nora, our guide, was as usual a liar, when my shikari suddenly stood stock-still near a small narrow open bit of ground, and whispered, ' Zebra !' But stare as hard as I could, I saw nothing but an open plain, surrounded by thorn-bushes. My shikari literally shouted in my ears, ' You never see it, you no see the zebra ?' as he pointed with both hands.

' No, I never see it,' I answered, staring my eyes out in the direction indicated by him.

And I verily believe I might have stared for hours, had he not heard my shikari and turned end on to stare at us. When he moved I could hardly believe my eyes. I had been staring at him as he stood broadside on to me quite close, and had not until now seen him! So marvellously does the skin of this animal blend with the colour of its surroundings. I was so taken aback with surprise that I fired hurriedly, hitting him too low down, between the fore-legs, when he went off at a lumbering gallop. With the second barrel I knocked him over.

What struck me most, on seeing my first zebra lying dead before me, was the beautiful colouring and gigantic proportions of the broad ears, rounded at the tops, the huge girth of the animal and the thick short legs. Grévy's zebra is truly a magnificent animal, and must not be con-founded with Burchell's zebra seen in circuses at home. The latter animal is a miserable-looking little thing in comparison.

Leaving the men to finish skinning the animal, we proceeded until we reached some rising ground to the south; below this small hill stretched ten miles of trees away to the Nagob hills. Here and there were large grassy open places, some about two miles long by half a mile broad. It was to the other side of one of these open plains that the wells lay to which we were to wend our way. On descending the ground altered. Instead of the red sand, the colour of the earth was yellowish. Instead of high, monument-like ant-hills, at every 20 yards or so were to be seen dome-shaped ant-hills of a dirty-yellow colour. The grass here was scanty and dried up, and scattered over the ground was a green plant which looked like a young cabbage.

Suddenly out of the bushes ran the first wild wart hog I had ever seen, with his tail cocked up straight in the air, looking a most ridiculous object. I was out of the saddle in a moment, and seizing my rifle (even if I had had a spear, the bush was too thick for riding), I crawled to a bush, from which I could make out two pigs partly hidden in the bushes. Bang! The bullet ploughed up the dust just before it reached him. Mr. Pig had just saved his bacon! At length we reached the well, just in time to see

GAME ON THE FEROLI BUN.

[To face p. 85.

a black object disappear behind a tree to drink. Presently a most amusing sight presented itself. Out of the pit of water surrounded by trees ran four little wart hogs, followed by their mother and father, every one holding his or her tail on high. Run, run, run, and squeak, grunt. squeak they went. I laughed so much at the funny sight that I clean missed the old boar, who brought up the rear, and who possessed a very handsome pair of tusks. We descended a small bank, and after drinking I had a most refreshing bath in the yellow muddy pit. On the trees around this water-hole I noticed some beautifully plumaged weaver birds, which looked like bits of brilliant orange and black plush hopping about. Round the water we found the tracks of hundreds of zebra and rhinoceros.

We then retraced our steps across the open plain to where our camp had been pitched. After breakfast I sallied forth to sit near one of the wells to wait for zebra to come for their afternoon drink. Directly I got outside my tent I beheld a grand sight ; the grassy plain was what my headman called ' covered up with game.' Sitting down, with my telescope I counted over 100 zebra quietly feeding towards the water, and ' owl ' gazelle on all sides wherever I looked. We walked across the plain, the gazelle slowly walking out of our way on either side of us, and standing to stare at so unaccustomed a sight. We sat down close to the well. But what with the flies, and what with the heat, and one thing and another, I soon voted it not good enough, and walked forth to meet the incoming zebra. But there they stood, right bang in the open, under two or three solitary trees, a long, long shot. There they stood, and refused to budge, standing in couples, facing both ways. At length I determined to try to reach a bush about 100 yards from them, and in order to accomplish this I was obliged to crawl in full view of them for some 50 yards. My lazy shikari, however, would not crawl, but, squatting down, he walked crab-like. waving the rifle about on high as he proceeded. Turning round, I beckoned to him to crawl, but it was too late : the zebra had noticed him. They began to walk slowly away. I snatched the rifle from my shikari, and ran through the bushes to try and get level with them, or, if possible, in front of them, as they walked parallel to the bushes. They were not seriously alarmed, but trotted quietly towards the bushes, instead of keeping to the open plain, where they had been standing safe for so long. I raced on parallel with them, until they suddenly came to a standstill to stare about them. I sat down, hot and very shaky, and fired ; the animal aimed at ran on about 10 yards, and then fell over stone-dead. I raced on through the bush, to try and keep up with the cloud of dust as the whole hundred dashed away. At length I heard them stop, but at first the dust was too thick to see them. At last, however, the wind blew some away, and disclosed a sight I shall never forget. Surrounded by a halo or vignette of dust stood this magnificent herd, making the most perfect picture, framed all round with dust, it is possible to imagine. I sat down, but could not then see over the edge of the frame ; so again standing, I fired, as it were, through a hole in the dust cloud, and then raced through the cloud, yelling for the pony, which, after a gallop of a few hundred yards, succeeded in stopping a zebra which I had hit in the middle. Before I could come up, the animal lay down and died.

About a mile off could be seen a great yellow cloud, as the remaining animals made good their escape, looking like the steam from a locomotive wending its way through trees and open plains as far as the eye could see. When I got home I could see, with the aid of my telescope, a huge crowd of vultures feeding upon the carcase of the first zebra, which lay right out in the open about a mile from camp. Behind them walked a huge herd of ' owl,' making a very pretty panorama. As I looked through the glass, I saw two jackals stalk through the grass towards them. All the vultures' heads went up in a moment, and the cowardly animals made off at once, with their tails between their legs.

After watching the sun set, I turned my chair to the right about to see the full moon, like a huge golden sovereign, slowly peep over the range of hills in the east. I soon witnessed what appeared to me a very singular phenomenon. There appeared on the left-hand side of the circumference of the moon, as it were, a huge black crack, penetrating far into the centre of the disc. This suddenly vanished, and another large black crack appeared lower down, completing a segment of the circle. This likewise vanished in a few seconds. I may add that at the time the whole sky was perfectly clear of clouds. Below is a sketch of the moon as she appeared during those few seconds.

The name of this place was Bun Feroli (the Zebra Plain).

Upon and around this plain game simply swarmed, and I had great sport, shooting one day four oryx, not a pound of the meat of which was wasted.

One morning I went to the well to look at the tracks, and found that a rhinoceros had drunk there the night before. His spoor led back again, across the plain, towards my camp. We followed that spoor from 5 a.m., across sandy ground, over stony ground, through thin bush, up a steep rocky hill, and down into an open plain on the other side, until 8 a.m., when, on going through some thick bushes, he got our wind, as he was lying down, and, jumping up, ran fast to my right. I fired the elephant rifle at him as he dashed past; but although he stumbled as I fired, and squeaked out, as my shikari said, 'like a smarl stimboat,' we found no blood-track. Shortly after we saw him walk quickly into another patch of bush ; but he escaped us, and finally we lost his track among boulders and stony ground, and had to give up the chase. Coming home, I spotted an ostrich in splendid plumage, with six or seven young ones, on a small sandy plain. I mounted the pony and gave chase, but they all got clean away from me in the long grass on the opposite side of the plain. We searched all over the grass, thinking that the young ones were squatting, but could not find them.

My knees, which were terribly barked by the long crawl the day before, now gave me a good deal of pain and trouble, as my clothes would insist on sticking tight to the sores. In the afternoon I tried another oryx drive, but it was not attended with any success. Soon after we came across a lot of vultures, sitting in some thorn-bushes, and walking up, we found the rotting carcase of a wounded oryx of the morning before, with a bullet-hole in its middle. The smell was overpowering, but we managed to cut off the head, which I took home as a trophy, making the bag of the day before up to four oryx. The vultures here were very tame. By taking aim above their heads, with a stone I could hit them hard in the body as they rose, nine times out of ten, so close would they allow me to approach them. That night I slept in a zareba by the water-hole. Hyænas came and howled, and lapped water all night round the zareba, but I could not see to shoot at them, until an extra large one came and stared at the donkey. I could not resist the temptation, when the moon came out from behind a cloud, so put a bullet through his right eye. He turned out to be a fine spotted hyæna, of very dark colour. He possessed positively immense jaws and teeth. During the rest of the night jackals made their curious ferret-like noises, and zebras galloped about and neighed, but did not come in sight. Oh, the mosquitoes ! I was nearly eaten alive, and the noise of chirping grasshoppers and frogs was almost deafening. I was very glad when morning broke at last, and the men came to let me out of my little prison.

After a cup of coffee, I went out again to try and get a wart hog, where we had seen them before; but although we saw plenty of tracks, which were by no means old, we saw no pig. We saw three zebras and several oryx, but could not get near them. When I got home to breakfast, some men came in, having driven past the camp an enormous number of camels, and reported Abyssinians in my guide's village, who were asking to see him. So far we had been lucky in not meeting with these gentlemen.

In the afternoon I found a young 'owl' gazelle, which I caught, and as we had no milch goats with us, it was of no use attempting to rear it, so I tied it with a bit of rope to a tree, and hid in the bushes close at hand. The gazelle began to bleat, when up ran a large herd of 'owl.' When within some 15 yards of me they got my wind, and would come no nearer, but stood sniffing and craning their necks to look at the baby antelope. I watched this pretty sight for upwards of half an hour, the herd consisting for the most part of mothers and babies, with a few old bucks with good heads. At last I showed myself, and they ran away, and stood again about 300 yards off. I then let loose the baby 'owl,' and with a few frantic kicks and jumps in the air he galloped off, bleating, to the herd, which also advanced to meet the recent prisoner, receiving him with joy, and licking him all over.

We then went a long round without seeing anything worth a shot, until we came to an open plain which we had not visited before. Here we found a herd of almost 100 zebra, a great many oryx, and countless herds of 'owl.' The zebra caught sight of my shikari, who, as usual, absolutely refused to crawl, and for several seconds I could see nothing but dust, and hear a great rumbling noise of retreating hoofs. Coming home, I saw an 'owl' with an extra good head, at which I determined to expend one cartridge, as I had been firing away my ammunition rather recklessly of late. I broke one of his fore-legs, and, seizing a spear from my syce, mounted my pony, for what turned out to be one of the grandest chases I had ever had. For a long time the wounded beast kept up with the main herd, but at length, by digging my heels into the pony's flanks, I separated the antelope from the main body, and turned him straight for camp The ground was open and level, and we went at a racing pace. I got level with the beast, but he would not stop, and as we neared camp the whole of my men turned out to witness the truly exciting scene. The pony ran right up to him against the very walls of the zareba, and when I ran the spear through behind his shoulder he fell dead, amid the plaudits of the crowd. I certainly possessed a grand pony for pace and endurance. He went out every day and all day, never got any thinner, and was always ready for a long, hard gallop. Without this pony my bag would have been but half what it was up to that day. My guide now told me that he would not leave me if I wrote a letter to the Abyssinians, saying that he was with me simply and solely to show me game. The men reported seeing a leopard upon the plain to-day. The game seen whilst we were encamped at Bun Feroli included the following : oryx, ' owl,' gerenook, zebra, jackal, fox, ostrich, hyæna, wart hog, rhinoceros, dik-dik, koodoo, leopard, and lion, the latter reported at a near village.

Next day I went to the place where we had seen so much game the day before. We found four or five zebra and a lot of ' owl,' but no oryx. The zebra made off, but I managed to put in a bullet somewhere in the middle of the hindmost. My legs were quite raw after the stern chase of the day before, so I sent my syce away after the animal on the pony. I myself followed the spoor on foot slowly. After going about a mile and a half I heard shouts and yells from behind me. I didn't know what to do. It might be other Somalis. Surely, I thought, the zebra had not gone back to the place whence he started ? However,

Caldwell 1899

HE LUMBERED ALONG IN FRONT OF ME AT A GOODLY PACE.

[To face p. 91.

I turned back, and had not retraced my spoor very long,
when I heard a shout a long way ahead of me, shortly
followed by a second. I sent away my shikari running on
the spoor, and after going a little further, heard shouts.
Coming through the thorn-bushes I found the pony, syce
and shikari standing over a dead zebra. They had had a
very long chase among the trees, the zebra having gone
right back to the place he was in when I fired at him.
Leaving two men to skin him, I sent back the others for a
camel to carry the meat, and proceeded with my shikaris,
but as we got hopelessly lost in thick bush, we did
nothing more. It was hours before we found camp
eventually. In the afternoon I saw the same sounder of
wart hogs, so mounting my pony, and seizing one of the
Somalis' spears, I thought I would have a little pig-stick-
ing. But after a hard gallop the old boar gained the thick
bushes, which put further riding out of the question.

We next approached an open plain, upon which we saw
oryx feeding, and I was just contemplating how I should
best get a shot at them, when a huge animal stole out of
some high grass into the open, and slowly walked towards
the thick bushes surrounding the plain. We all shouted
'Libah, libah!' (Lion, lion!). Catching hold of my ·450, and
vaulting into the saddle, I rode at him as hard as I could
get the pony along. I soon discovered that I was riding
after a large leopard, and not a lion; and as he lumbered
along in front of me at a goodly pace, I saw it would be a
frantic race to the bushes. Turning the pony's course, I
steered straight for the bushes, to stop the leopard from
entering. Just when I thought he must reach them in
spite of me, he stopped dead, screwed himself up into a
ball, and, showing his pearly teeth, snarled at me hoarsely.
I thought he was about to charge, and stopped the pony
to fire at him, when he turned and made off out into the
open as fast as his legs could carry him. I then knew that
I must either get him or he would get me. Laying the
reins upon the pony's back, and digging my heels into his

sides, he went off at a marvellous pace, considering the long
gallop he had only just finished after the wart hog.

We gained on the leopard rapidly, and as there was at
least half a mile of open to cross before the leopard could
reach the bush again, I let the pony go his own pace,
keeping to the right of the retreating leopard, which
lumbered along with its head nearly touching the ground,
and going at a great pace. At length I got close upon
him, when he stopped dead, and I dashed right past him,
not being able to pull up in time. Seeing this, the leopard
turned round and made off again. I half jumped, half fell
out of the saddle, and by the time I had the reins round
my arm, and the rifle up to my shoulder, the beast was a
good 100 yards away, and I missed him with both barrels.
Was I going to lose him, after all? I jumped into the
saddle again, my pony blowing like a steam-engine. But
the leopard was done too, and I easily overhauled him again.
When he saw I was gaining upon him, he turned round,
sat up, and looked the picture of fury. I pulled in, and
took a long aim at his chest from the saddle. When the
smoke cleared, and I had recovered my seat, which I had
nearly lost through the pony starting at the report, I
beheld a large spotted mass lying in a heap before me.
I trotted up, and found the animal stone-dead, but do what
I would, I could not get the terrified pony up to the beast.
At length my shikari ran up and held him, whilst I walked
up to examine my prize. The bullet had gone right
through his right eye, killing him instantaneously. He
had a beautiful skin, and I was mightily pleased with him,
after the grand sport he had afforded me. We lifted him
with great difficulty upon the pony's back, after covering
the latter's eyes with my coat, and carried him home in
triumph. On the way I saw an ibis and a huge marabou
stork.

Next morning I went out in an easterly direction, when
suddenly I heard a buzzing noise, and, looking up, beheld a
huge cloud of black-looking objects approaching me, and

flying through the air, straight on a level with my head, at a terrific pace. I had just time to throw myself flat on my face in the grass as they passed over me. They went so fast it was almost impossible to make out what they were, but I suspect they were some sort of large bee swarming. I asked my shikari what he called them, and he said ' shindy.' Yes, I thought to myself, a very appropriate name ! During the morning I saw six different herds of oryx, but got a chance at one lot only. I had a very long crawl on my stomach, and my poor barked knees, which were healing up so nicely, were made worse than ever. I got at last within 150 yards of them, and then missed them with both barrels. They stood staring at me, huddled close together, for over a minute, as I felt in vain in every pocket for another cartridge. I had none, and when my shikari was in the act of throwing me the cartridge-bag, the antelope all turned round, and with a whisk of their tails cantered off. Coming home I saw another sounder of ' big,' as my shikari called wart hog, but they got into thick bushes before I could mount. At noon the temperature was 96° in my tent, and 119° in the sun. During the afternoon two native policemen, in the employ of the Government, came in, and asked for cartridges, stating that the caravan they were escorting had been attacked near Milmil, and that, after terrific fighting, they had succeeded in killing one ' boney ' and badly frightening half a dozen men. I gave them ten rounds of ammunition each, and a letter to send to the coast, to be forwarded home.

Next morning I started south-east for a village where lion were reported to have been lately at work. We marched for five hours steadily uphill, through thick tree-jungle. As we neared the village of Godgodeo, we found the spoor of a lion, a few days old, but when we reached the village, which was one of the biggest I had yet seen, we found, as usual, that nearly all the reports about lions were lies : so that I had come all this way for nothing. In your intercourse with Somalis there are two maxims I

would impress upon the would-be sportsman : firstly, never
believe what you hear ; and, secondly, never do what you
are told. I had a zareba built between the well and the
village, and sat in it all night. A great deal of rain fell,
which did not add to the comfort of sleeping 'rough.' Of
course a lion was neither seen nor heard.

My head-shikari was not with me, as he had complained of
a bad headache, at which I had sniggered, but next morning
I awoke to find that I also had a headache, and felt so
stiff and slack, when let out of the zareba, that I could
scarcely walk. However, I determined to start back to
the main camp at Bun Feroli, and started at 4.30 a.m.
When I had ridden for two hours, I felt so weak I could
with difficulty sit in the saddle, and calling a halt, I sat in
the shade for half an hour. Hearing some camels roaring
about a mile off, I sent two of my men to try and get me
some milk ; but after drinking it I was violently sick.
After a five hours' ride, I at length reached Bun Feroli, and
as my tent had not as yet arrived, I threw myself under
the very inefficient shade afforded by a thorn-bush. I
was now seized with a very violent attack of fever, and,
the heat that day being very great, I had a poor time of
it. When my tent arrived and was pitched, I went to bed,
but I could neither sleep nor eat. At night I dosed my
shikari and myself heavily with quinine. Two lions roared
round the camp during the night, and made a most magnificent noise, which I should have thoroughly enjoyed had I
been well.

The whole of the next day I remained in my bed, feeling
very weak and ill. I ordered two small zarebas to be built,
and in the evening my two shikaris went out and watched
for lions in them. Somalis are extremely cruel to the brute
creation. I saw a man deliberately cut a huge slice out of
the ear of a donkey, which was going to carry some bedding to
one of the small zarebas. I made him understand that if
I saw him do it again I would take a slice out of his ear.
On asking him why he did it, he replied that he ' did it for

luck ; as the blood flowed from the donkey, so would the blood flow from the lion.' I suggested that the next time they went to watch for lions, they should cut their own ears instead of the donkey's for luck. A lion came near one of the zarebas during the night, but got wind of the men and decamped. Next morning I felt a bit better, and determined to clear away from the plain to higher and more healthy ground.

CHAPTER VII.

I STARTED from Bun Feroli at 4 a.m., and pitched for the
mid-day rest near some bitter-water wells, at which herds
of camels were getting their monthly drink. Here my
headman, of course, wanted to stay for the day; but I was
determined to get away to fresh air, and marched on. In
the evening I killed a sheep for the men, to show them
how to do it in a humane way, as I was perfectly disgusted
with the manner in which they butchered the poor brutes.
After I had killed the sheep, the men utterly refused to eat
it because they had not killed it themselves!

From cleanliness in sheep-killing, I pass to cleanliness in
teeth-cleaning, where the Somalis, in their turn, beat us
hollow. They are for ever rubbing at their teeth with a
green stick, which they cut from a thorn-tree. This renders
their teeth magnificently white. The stick, although green
to the core, is perfectly tasteless and harmless. I noticed
that my men, fearing Gallas, carried their rifles more than
usual about this time, instead of allowing the camels to
carry them. They had carelessly burst four of their rifles,
and knocked off the sights of some half-dozen. They
had broken nearly all my tent-pegs, and an extra strong
mallet bound with iron had been reduced by them into
matchwood. They got at my tool-roll one day, but I
rescued it before they had got further than breaking a pair
of pincers and two large gouges.

We encamped at 3.45 p.m. on stony ground, at a place

called Gonsali. I hoped that we had at length got rid of the villages for some time to come. I must not forget to mention a very dangerous practical joke played on villagers by my men. When approaching a 'woolidge,' and seeing some Somalis quietly watching their flocks and herds, they would rush at them, shouting at the top of their voices; they would then kneel down and point their rifles at them, when the villagers would all run away as hard as they could go, leaving all their sheep, cattle, and camels to our tender mercies, believing us to be a raiding-party of the dreaded Abyssinians. As I feared the villagers might make it very warm for us by mistake some day, I soon put a stop to this nonsense.

That evening we saw the first spoor of an elephant, but several days old. Here we decided to remain before proceeding to Biermuddo (the Black Water Hole). A man brought us in some honey of most excellent flavour, which I bought for some tobacco. Next morning, piloted by our guide, we went out early to look for elephant spoor, near some wells of which he knew. We soon found the very old spoor of a large bull elephant, and plenty of fresh rhinoceros spoor. We went on, however, to visit a second well, before following any track. We walked up a dried-up river-bed for about a mile, until we came to a pool of water, round which were the tracks of some half-dozen 'rhinos' and a few old elephant tracks. We singled out what appeared to be a really fresh track, and followed it. The spoor soon left the river-bed, and we quickly lost it in the rocky ground bordering the channel. I was pottering about, trying to find the tracks again, when I caught sight of a rhinoceros, slowly walking through the thin bushes, about 300 yards from me, up a bank. I had with me half a dozen men and my two ponies, as I expected every day to fall in with elephants. Leaving three men and the ponies behind, I followed the rhinoceros, and presently saw the beast again fairly close. I began to stalk him, making, however, a great noise in some thick bushes and on the stony ground.

7

The animal seemed to be walking very quickly, and I found it almost impossible to get along on the uneven ground, over little dried-up watercourses, interlaced with thorn branches. Suddenly coming over a small rise, I beheld, barely 20 yards away, with their backs towards me, not one, but two rhinoceros, one a large animal, the other a little smaller. I cocked the elephant rifle, and crouched along through the thorn-bushes until the big one, hearing us, suddenly turned sideways, held his head high in the air, cocked his ears, and snorted and sniffed loudly. Kneeling upon one knee, I aimed for the heart. Bang! The bullet struck him in the shoulder. There was a great snorting and rumbling of stones as I fired my second barrel at his retreating form, when, through the smoke, I became aware that the smaller animal of the two was charging down upon us. However, by some miracle we all dodged behind bushes, and he thundered off to follow his friend, my men letting off their Sniders, presumably at him, although in reality most of the muzzles were pointed up into the air! I loaded, and ran on the big one's blood-spoor, which was only too evident on the rocky ground. We soon found him, standing behind a bush, breathing heavily, when I took a steady aim and fired. It then became evident that the wounded beast meant to charge us. He tossed his head, and looked defiantly at us. He was standing on very rocky and uneven ground, thinly scattered here and there with 'wait-a-bit' thorn-bushes, on a steep slope 25 yards above us. Suddenly, with a shake of his ugly head, he made a most determined charge straight for the middle of the four of us.

Seeing him coming at a terrific pace, and so close upon us, I yelled, 'Fire!' and at the same instant fired the left-hand barrel of the big rifle I held in my hand. The next thing I remember was a huge dark head coming through the smoke. Whether I fell, jumped, or was thrown out of the way, I don't know, but I saw the huge beast dash past me, and felt the wind from his nostrils in my face. My

THE RHINOCEROS TOSSED HIM AT LEAST FIVE FEET UP INTO THE AIR.

[To face p. 90.

second shikari and another man had thrown themselves behind a bush to the left. For a second after I was conscious of nothing but a huge cloud of dust and smoke, and a loud rumbling of stones. The next second I saw two men crouching behind bushes, but I was horrified to behold my head-shikari racing downhill, closely followed by the infuriated rhinoceros. I yelled out to the man to dodge. But straight on down the hill he kept, until he reached a bush, round which he appeared to stumble to the right, the rhinoceros gaining upon him at every stride. As the man stumbled, the rhinoceros, which, marvellous to relate, had turned the sharp corner with as much dexterity as the man, caught the poor fellow with his horn, behind, and tossed him at least 5 feet up into the air, my Express, which the man was carrying in his hand, going up perhaps double that height. My shikari, being a very heavy man, was turned literally head over heels in the air, and landed on the side of his head and shoulder, through a very thick thorn-bush, on the rough, stony ground, before the very nose of the rhinoceros, which had stood calmly waiting for him to fall. When the man fell he lay perfectly still on his side, and I quite gave him up for dead. The rhinoceros now commenced to give the man's head and side a series of terrific rams with his horn.

Although all this has taken a long time to tell, the events related all happened in a few seconds. Meanwhile all the men remained crouched behind trees, calling upon Allah to save the wretched shikari. Picking up my rifle as soon as I could, I rushed towards the huge brute as he was still butting at the man, yelling with all my might. I dared not fire at the animal, as his head touched the man, and as he stood below me I could see nothing else to fire at when he faced me, so, picking up some large stones, I threw them high, so as to land, if possible, on the animal's back, and not touch the man. At this he stopped mauling the man, and, raising his huge ugly head, stared at me, as though in doubt whether to charge me or not. I loaded quickly

for him, and at length he made up his mind to bolt, and
galloped away to the left. I fired both barrels at close
quarters into his ribs, before he vanished in the thick
bushes. I now rushed down to my shikari, when I was
surprised to see him sit up, and I saw that blood was flowing from a large cut on the side of his head. He was
utterly unconscious, and after stopping the flow of blood
I left him with my water-bottle and two men, and rushed
to avenge myself on the infuriated 'rhino.' About 100
yards off we found him behind a bush, standing above us,
with his head towards us. This would never do; so
retracing my steps, and making a short détour, I got
behind a thick bush, with him broadside on. Fearing
further disaster, I ordered a volley to be fired at him.
All taking aim through the bushes, I said ' Fire !' at the
same moment firing both barrels of my eight-bore simul-
taneously, and then picked up the Express. This moved
him 50 yards further up the hill ; stalking again, I got closer,
and taking careful aim, we fired a second volley, which
made the beast plunge about, but he did not shift his
position. After this I waited a few seconds ; then, seeing
the game was nearly over, I advanced out into the open,
within a few feet of him, and planted a ball in his neck.
He still stood. I was aiming again, when, with two or
three shakes of his ugly head, he fell heavily over on his
side stone-dead. Thus died one of the most aggressive
animals I have ever had to deal with, its great tenacity
of life being simply marvellous. I counted eleven bullet-
holes in his skin when dead, my first ball having gone right
through his heart : how he survived this so long I cannot
imagine.

I did not stop more than a minute looking at the great
brute, but rushed back to find my shikari still unconscious,
in the arms of the two men I had left with him.
I examined his head, and found he had a frightful-
looking cut, about 7 inches long, round the right side of
his shaven head, the gaping wound displaying the bone of

the skull. On his temple, which was much swollen, he had a small indentation. He jabbered away, half in Somali, half in English, but what he was talking about it was difficult to know. We waited by him for a bit, as the blood had stopped flowing, when suddenly he regained consciousness, and I asked him where he felt it most. He replied, ' On my behind.' I turned him over, and found a small bruise only, where the horns of the ' rhino ' had lifted him. He had a large bruise on his shoulder, which, however, was not broken. I had him carried home on a pony. When we got him home, the Somalis made a terrible din, jabbering nineteen to the dozen. The man's skull was not fractured, for I could get my finger right through the gaping cut and feel all along the bone of the skull. I pulled the sides of the cut together, sewed them up, and put strips of plaster across to keep them well together, the Somalis trying to spoil all my work by pushing a great piece of dirty wood into the wound, and then tying it round the patient's neck with a piece of string, offering up all the while a kind of prayer for his safe recovery. After breakfast I ordered a camel to be got ready, and started away to cut off some mementoes of my first rhinoceros. Thinking that the other rhinoceros might still be lurking about looking for its companion, I took the rifles with me. On reaching the dead animal, we found the inevitable vultures in hundreds round the corpse. I took some photographs of the animal, and with great difficulty the Somalis cut off his head, his four feet, his tail, and a large piece of his hide, and loaded the camel with the spoils. The length of the rhinoceros was 10 feet 2 inches and the girth 7 feet. The horns were short, $11\frac{1}{4}$ inches and $5\frac{1}{2}$ inches long respectively, and were very rounded at the tips, otherwise I think my shikari must have been killed.

Coming home, we found the track of a lion of the night before going to the water. I had a bathe in one of the ' wells,' and then went and dressed my shikari's wounds again before dark. The severance of the horns from the head of the ' rhino' caused my men endless trouble, several of my tools being broken during the operation. At length I made them cease hacking at it with knives, etc., and sawed it off with a big saw in a minute. Of course they

AUTHOR ON DEAD 'RHINO.'

wanted two sheep killed in honour of the occasion. I had a row with my headman about the number of *tobes* he had got rid of in exchange for sheep, *harns*, etc. A *tobe* of *merikani*, or Massachusetts sheeting, is measured by a man's hand and arm to the elbow. Seven of these lengths

go to a *tobe*, or ' clothes.' Next morning I went down to
the river-bed, Gonsali, to look for spoor. I walked along
the river-bed for several miles, seeing old elephant spoor,
some fresh ' rhino ' spoor, and that of one or two lions. We
next climbed a high hill, overlooking the river, from which
we got a good view of the country, but saw no game.

I came home by a very rough route, through nullahs
covered with rock and stones. In the river-bed I found
some beautiful clear water in the hollows of the rock, at
one of which I knelt down determined to have a good
drink, when, ugh! I found it fearfully salt. The water in
a ' well ' near camp becomes perfectly black when agitated,
and smells very strongly of soot. It was most disagreeable
to wash in, and to drink it would have been certain death.
Marvellous to relate! my rifle which my shikari threw up in
the air when tossed by the rhinoceros escaped comparatively uninjured, with the exception of a few scratches and
a large indentation of the file-like ridge running between
the barrels.

In the afternoon I went out and had another long walk,
but saw nothing. The day after we pottered about in the
river-bed among a perfect maze of ' rhino ' tracks, and after
following one, which left the river, for upwards of four
hours, we ultimately lost it in thick grass. Coming home,
we saw a splendid cock ostrich, in beautiful plumage, and
two hens, on a small piece of open ground, but, as usual,
they made off before I could get within range of them. I
found elephant spoor two days old all over the country,
and sent my guide and pony after it, to see if he could
make out where they had all cleared off to. Next morning
we struck camp and marched to a place called Biermuddo
(the Black Water Hole), over rough stony ground covered
with the everlasting ' wait-a-bit ' thorn-bushes and very
little grass.

About 9 a.m., as we walked along, I saw some old wart
hogs, with some squeakers; but just as I was in the act of
taking my Express, I saw a larger pig-like animal, in the

shape of a huge rhinoceros.   Exchanging my Express for
the eight-bore, and getting behind some bushes, we crouched
down to witness an extraordinary performance.   The big
beast had evidently got a whiff of our wind, for he careered
about in a most alarming fashion, rushing up in this
direction, and then turning and galloping off in that.   At
length he rushed straight for the very bush behind which I
was concealed.   I half turned round, and beheld my brave
followers doing a ' guy ' as hard as they could go.   When
the ' rhino' got almost up to the bush, I could wait no longer,
but stood up and flourished my rifle in its face, when it
turned sharp to the right and bolted.   Taking aim off the
shoulder, I fired the heavy gun as he galloped away, which
caused him to spin round and round as hard as he could
move five or six times, like a huge top, and kicking up
clouds of dust.   He then bolted off quietly into some thick
bushes.   Now came the most unpleasant part of dangerous
game-shooting, *i.e.*, following wounded game in thick bush.
However, after peering about in the bushes for a minute or
two, we found the animal on the other side in the open,
standing under a small thorn-tree.   As I looked, he lay
down and expired.   The wart hog then reappeared close to
the ' rhino's ' body, and, taking a shot at a large boar, I was
unlucky enough to hit a smaller one, which walked past its
companion as I was in the act of pressing the trigger.   It
fell dead almost at the hind-feet of the ' rhino.'   It possessed
poor tusks.   Running up to them, I found the ' rhino ' a
much larger beast than the first, and very much older.   He
measured 11 feet 6 inches from tip of nose to tip of tail,
and his girth was 9 feet 6 inches.   He had larger and more
pointed horns than my first, the front horn, which was
cracked, measuring $11\frac{1}{2}$ inches round the curve.   I found I
had made a very good shot behind the shoulder, the bullet
probably penetrating the animal's heart.   In the afternoon
I photographed him, and on skinning him I found a large
flattened spherical eight-bore bullet implanted between the
skin and the flesh of his neck.   How long it had been there

it was, of course, impossible to say, for the wound had healed up entirely. We took off his head, feet, tail, and part of his hide as trophies of the great beast, and left his huge carcase for the vultures.

The whole of the next day we found ourselves among a labyrinth of 'rhino' tracks, and followed two, both of which, however, got our wind, and went crashing through the bushes before us. The heat was very great, my thermometer registering 122° in the sun. Early on the following morning I found a rhinoceros lying down under a thorn-bush in very open ground. I had had enough of 'rhinos' at close quarters, so tried a long shot and missed, when he jumped up, and stood broadside and stared at us. I could not load quick enough, however, owing to the stiff action of my gun, and he thundered off. We followed the track for upwards of twenty minutes, when we suddenly came upon him standing broadside in thick bushes. I caught him a good smack in the side, but he wheeled round, and went off very fast, nodding his head up and down as he went. There was not much blood to follow, except under some trees, where he had evidently stood to listen. On reaching the top of a stony hill, we spied him walking quickly along at the bottom. We ran down the hill as fast as we could after him, and soon saw him again, running and dodging round the bushes. After this we lost him and his track altogether. I then walked up to the top of a small rise, to have a look round. Below me stretched a circular valley, or huge pit, four or five miles in diameter, like a huge extinct volcano crater, covered with very thick thorn-bushes, and surrounded by short but steep and rocky hills. The rocks were piled one upon another in huge fantastic shapes. There was not a breath of wind, and not a sound to be heard. The place looked weird and uncanny in the extreme. Presently I perceived below me two oryx glide softly from behind some bushes, and vanish again in the thick bush, like two gray spectres.

Leaving the pony behind, and telling my shikari to carry

my Express, I descended the hill into the crater covered with thick bush. When at the bottom, we could not see more than 10 yards ahead of us in the most open places. However, by tracking we soon found the oryx quite close to us, and I began to walk over the stony ground in tennis shoes and on tiptoe towards them. Not a sound could be heard. I was getting very near them, and was in the act of stretching out my hand for my rifle, when, on crouching cat-like round a bush, I suddenly became aware of an enormous head and horns about 3 feet from my face, and realized that I had literally walked into the face of a huge rhinoceros, which was standing under a bush within an arm's length of me, perfectly rigid. My shikari, who was carrying my rifle behind and a little to the left of me, stood with open mouth, as if petrified. I gave one glance at his horror-stricken face, and another at the ugly 'mug' of the 'rhino,' and then backed slowly away from the huge beast round a bush. When I turned round to grasp my rifle, I caught a glimpse of my shikari running hard away on tiptoe through the bushes with my rifle, gesticulating and point-ing back towards the rhinoceros. This made me turn round again, when I beheld the rhinoceros slowly advancing upon me without a sound, having evidently got my wind when I was almost touching him. It was now my turn to run, and my name was 'Walker' until I had reached my men and snatched up my big rifle, when I again went to the attack; but look as I did all over, I failed to see him or his tracks anywhere, and at length stood and rubbed my eyes, to see if I was dreaming or had seen a phantom. On open-ing my eyes again, I sighted the same two oryx close to me, and had again begun to stalk them, when my shikari suddenly stopped, and, looking as if he had seen a ghost, whispered, 'The rhino!' There, sure enough, about 20 yards off, stood the rhinoceros, which seemed to haunt us like a huge demon. Before I could attempt to raise my rifle, I felt myself violently clutched by the arm, and dragged off at a great pace by my now utterly terrified shikari, in spite of my struggles and curses in an undertone upon his head. Nothing would now induce him to return, as he kept saying : ' Leave lone, sahib—leave lone. It am de debil—you no kill him !' I turned round, and, reluctantly followed by my other men (my shikari remaining behind with the pony), I again sought the phantom ' rhino.' I soon discovered him musing under a thorn-bush some few yards below me. Taking careful aim for his shoulder, I was in the act of pressing the trigger, when he whisked round, and without a sound vanished into the bushes in an instant. This was more than my men could stand. On looking round, I perceived that the superstitious devils were all taking to their heels as if for life. I never saw the phantom ' rhino ' again, and didn't want to, for, although I am by no means superstitious as a rule, it was a curious fact that this animal, which I saw three times, never made the slightest sound, and we could find no spoor of him, perhaps owing to the rocky nature of the ground. We left the wild and uncanny spot, and reached camp as the sun was setting.

CHAPTER VIII.

Large 'rhino' shot—Down a precipice after koodoo—The Webbi Shebeyli —Tracks of elephants—Abundance of insect life—Nest of bees.

NEXT day, we had gone barely a quarter of a mile from camp, when I saw a rhinoceros, which bolted on our near approach. Shortly after I saw another, with a poor head, which I let alone. Number three dashed away out of some bushes in which it was lying asleep, and as the men walked along, talking and making a great noise, my second shikari spotted a fourth within an hour. He excitedly exclaimed : 'Come down from the boney.' I stalked the 'rhino' until I got fairly close, took a careful aim, and fired. There was a tremendous commotion, and for a second or so I saw only a cloud of dust, out of which suddenly dashed the monster, across an open space, at a tremendous pace. He certainly looked very awe-inspiring, galloping off with his head stretched out and nose high in the air, the dust flying behind him like a whirlwind. We ran to the spoor, and found a good deal of blood, which we followed, and in a few minutes found the great brute snorting under a thorn-bush. Creeping as close as I dared, under the cover of some thin bushes, I fired the big gun at him again, and evidently hit him, for he plunged about violently, but did not leave the thorn-bush. As he kept turning round and round, and would not keep still, I waited. At length I fired again, and hit him right behind the shoulder. Feeling for more cartridges, I found I had not one left, and as my men were some 20 yards behind me, I had to sit still and await results, as I dared not move back, fearing he might see me and charge. At last, after what appeared to me to be an age of suspense, he lay down. My men began to talk, when he stood up again and began snorting loudly. At length he lay down again in a kneeling position, when I quickly shifted my position and got my Express. I fired one shot at him at long range, but as he did not move, I walked up to him shouting. As we got up to him, he lifted up his huge head twice in the air, and let it down again upon the ground with a bump, making us all start back; but he never moved again, and we cut his throat, and left him looking most natural and life-like, as he knelt with his chin resting upon the ground. Coming back a couple of hours afterwards, we found that, owing to the absence of blood and his life-like appearance, not a single vulture had as yet arrived. He proved to be the finest specimen I had as yet shot, measuring 12 feet from tip of nose to tip of tail, and 9 feet 10 inches in circumference. His front horn measured $16\frac{1}{2}$ inches round the curve, rear horn $7\frac{1}{2}$ inches; circumference of front horn $17\frac{1}{4}$ inches, and of rear horn $15\frac{1}{2}$ inches. It shows that this animal was here very numerous, when in one short morning we came casually across four without any tracking.

The guide returned in the afternoon from investigating some wells half a day's march off, and reported further elephant and 'rhino' tracks by the dozen. During the night two lions roared round the camp, causing a general stampede as usual among the camels, which came crashing into my tent and through the thorn zareba. They were with difficulty and no little danger found, secured, and brought into camp again.

Next day I took a rest, it being Sunday. I sent out the men to look for lion spoor, but it was utterly impossible to find it in the rocky ground. At five next morning we struck camp and marched to Boholo Deno (the Blocked-up Water Hole). On the way we saw some oryx, one of which I killed with a good shot through the shoulder at long range. We then walked up a small river-bed in which we found a number of holes in the rock full of water, most of it tasting very salt, and salt was deposited on all sides on the rock in the river-bed, looking exactly like a thin covering of snow. Here we found elephant tracks, some two days old, innumerable 'rhino' tracks, and what made my men look grave, namely, tracks of Abyssinians of the day before. There was no mistaking them, their feet giving a totally different imprint in the sand from those of Somalis. I sincerely hoped these robbers would keep out of my way, as the pleasure of shooting and collecting ceases when the hunter becomes the hunted either of man or beast.

Coming back to where the camp was pitched we found fresh lions' spoor. It was extraordinary we never came across lions in this desolate country, although we frequently saw their spoor, and they roared round our camp nearly every night. It was amusing to see how my men now stuck to their rifles, even when going down to the well, which was barely a couple of hundred yards off. The two donkeys would have an escort of four or five men, as the men feared Gallas and Abyssinians, to say nothing of lions, elephants, and 'rhinos.' To-day my head-shikari turned up on the field of action for the first time since he had been tossed by the rhinoceros.

Next morning we found very fresh spoor of four elephants in the little river-bed close by camp. We followed it west for several miles. From the top of a small hill we saw two rhinoceros, but, as I was after bigger game, I left them alone.

On and on we went for miles. The elephants had made a pathway which could not be mistaken, strewing the ground all the way with branches of thorn-bush which they pulled off to eat as they walked along. We tracked them to the Daghato River, a river running at the bottom of an immense gorge. The elephants evidently knew their way, for they passed down a precipitous and narrow rocky path, the only pass we could find down to the river. Across the river they went, and right up the other steep side of the nullah, where, as darkness was coming on, we were forced to leave them.

Coming home I shot a large marabou stork which was scavenging round the camp in the dark. This bird has a very large and strong beak, and a naked head and neck, with the exception of some fluffy, fur-like feathers at the back of the head. Where the neck joins the body there is a huge crop, bag, or pouch of skin hanging down in front. The look of this bird is most gruesome, his face appearing to frown at one as he turns his back and slowly stalks along with his thin legs, and screws his huge head and beak round to gaze at you. The skin of the sides of his face is red and yellow, spotted with black, and the naked skin of the neck is bluish-gray, except where it joins the body at the back, where it is a brilliant vermilion.

Next day I went west again to look for elephants, and as we walked along the top of a range of hills we spied some koodoo far below us. There were two females and a magnificent male. They were feeding quietly, so I made a huge détour and came up above them. We found that they had moved, and for a long time could not see them. At length I spied a cow watching me intently, and soon after a large bull walked up to her and stood broadside on. My rifle shook with excitement! A chance like that occurred perhaps once in a lifetime. A huge drop of perspiration fell from my forehead into my eye as I pressed the trigger on one of Africa's grandest animals. I heard the bullet 'phut' on him, and a moment later saw that I had fired too far back. I fired again as he bounded away and disappeared headlong over the precipice. I ran as hard as I could over the loose rocky ground, and reached the edge of a yawning gulf. Not a sign of the koodoo was to be seen. There was not a sound to be heard in the stillness of the morning. We soon found, however, a spot of blood, and then began one of the stiffest and most dangerous descents I had ever experienced. Down, down, down the mountain-side we went, following the blood spoor, now losing the track, now being obliged to make a détour to get round an impossible precipice.

After an hour of this sort of thing my throat became parched, and my water-bottle was by now miles away behind. The sun came out strong, and I longed at that moment to be following red-deer in a country where one treads on water at every step. We were still far from the bottom of the huge nullah, where I saw a ' tug ' (dried-up river-bed) wending its way through the hills. A river-bed ; but how far should we have to dig to find water ? We had now lost the blood spoor, and shouted to the men above us for the water-bottle. Not a sound broke the stillness after the echo had died away in the valley. Down and down we went on recovering the blood track. Soon after there was a rushing of loose stones below us. We raced down the precipices, but saw nothing among the thick bushes and huge boulders.

We next came upon a great quantity of clotted blood, and knew that we must see the game again ere we reached the bottom. Creeping, crawling, sliding, and slipping, we slowly wended our way down the steep mountain-side until we came to a place where the koodoo had evidently fallen. On tip-toe we crept on, when up jumped the antelope out of some cactus bushes, and immediately disappeared again amid a rumble of stones. I was nearly played out, and fell twice on the uneven ground in quick succession. I was obliged to stop and take a breather. By this time we were within 500 yards of the bottom, having come all the way down in a slanting direction.

On restarting more blood became apparent, and at last I caught sight of the beautiful animal's head crouching among the rocks facing us. My shikari in his excitement fired my rifle before I could stop him, and the bullet whizzed over the animal's horns ; but the poor beast was now too done to get up, and, seizing the rifle, I put a merciful bullet through its neck. What a truly magnificent animal he was ! His great spiral horns measured 42 inches in a straight line, making a record head from Somaliland. Soon after the fall of this monarch of the mountains the men came down the hill with the precious fluid, and I sat under the shade of a tree during the skinning operation, and thoroughly enjoyed a good pull at my bottle. After a long and very arduous climb we reached the top again, and did not reach camp until after dark.

Early next morning I started for the Webbi Shebeyli, or Leopard River. After following a small dried-up river-bed for several miles, we reached a large pool of water in it shaded by trees, and seeing tracks round it of countless game, we walked over the river-bank, and immediately saw two oryx staring at us about 120 yards away. They were kind enough to allow me to dismount, load my rifle, sit down, and take a steady aim, when I struck both, right and left, but we eventually lost one of them.

After this we passed over the everlasting rough, stony ground until we came to a cone-shaped hill with the top cut off. The remaining top was covered with a light yellow stone, whereas the base was dark, and at a distance it reminded me exactly of the great Fujyama, the sacred volcano of Japan, on a small scale. From the top of this cone we got a grand view of the surrounding country. To the south of us was a huge gorge, or nullah, at the bottom of which ran the great river of Somaliland, the Webbi Shebeyli. To the east stood out the great mountain range called the Nagob, and south of it the curious-shaped Mount Culdush. As I looked upon the vast sea of trees below me, there emerged from the bushes two zebras, which majestically walked past the cone-shaped hill I sat upon ; but I let them pass unharmed, as I could not find the heart to spoil so grand a picture.

Coming down from the hill, we soon reached a huge nullah, at the bottom of which trickled a small river which joined the Webbi Shebeyli close at hand. To the bottom of this nullah we essayed to march, intending to follow its course to the big river, which we wished to cross. But we

utterly failed to find a pass for the camels to get down.
We set to work to make one. We made stepping-stones of
rock where it was steep, we hauled rocks out of the path,
we cut down dozens of trees and cleared huge branches and
roots out of the way to make a road ; but do what we would,
the camels utterly refused to come down, and after pushing,
pulling, hitting, coaxing, and swearing at them, in turn, we
had to turn round (a matter of great difficulty in the
narrow path down the precipitous rocks), and go up again
and encamp at the top of the nullah. There I found that
my bearer whom I had sent to look for game was missing,
but he eventually turned up and reported having seen
water-buck at the top of the nullah.

In the afternoon I walked down the side of the steep,
rocky nullah to get my first sight of the Webbi Shebeyli.
The rock here was covered with cactus as in the Daghato
Valley. As I neared the river I found the water entirely
hidden from view by a dense forest of rich trees, including
three sorts of palm, the first of their kind I had as yet seen
in Somaliland. The scenery here reminded me of the rich
vegetation of Ceylon, one of the most beautiful countries
after Scotland, to my thinking, in the world. Butterfly
life swarmed here, and setting two men busy with nets,
I proceeded to the water's edge with great difficulty
through the almost impenetrable jungle which lined the
river-banks.

The river Shebeyli was here about as wide as the
Thames at Reading, and flowed about 4 feet deep. On
either side of the river towered steep rocky hills covered
with bush. On the sandy bank of the river I noticed the
curious spoor of the hippopotamus coming out of the water
at night to feed on the luxuriant grass growing on the
banks of the river. I had a most delicious bath in some
shallow water, which was marred, perhaps, by suddenly
discovering the distinct form of a large crocodile imprinted
on the sand just where I had left my clothes ! There it
was, head, tail, feet—a perfect fossil-like spoor ! The im-

print of the foot, which had four toes, measured 3½ inches long by 2 inches broad.

After fetching down some nuts from the palm-trees, which turned out to be as hard as bricks, and photographing the river, I wended my way through a beautiful little forest of palms, and then went through another almost impenetrable thicket of trees, creepers, and undergrowth, under which we were often obliged to crawl on our hands and knees. Coming to more open ground, I disturbed a small herd of water-buck, and was lucky enough to get in a shot at the old male, bringing him down with a crash. He had a long shaggy coat and fine horns.

The next day I sent men all along the top of the gorge, to look for a pass down which we might take the camels, in order to cross the river. Others I sent in different directions to look for elephants, and collect birds and butterflies. I went out myself in front of the men along the top of the nullah. It turned out to be a very hot day, the temperature at noon reaching 117° Fahrenheit. From the top of a small hill we spied a rhinoceros slowly walking along. We descended, and found him still on the move. It was very difficult to keep pace with him on the rocky ground, as if one advanced too quickly the noise made would be sure to scare off the game. At length he stopped to feed where the bush was very thick. As I could see but his head and neck, I crawled within a few yards of him, and took aim at his neck; but my rifle shot high, and I suppose the bullet went over it, for he went off snorting loudly, like a steam-engine, and raising clouds of dust as he rumbled over the stones. We found no blood, yet I could hardly believe I had missed the huge brute at such dreadfully close quarters.

I found rhinoceros-shooting very exciting and dangerous work. After the shot you never knew in which direction he would make his headlong charge to get away; and as his sight is always extremely bad, he was just as likely to make straight for you as in the opposite direction. He is certainly very easy to stalk, if the wind is blowing from him to you.

A minute or two after firing at the rhinoceros, we came to a hole in the rock, full of very brackish water. We were talking loudly round it, when suddenly, from behind some thorn-bushes, about 15 yards off, sprang, or rather blundered, two rhinoceros, which careered away at a great pace. We could hear the rumbling of stones for several seconds. Whilst kneeling down and peering under the bushes, I beheld them staring in every direction, but before I could get close enough to make a certain shot, they made off among the bushes. After this we walked along a dried-up watercourse, as far as the foot of Mount Culdush, a path probably untrodden hitherto by white man's foot. Here we found that a large herd of elephants had been at work two or three days before, scratching holes in the sandy river-bed, searching for water.

The havoc made by these animals was extraordinary. Branches torn down and stripped of their bark lay in every direction. Large trees had been literally torn up by the roots and hurled aside, and were left to die stretched lengthwise on the stony ground. Every now and then the elephants had rested in a small patch of thick bush. Here was a pretty mess. Branches all over the place, and the grass all trampled down.

Everywhere we went we found elephant spoor, but we were two days too late. Not an elephant remained behind, and we wended our way home, hot, tired, and disappointed. At night, when the camels came in, they were followed by a perfect swarm of tsetse fly. The sting of this fly, though harmless to human beings, is very painful, and made me jump every time I was bitten, as if a needle had been stuck half an inch into my flesh. One of my ponies was badly bitten on the 'billy,' his tail not being long enough to whisk the pests off. The Somalis said the pony would live until the next rain. We rubbed sheep's fat on the ponies and the camels every day.

It is an extraordinary sensation, coming into a belt of ' fly.' There may be but a tiny river-bed. On one side of it not a fly will be encountered, but walk a dozen feet and they suddenly come buzzing by one in hundreds.

We stayed by the river Shebeyli for some days trying to get the camels down the nullah, but all to no purpose ; we could not find a suitable place, and after having good sport with oryx, bush-buck, water-buck, and other game, I decided to go back, my supplies getting short, and many of my followers contracting fever by the river. So, breaking up the camp, I marched away from the river northwards again, after being greatly disappointed at not being able to find one single elephant. We had not proceeded far when we cut the fresh spoor of a rhinoceros, which I determined to follow. The spoor led us east for a long way through pretty thick bush. At length, when I was beginning to get tired out, I caught a glimpse of Mr. Borele quietly walking along in front of us, his great gray back showing up well in the sunlight, and his armpits and parts of his neck tinged with a faint blush of red, which showed up stronger in some lights than in others. On and on he walked, heeding nothing, and never lifting his head. How unlike an antelope, now nibbling a blade of grass, now quickly raising his head, and ever on the *qui vive !*

We continued to walk close after him, as quiet as mice, as if we were part of a funeral procession following a huge hearse, instead of a party of men stalking big game with beating hearts and full-cocked triggers. At last he slowly turned and offered his broadside. The anxious moment had arrived. Quickly kneeling and ' drawing a bead ' for his heart, I pressed the trigger. Looking under the great volume of smoke, I saw that I had knocked him backwards upon his haunches. Bang ! and another spherical ball went crashing through his ribs close by the first. This last knocked him clean off his four feet, and he lay on his side, plunging, snorting, banging his huge head and horns upon the ground, and kicking up the dust in his vain endeavours

to regain his legs.   But he was by no means done for yet.
I sent a ·450 solid through his neck, which quieted him,
and my shikari ran down to cut his throat.   But no!
With a fearful effort, the huge beast almost regained his
feet, and, falling back into a half-sitting position, brandished
his formidable-looking horns about in threatening fashion.
Fearing if he regained his legs there might be trouble in
store for some of us, I again seized the eight-bore, and,
running right up to him, finished his awe-inspiring struggles
with a bullet through the neck.

As we were now a long way from the main caravan, I
sent my syce on the pony to fetch a camel to carry his
head and hide.   This animal measured 11½ feet long ; girth
9½ feet.   His anterior horn measured 16½ inches, and the
posterior horn 7 inches, in length.   Whilst following the
caravan we fell in with an incredible number of 'rhino'
spoors, and a few old elephant tracks.   The latter had
evidently left the country.   In the west the lightning was
flashing every night, and this the elephants had followed.
For lightning means rain, and rain means fresh green grass
and tender shoots upon the thorn-trees, whereas here it
was all burnt up, and there was a general atmosphere of
drought.   As my shikaris truly said, ' Dar aliphint is all
same wind, now here, den dare.'   We at length found the
camel's spoor, and after tracking it for several miles came
upon the camp pitched near Boholo Deno.

After several hours of sawing, hacking, and cutting at
the 'rhino's' head, my men managed to sever the horns
from the skull, not before they had broken my saw and
snapped a heavy chisel into two pieces!   They were
getting tired of work, it was easy to see, by the grumbling
and growling that went on every day, and the careless way
in which they loaded the camels and attended to the big
game trophies.   I was obliged to watch the latter with the
greatest care, as the ravages made by a little beetle-grub
upon the skins were terrible.   I also discovered that part
of the head of one rhinoceros was going rotten, and was

full of maggots, and I only saved it in time with hot wood-ashes mixed with alum and saltpetre.

After leaving the river butterflies were scarce, but other insect life positively swarmed. There were black ants from $\frac{1}{8}$ inch to 1 inch in length; there were brown ants, red ants, and cream-coloured ants. There were grasshoppers innumerable, one of which reminded me of a yellow-underwing moth. Another beauty had its upper wings of a brilliant emerald green; another had its upper wings of green and chocolate brown, with under wings of a fiery red. Unfortunately the colours of these fade dreadfully after death. Then there were the marvellous 'stick' insects, which you would never see unless they moved, so much do they resemble a piece of stick, the branches of which are its legs! The longest I caught measured 5 inches.

Spiders were 'very fine and large;' one monster of a dull reddish-brown which ran across the floor of my tent at Berbera I have never ceased to regret not having been able to capture. Another common but very local spider, which builds a huge web strung between two bushes, has a black body with yellow bars meeting in the centre of the back. Beetles in Somaliland are very numerous, reptiles few, with the exception of small lizards in the sand. There are but three common snakes, two of which were said to be very deadly.

According to the Somali, the Webbi Shebeyli flows into Egypt's Nile. This, of course, is ridiculous, as it flows towards the east coast of Africa, in entirely the opposite direction. It is supposed never to reach the sea, but loses itself in a large swamp know as Lake Batti.

A word about storing insects. Butterflies travel best in little triangular pieces of paper. One butterfly only should be put into each paper. Moths and insects with long brittle legs and antennæ should be pinned in store boxes on one side of the box only, the other side having a sheet of cotton-wool pinned to it, in which, in the event of a moth or leg of a beetle becoming detached, it will be caught and kept from being broken.

Next day we marched towards the zebra plain again, and as we proceeded down-wind the whole day, sport was in consequence but poor. We tracked a rhinoceros for a long way, but he ultimately got our wind and decamped. The same thing happened when we saw four zebra. As we marched, one of my camels, which had contracted a bad sore back from being carelessly loaded, fell down and utterly refused to get up again. I was obliged to shoot it and march on. I took its head as a trophy. This was the third camel I had lost since leaving Berbera. My caravan always looked an imposing spectacle when on the march, the camels being tied together in long strings, the tail of the foremost being attached to the head of the second, and so on down the line, which often reached a distance of upwards of half a mile.

Next morning we marched north and crossed the spoor of three ' rhino ' all walking together, but the noise of the camel-men, who were not far behind us, must have disturbed them, as we soon afterwards found by the tracks that they were running on ahead of us. At length we emerged out of the bush upon an open plain, and saw three full-grown rhinoceros at full gallop enter the bush on the opposite side. As there was a large herd of oryx on the move on the plain, I left the bigger animals, having had quite enough of ' rhino '-shooting. The oryx had fled from the ' rhino,' and would pass us some few hundred yards off. I ran hard to get to some bushes, from which I should have had a grand chance, but I could not get there in time. When I reached the shelter, they had all gone past, and firing at their retreating forms, I missed clean both barrels !

Whilst we were looking at the track to see if we could find any blood, Nur Telegrapho (or whatever our guide's name was) suddenly ran away from us with all his might. When I asked for an explanation of this extraordinary performance, my shikari said that he had heard a bird

' calling,' by following which he hoped to find honey.
Presently we heard a whistle, and running up found ' Nora'
contemplating a tall ants' nest 8 or 9 feet high, with
a huge grin on his ugly face. On closer inspection I
perceived a lot of bees crawling in and out of holes in the
pillar of the old ants' nest. We were soon at work collecting dry sticks and grass, and lighting two bonfires to
windward of the pillar. We then by our collective weight
broke the pillar in two, and bolted as hard as we could go,
followed by a perfect swarm of bees, which stung us all over
from head to foot. Then, armed with torches of burning
wood and sticks, we approached the base of the ants' nest,
and with the aid of an axe got at some honey, which we
lifted out.

The fires had now caught the thick bush round the nest,
and, blazing up to an immense height, forced us to beat a
hasty retreat, with the exception of ' Nora,' who, armed with
his axe, and standing absolutely naked, surrounded by
flames, remained hacking away at the ants' nest, and every
now and then putting his hand into the hole and producing
more honey, whilst above and upon his head swarmed the
bees. Up his naked back they crawled in hundreds, and
little did he seem to care or notice the stings, except that
every now and then he would stop for a second to scratch
himself.

The base of the hill was so hard that it was impossible to
break it, so we left what honey remained in it to the busy
little workers. After dusting off the bees which crawled
over the immense quantity we had collected, we put it in a
tobe, and as we walked away an onlooker would assuredly
have laughed heartily at our comical appearance, as we all
scratched away at the irritating stings we had received.
It was quite the most delicious-flavoured honey I had ever
tasted, but, then, the circumstances attending its capture
gave us a greater relish for it.

In the afternoon we encountered a lot of game, but as
we were going down-wind the whole time, and the caravan

was always close behind us, we made nothing of it.   Twice
our stalks after oryx and zebra were spoilt by my noisy
camel-men.   At length we reached the Bun Feroli again,
and saw upon it 'owl' gazelle in hundreds, and a few herds
of oryx; but as the water about here had nearly dried
up, the zebra had shifted their quarters.   On the way I
noticed very curious clouds of sand, sent up sometimes to a
height of 400 feet into the air by a whirlwind.   This sand-
cloud would often remain at this immense height in one
huge pillar, which would slowly drift along, not dispersing
for several minutes.   The great quantity of dust was caused
by the huge herd of camels which had lately been driven to
and from the wells at Gonsali.

CHAPTER IX.

Long crawl after oryx—Return of caravan from Berbera—Abundance of
game—Somali method of hunting elephants—Abyssinian zareba—
First encounter with Abyssinians—Fight with Midgans—Camp at
Jiggiga—Huge herds of game—Shooting hartebeest.

NEXT day I walked over an immense area of ground
where, when I was here last, I had seen a great number of
oryx. To-day there was not one. They had all been
disturbed by the large villages established just before I
left the place for the Webbi Shebeyli. The 'owl' were
also so wild that I could not get near enough for a shot.
I sent four men to the Nagob Mountains, to look for koodoo
spoor, as on asking my shikari if koodoo lived there, he
answered : 'Nobardy go, nobardy know.' My head-shikari
now got fever badly, and had to be left at home.

On looking over my trophies, I discovered to-day that
another of my 'rhino' heads, which utterly refused to dry,
had become infested with maggots, and the skin had begun
to 'smile' badly, as my shikari put it. I was just in time
to stop it going altogether with alum and saltpetre. Whilst
attending to my skins I saw an ostrich strutting about upon
the plain. I sent the pony round him to try either to over-
haul him or drive him round to me. You might just as well
try to stop an express train. He was off in the twinkling
of an eye.

I went out in the afternoon upon the plain, and saw four
oryx, which I stalked, or, rather, crawled at, in the open.
I crawled about 400 yards in full view of them, enduring
agonies the whole time from thorns in my hands and knees.
Thump, thump, thump went my heart against my ribs with

excitement, as I tried at last to get a steady aim upon one. I pulled the trigger, and the oryx fell as if struck by lightning, and never moved again. I deserved a kill after such a crawl. The oryx had a magnificent head, its horns measuring 32 inches in length, my best having been 33½ inches. The bullet had gone right through the shoulder, which in my experience kills much quicker than a bullet placed *behind* the shoulder.

On coming home I found I had three men and a boy in hospital with fever, and two men with sore legs, and several others I physicked because they had shown temper.

Next day I walked through thick bush and disturbed an oryx, which I perceived was wounded in one of his fore-legs. Seeing he was making for an open plain, I sent my syce after him on the pony, and so well did the boy make him gallop, that he stopped the oryx right in the middle of the open. I was running hard after my second shikari, who was carrying my rifle, when the silly idiot of a man let a large bush swish back right into both my eyes, rolling me head over heels backwards. I felt as if I had been suddenly struck blind. I sat down, and for upwards of half an hour I could not open my eyes, and when at last I did so I could see very indistinctly.

As I sat in agony, up came my syce with a distressing story of how the oryx had broken bay, that he had again run it to a standstill by the edge of the bush, and had then shouted for my shikari to come up and shoot it. The fool of a man, instead of stalking it—which he could have done with the greatest ease under cover of the bushes—ran right out upon it in the open, when it broke the bay again, and slowly trotted into the thick bush, where it was impossible to follow it on horseback. I then rode the pony, which was led for me, home. After several hours of intense pain, I managed, by drawing all the curtains of my tent, and so keeping out the strong light, to get a little sleep. When I awoke I could see fairly well up to 30 yards or so, but after that all was blank.

Being very much put out at losing the oryx, and knowing there were more about, I perhaps rather imprudently
sallied forth again about 4 p.m. The sun was very trying
to my eyes, and I was thinking of returning, as I rode
along with my eyes shut, when the eagle eye of my syce
spotted a herd of oryx near some bushes, a long way out
on the plain. Getting him to lead the pony towards them,
I shut my eyes, to save them for the shot. We were
obliged to remain behind some bushes several minutes, to
allow some ' owl' gazelle to pass. On proceeding, my
shikari suddenly shouted, 'Come down from the horse!'
and after crawling through some bushes exclaimed, ' There !'
I opened my eyes, but could see nothing. I blew my
nose : still I saw no game. Everything seemed to wobble
in the hot sun. At last I made out an indistinct form in
the haze, and, straining my eyes to the utmost, fired at it,
after which I could hear nothing but, 'Well done, sare !
your bullets is good, your bundook is good,' and a great
rumbling of hoofs, as the herd galloped off. Thoroughly
pleased with my blind shot, I went and hid my aching eyes
in the middle of a thick thorn-bush, out of the hateful glare
of the merciless sun. On opening them half an hour afterwards, I was delighted to find I could see much better, and
rode home with the oryx horns tied on the back of my saddle,
and sticking into my back at every step, in the best of spirits.

During the morning I saw a koodoo, with fine horns, in
the thick bush by the edge of the plain, and stalked an
ostrich out in the open, without success.

When we were all in camp in the afternoon, we heard a
shot fired a long way to the north of us. Fearing it was
Abyssinians, I sent out a scouting-party, which soon returned
with the caravan of four camels I had sent to Berbera a
month ago for fresh supplies of food. The men came in
and pressed my hand, saying : ' Salaam, sahib.' They
brought me a whole budget of letters from Europe, Asia,
Africa, and America. I got my hair cut by the cook, who
had improvised a comb of porcupine quills he had picked

up for the occasion.   My word! it was a painful operation.
He would persist in sticking the sharp quills well into my
head ; he also had a knack of taking up a lock of hair
with the comb, cutting half of it off with the scissors, and
pulling the other half out by the roots!   When it was
over, and I looked at the result in the glass—well, I never
was a beauty before, but now—' Larf! I thought I
should 'a doid !' There was no hair left.   Between rows
of long white furrows a few short bristles stood up, as
though to mock me.

Next day I spent the whole morning tracking the fresh
spoor of a lion, but could not find the animal himself.
Coming home I disturbed a huge spotted hyæna, which
was crouching in a bush close to my sheep.   During
breakfast the men had a row among themselves about
the ownership of the sheep-skins.   The cook, seizing a
large carving-knife, and brandishing it on high, shouted
in a loud tone that they all belonged to him.   Before he
had stood there two seconds, about half a dozen men fell
upon him, knocking him head-over-heels into a cooking-pot
of boiling water, and throwing his carving-knife right over
the zareba.   A general mêlée ensued, some taking the cook's
part—goodness only knows why—and some taking the
opposition.   Knives were used freely, but I managed, by
rushing in between the parties unarmed, to quell the riot
before any serious damage had been done to anybody.

As we were short of meat, I devoted my afternoon to
riding down ' owl ' gazelle, and shooting from horseback.
Singling out a large herd of old bucks, I soon cantered up
level with them ; but as the pony refused to be brought to
a standstill, I was obliged to fire at them at the gallop.
After several ineffective shots, I got in a marvellous right
and left, both animals dying instantaneously, and after
another long gallop I shot a third.   Having now enough
meat for the men, I returned home, much pleased with the
behaviour of the pony under fire.   On coming back I
wished to see the new bags of rice, and found that they had

brought three less than I had ordered them to bring. Then
came a grand story, how the caravan had been attacked by
Midgans (a low-caste tribe of Somali), who had stolen the
three bags of rice, how my men had fired at them, and
eventually they had dispersed, leaving behind them a
quiver full of poisoned arrows, which they now brought me
as proof of the veracity of their statements. My boy, who
was the only man with any pretensions to truth, honestly
told me some days after that this story had all been
arranged for the men by my headman, who had ordered
them to sell the three bags of rice and give him the pro-
ceeds !

The arrows used by the Midgan hunters have a barbed
iron head ; under the barb the poison is stuck on like black
glue ; the shaft is then stuck into a thin stick, and made
tight with a bit of hide. The quivers are made of wood,
with gerenook-hide sewn round them ; to the quiver is
attached a knife in a sheath, a stone for sharpening arrow-
barbs, and a pointed tool for mending sandals. The bows
were ordinary pieces of bent wood, with the gut of some
antelope for string. The poison used on the arrows is
obtained from the sap of a certain tree.

Next day I left Bun Feroli an hour before sunrise, and
when it was light we found ourselves surrounded by game
—three lots of oryx, gerenook, ' big ' or ' pork ' (wart hog),
zebra, and endless herds of ' owl.' I stalked a herd of oryx
with great care, and knocked one over, when they dashed
off in every direction, with the exception of one old fellow
who, after staring at me for a moment, put his head down
and his tail up, and charged me at a gallop ! I had but
one cartridge in my rifle, so I waited until he was close
upon me, when I put the bullet in the very centre of his
chest, knocking him right back upon his haunches, and then
he fell over on his side. I never saw an antelope charge in
such a deliberate manner before, and I think I had a very
lucky escape from being badly hurt, if not killed. On
looking for the first which I had knocked over, we failed to

find him or a blood track anywhere, and were at length
obliged to give it up.   The zebra (three of them) watched
our approach from the very centre of an open plain, but I
could not get near enough to make sure of killing and not
merely wounding, so I did not shoot at them.   One stallion
left the others, and went off into the bushes.   I pursued
him for a long way, seeing him every now and then, but
he finally dodged me on stony ground.

Next day we encamped in my guide's village—a place

called Affira.   I wanted to buy a pair of elephant tusks he
had here, but he would not sell them, as he feared the
Abyssinians, who considered that any ivory killed in
Somaliland belonged to them.   Here I saw incredible herds
of camels.   In the evening we reached the river Sucut, and
found a little water.   We watched for zebra at night by
some wells, but none came to drink, and the mosquitoes
finally drove me away.   I paid off my guide, Nora Telegrapho Korfdrop, and gave him a present.   He was a most
amusing old man, quiet, and a good tracker—a totally

different character from Somalis who have much intercourse with white men. Four of my men now had fever, and had to be carried on camels, and I suffered terribly from diarrhœa and prickly heat, which prevented my sleeping at night.

In the morning, through bad stalking on the part of my shikari, four zebra got our wind and made off. Owing to bad shooting on my part, soon after the same zebra escaped again.

After seeing a great number of koodoo tracks without seeing the animals themselves, we pitched for the mid-day rest on the bank of the dried-up river Sule, which runs into the Daghato River, which runs into the Shebeyli River, which runs—goodness only knows where ! By means of digging with spears for the space of an hour, we made a hole upwards of 4½ feet deep, and produced some of the dirtiest, sandiest water I ever beheld.

It is a pretty sight to watch the men baling out the water into buckets as they sing or chant, when up trot the ponies, sheep and donkeys to be watered, all knowing the song so well : ' Ho-a ho-ah, te da ta jummy, eh ali ya ha, ho elli yo ha !' (Drink, pretty creature, drink !)

We had not had a drop of rain for a month. Here I met a Somali elephant-hunter. Their manner of hunting these great pachyderms is as follows : Several men, each mounted on a good fast pony, approach a herd of elephants as near as possible, when they all throw their spears at one they have singled out. The infuriated animal then charges and pursues one of the mounted men, when another man with a long Abyssinian sword gallops up behind and endeavours to hamstring the elephant. If the elephant turns round and pursues this man, the first man pursues in his turn, and endeavours to disable the brute from behind. At length the poor bleeding animal sinks to the earth, and is despatched with the stabbing spear, but woe betide any man who approaches too close to the dying beast's trunk. With the great influx of hunters into Somaliland in the last few years, the game has shifted further and further

west, and he is a clever and a lucky man who kills an
elephant now in Somaliland.

That evening, as I was having my bath, my shikari
suddenly seized my rifle, and, shouting 'Hyæna coming
wells!' dashed out of my tent. I followed clothed in a pair
of slippers, but when we got to the wells the hyæna had
vanished.

I was driven nearly frantic every night now by prickly
heat, which was worse than a hundred thousand mosquito-
bites! At this place I killed the very curious Paradise
Whydah bird, a pretty little black and buff bird with a
long tail of four feathers, and two rounded feathers where
the tail joins the body. This bird flies very slowly through
the air, beating its wings with great rapidity, as it would
appear, to propel its enormous tail along.

We marched the whole of the next day along the dried-
up Sule River bed, and disturbed three koodoo cows which
were grazing on the bank.

During the morning we met a caravan which reported
that a lion had killed two women the night before in a
village half a day's march off. One of the women he had
taken bodily off and eaten for his supper. We saw several
lion tracks in the river-bed, but the animals themselves still
kept out of my way.

At night six of my men were down with fever. As they
all had to be carried, the camels were in consequence
terribly overladen, rendering quick marching impossible.
My stock of quinine was now rapidly diminishing every day.
The whole of the next day we marched up the Sule River
bed. Early in the morning a hyæna ran across the river,
but I missed him as he was disappearing in the bushes on
the opposite side. After this we did not see a single head of
game for the remainder of the day.

At mid-day we rested and watered the camels at some
deep wells dug in the river-bed at a place called Megadaha-
mado. Here was to be seen a large and well-built zareba
which had been erected by Abyssinians some six years

before, when they wished to annex this territory. The zareba had been built of very high trunks of thorn-trees, stuck firmly in the ground close together. Within the zareba were a number of beautifully-built huts—one might almost call them houses, some were so large. They were all built of bent thorn branches tied together. These huts were of various shapes and sizes, according to the rank of the occupants. The headman of the embassy had a magnificent hut, large and roomy, and supported in the middle by huge tree-trunks. The second in command of the expedition had a smaller one, and so on, down to the ordinary huts of the camel-men. All were carefully thatched with grass. There still remained the seats erected outside the huts, where the men sat in the morning and in the afternoon out of the sun. Everything looked as if built but yesterday, except that the roof of the headman's hut had fallen in.

A large caravan of camels, sheep, goats, cows and calves, came to these wells to drink. The wealth of animals possessed by the Somalis is astonishing. No wonder the Abyssinians find it a paying game to come down upon them and loot them. One of my men brought me a chameleon fixed firmly at the end of a stick, with its claws and tail clasped round it. All the men went in great fear of it, and were much surprised when I handled it. As I had no spirits to bottle it in, I was obliged, in order to skin it, to hit it on the head, when from a bronze colour it turned perfectly green, as well it might, poor beast! The skin of a lizard sticks with remarkable firmness at the back of the neck and on the head itself, and you are indeed a good skinner if you can take off the whole skin without tearing it.

In the afternoon I went out bird-collecting, as there was no big game about to 'mek blued' (kill). Early next morning we at last left the Sule River bed.

Jiggiga, a place situated on a large plain, to which I was bound, was now reported five days' march off. During the

day I saw several fresh rhinoceros tracks, but not a head
of game did I encounter. On the following day a very
strong wind blew all the morning, and it turned out to be
the coldest noon I have ever experienced in Somaliland. I
literally shivered in the shade at breakfast-time. Light,
fleecy clouds did not entirely obscure the sun's rays, so I
was at a loss to account for the sudden change of temperature. The country had changed from thick bush to hills
covered with long, burnt-up grass, with a thin sprinkling
of trees. In the afternoon we descended several hundred
feet, when the temperature rose again, until it became
unbearably hot. During the day we saw very little game.
Fever was now rapidly abating in our ranks, but I was
still obliged to tramp it on foot and allow one sick man to
ride a pony, the other pony being sick. All next day we
marched through the most game-forsaken country I had
ever had the bad luck to pass through ; there was not even
a game-bird to be seen. I had now traversed some hundred
miles without bagging a single head.

From the top of a considerable rise we got a good view
of the surrounding country. Range upon range of hills,
thickly covered with trees, stretched out before us, and in
the valleys were open plains covered with long, burnt-up
grass. I thought to myself : ' Well, at any rate, we shall
see game this afternoon.' We now heard two signal-shots
fired by the main caravan, but it was utterly impossible
even then to make out where they were, in such a labyrinth
of nullahs on all sides. I told my boy, who happened to
be with me, to fire my shot-gun as a signal. ' Ba—bang !'
went the gun, and the next thing I saw was Master Ali
Deria sprawling on his back ! He had fired both barrels
off at once, which had knocked him clean off his pins ! At
length, on descending, we found the caravan and pitched
for the mid-day rest on a long, open plain, covered with
dried-up grass. Here, probably owing to the absence of
dew and rain, not an ' owl' gazelle was to be seen,
although it appeared to me to be an ideal place for them.

We had just finished unloading, and had turned the camels off to feed, when my cook, whilst lighting a fire to cook my breakfast, set fire to some long grass to windward of my whole kit. The grass being extremely dry, enabled the fire to literally race along. All my stores, food for the men, trophies, camel-mats, water, everything, appeared in the utmost danger of being consumed. Yelling at the men, I managed to collect them all together, when we kept up a perfect storm of sand upon the flames, as they crept closer and closer to the stores. Would it reach them ? I urged on the men with shouts and cheers, and working with a will, we just extinguished the flames when within a few feet of the whole of my effects !

All the afternoon we marched through the grassy plains, but not an antelope did I set eyes upon. I noticed, however, some old tracks of elephants and a few rhinoceros. Owing to prickly heat I could not sleep a wink, and next morning, after marching through open grass plains again, we reached a large village, called Abbas Gool, south of the Webbi Jerrar. Around this village I saw enormous herds of sheep, goats, mules, horses, donkeys, and cattle. There must have been several thousand milch cows ! Here we fell in for the first time with Abyssinians. They were a party of soldiers collecting taxes in the shape of cattle, sheep, and camels, from their wretched subjects, the Somalis. The Somalis were delighted to see us, and of course wanted us to join in an attack upon their persecutors. However, things went fairly quietly, the Abyssinians being very pleasant. I sat in state and held a levée, when the headman of the Abyssinians, followed by the whole of his armed force, approached, bringing me as a present two very fat sheep and several gallons of cow's milk, all of which, by-the-by, they had looted from the Somalis ! I placed two sentries to see that there was no ' hokey-pokey,' and offered the Abyssinian headman some *tobes* and a bottle of ' fizz.' But the headman shook his head and refused to take anything. He was a very handsome man and very tall, as was also his interpreter, but I cannot say the same of his followers, who presented a ridiculous appearance, dressed half after the manner of the East and half European. They carried rifles and scimitars, cartridge-belts full of long, steel-bulleted cartridges, dirty white trousers which reached a little below the knees, large rings in their ears, Oriental *tobes*, and white sun-helmets. They reminded me somewhat of the ridiculous figures cut by the Japanese of to-day, who walk about in long flowing dressing-gowns and sandals, with crushed-in billycock hats upon their heads. After a long conversation, spoken in a mixture of Abyssinian, Somali, French, English, and Italian, about where we were each going, and from whence we had each come, the Abyssinians informed me that they were going to fight all those Somalis who refused to pay taxes, and annex their country ! They departed at length after a great deal of salaaming, bowing and scraping, shaking of hands, and saluting.

In the afternoon we marched from the village. I was about to mount my best pony, when my syce said : ' No, dar boney got bit smarshed !' On examining him, I found he had contracted a dreadful sore back. After several false starts we were obliged to take a guide, and pitched for the night at the Webbi Jerrar. Here we found that the lioness reported with ' four little boys ' (cubs) was, as usual, a Somali fairy-tale, but a lion had been heard of a month ago, or a year ago—it was not quite clear which ! Early next morning (about 3 o'clock) we marched in the moonlight, accompanied by a pack of howling hyænas.

When the sun at length rose, I found we were still in fairly open country, covered with long grass and a thin sprinkling of trees. During the morning we saw several herds of gerenook, mostly females, and one herd of oryx, which were very shy. After the mid-day rest the heat became terrific, and I walked along, panting and perspiring out of every pore. Thick clouds appeared to the north of us, and it soon became apparent that we were walking into a thunderstorm. It suddenly burst upon us with a terrific downpour of rain, the first rain we had experienced for thirty-six days.

In five minutes after parting with the intense heat, I was shivering with cold, wet through and through. As we were obliged to wait for the camels to come up, I sat under the partial shelter of some trees for two whole hours. The lightning seemed to run along the ground all round us, and hiding my rifle under a bush, I kept at a respectful distance from it, expecting, nevertheless, to be struck at every moment. The camels at last coming up, and the rain ceasing, we pitched camp, when I was very glad to change into dry clothes. Shortly after rain fell again in torrents, which so soaked the whole of my kit that next morning we were obliged to wait until 9 o'clock before we could load up.

Some of the camel-men now gave a lot of trouble, and attacked, for some unknown reason, a party of Midgans whom they happened to meet. I was ahead of the caravan at the time, when I beheld the Midgans running hard after us. We stopped, and, loading our rifles, awaited events. They dropped their bows and poisoned arrows, and, walking boldly up to us, showed us a man with a tooth knocked out, and another with a spear-hole through his hand. I waited until the caravan came up, to discover if what they alleged was true, as the Somali is always a champion liar when he thinks he can make a little backsheesh. I found out that it was about six of one and half a dozen of the other, and there seemed to have been a considerable fight, in which my men had with difficulty held back their fire. I ultimately settled their disputes and marched on, lecturing my men well, in spite of their swearing that they had been first attacked by the Midgans. Shortly after this I caught my donkey-boy brutally ill-treating one of the donkeys, so I had him tied up to a tree, and gave him a thundering good hiding with a whip made of a rhinoceros hide.

After passing a large village called Bertira, which possessed

a large flock of ostriches, both old and young, I shot a
couple of guinea-fowl for the pot, and at length, after an
eight hours' march, reached Bun Jiggiga, an enormous
open plain bounded by high hills on the west, behind which
lay the Abyssinian town of Harrar.   Here I determined to
remain for several days to rest, as we had been on the
march for eleven days, during which time we must have
traversed upwards of 200 miles, through a game-forsaken
country.   We encamped on the face of an incline, overlooking the great open plain, and saw below us a large
encampment of Abyssinians, surrounded by a stockade.   We
had been pitched but an hour, when some men I had sent to
the wells with camels for water came running back, saying
they had been attacked by Abyssinians.   The latter had
drawn their swords, rushed at them, and tried to prevent
them from drinking.   Daggers were drawn, and a hand-
to-hand battle took place ; but, luckily, very little blood
was shed on either side.   That was the beginning of our
stay at Jiggiga.

Shortly after I saw the headman of the Abyssinians
emerge from the stockade followed by a large escort.   'Now
for it !' I thought, as I bustled about, looking to the rifles
and ammunition.   But on their nearer approach I perceived
that they came in peace, and not for war.

The headman came into my tent and said ' Salaam ' in a
most pleasant manner.   He said he was much annoyed at
his men's conduct, and was going to punish them.   He said
he was very glad to see me, and asked what I had come for,
when I explained that my only object was to shoot big game
upon the open plain.   He told me I was quite welcome, and
hoped I would stay a long time with him.   He then took
his departure, followed by his escort.

' Well, that's a bit of all-right,' I said to myself on his
departure.

He had hardly got outside the zareba, when another
terrific thunderstorm burst upon us, and before I could say
' knife,' a small river ran through my tent and wetted

everything through and through. Oh, how utterly
detestable rain is when living in a tent! Damp clothes,
rusty rifles, damp blankets, and a cold supper. I awoke
after a very damp night to find it still raining. It was also
extremely cold, and I sat in my tent enveloped in a 'sweater'
and great-coat, feeling very miserable.

I kept an eye outside the zareba, where, the night
before, I had seen two very daring jackals. Presently one
walked slowly round the zareba. Picking up a rifle, I
knocked him right over, but after giving vent to a series of
sharp barks he made off, hotly pursued by half a dozen
Somalis armed with spears. But he finally ran to earth
before they could stop him.

Soon after this the sheep and goats ran bleating into the
zareba, closely followed by three red-and-white dogs. I
was in the act of seizing my rifle, when my headman
shouted that they belonged to the Abyssinians. They were
very like Chinese 'chow-chow' dogs, or collies, with long,
bushy tails curled over their backs. We drove them off at
the point of the spear, fearing they would make off with
what little meat we had hanging up in camp. On sighting
the dogs, the donkeys cocked their tails and ' did a guy,' and
brayed as if their hearts would break.

The next little bit of excitement on this otherwise dull
day was the arrival of the headman of the Abyssinians
with his escort again, bearing as a present for me a very fat
sheep and several gallons of fresh cow's milk. I sat him
down in my only chair, and gave him half a bottle of ' fizz,'
as the poor old chap was nearly wet through with his walk
from the plain. He begged for some quinine for another
headman who had that day arrived from Harrar sick. I gave
him three dozen pills and some mustard plasters. After a
long parley through interpreters, he shook hands, said
' Salaam,' and departed, much to the delight of my wretched
sentries, who had been standing outside my tent in the
rain ' at the shoulder' during the whole of the interview.

The temperature at noon was 69° Fahrenheit. All the

afternoon it rained hard, so the Somalis set to work propping up sticks, over which they threw the camel-mats, and, having lighted small fires of damp wood in these extempore huts, sat huddled together shivering. I sent 'a present down to the Abyssinian headman, but it soon afterwards reappeared, having been declined with thanks. He sent a message asking me to send him down my vessels, when he would fill them with fresh milk every morning, and send them back again. My pony, which had been so badly bitten by the tsetse-fly, was now evidently dying. He became much swollen, especially round the eyes and belly. He kept lying down and getting up again, and when the poor beast cropped grass he let it fall uneaten out of his mouth. I wanted to shoot it, but the Somalis persuaded me to leave it alone, saying that it might possibly recover if the rain ceased.

After a very damp night spent in a very damp bed, I awoke to find it still raining, and the hills to the west were obscured in a thick mist. However, at ten it cleared up, and so I sallied forth, armed with thick clothing, for it was very cold. I hired four men and horses to scour the open plain for lions, and behind us followed a perfect multitude of men, women and children, who intended to follow us, hoping to be given meat. It was a long walk down to the open plain, past countless herds of sheep and cattle belonging to the Abyssinians, who had looted them from the Somalis. We soon spied a single hartebeest walking slowly along, looking like a huge donkey. But get near him I could not. At length, as he mounted an ant-heap and so showed up clearly, I let him have it at very long range. I hit him high up the fore-leg, but he got away at such an amazing pace that my pony never got within 100 yards of him, and when he ran down a gentle slope my syce very prudently gave up the chase, as we had a long day before us.

After missing two hartebeest at long range, I ascended a gentle slope, from the top of which I saw four herds of

WALLER'S GAZELLE.   ZEBRA SKIN.   SWAYNE'S HARTEBEEST.
SŒMERRING'S GAZELLE.   KOODOO HORNS.   ORYX.
WILD ASS. ORYX. WILD ASS. LION CUB. RHINOCEROS.
GRÉVY'S ZEBRA.

hartebeest, numbering respectively twenty, twenty-five, seventy-five, and eighty-five. I had wished to bring a camel out with me, but that devil of a headman had for once overruled me, saying that, as the camel-mats were all wet through, they would give the animal a sore back. The result was, I could get nowhere near these huge herds. On topping a second rise, I beheld a herd of upwards of two hundred hartebeest, accompanied by about fifty 'owl' gazelle. Such a sight of game I had but dreamt of. These 'owl' gazelle were a great pest whilst we were stalking hartebeest, as they were invariably the first to start off, quickly followed by the larger game. Thus it happened in this case. Off went the 'owl,' hotly pursued by the hartebeest. The former galloped past me, and, seeing that the hartebeest were bent on following them, I ran as hard as I could to try and get within range.

It was a truly magnificent sight to see those two hundred gigantic antelopes gallop past—a sight which will never fade from my memory. They were a long way out, but luck combined with skill struck one in the neck, and he fell almost head over heels, stone-dead. The hartebeest is different from the oryx and 'owl,' in that he never gives you a good second chance. When hartebeest cross you, and you fire, they invariably turn and gallop off away from you, presenting their haunches only, whereas the 'owl' and oryx still keep going in their original direction. Having skinned my prize, and taken the best of the meat for the men, I gave the rest to the multitude which followed. They fed upon what remained of the carcase, like vultures, and hacked and pulled away at it until nothing remained but a few blood-stains and the contents of the stomach to tell the tale of a kill. Lungs, stomach, and intestines were all greedily snatched up by these poor wretches, and as they walked along with grinning faces, one or two would be observed to munch away at the raw meat, unable to wait to appease their hunger.

After this we encountered another large herd of harte-

beest, and lying flat in the grass on my stomach, I sent my
men round to try a drive ; but not knowing exactly where
I lay, the silly men drove them all away from me instead
of towards me.   We passed some huge rocks, which looked
exactly like haystacks in a large field.   Behind one of these
rocks was a pool of water, round which we found the fresh
spoor of a large lion.

Coming home I saw some Egyptian geese, which were as
tame as domestic geese, and several yellow jackals, the hind-
legs of one of which I broke, when he began howling
exactly like a little child, as he made off at a great pace.
I was soon alongside him on the pony, and, dismounting and
dodging him round some tiny bushes, I knocked him over
the head with my rifle-barrels.   This jackal is of a dirty
yellowish-fawn colour, and not nearly so handsome as the
silver-backed jackal I shot between Berbera and Hargaisa.
The sun shone out about noon, and a cool wind blew off the
mist and unveiled the beautiful blue mountains in the
west.

As I approached the zareba, my headman appeared at
the entrance with a huge grin upon his satanic countenance,
which I knew by experience meant bad news.   He met me,
saying : ' Dar boney dead !'   His loss put a decided damper
on an otherwise extremely pleasant day.

When I awoke next morning, or, rather, when I got out
of bed—for sleep I did not, owing to the unearthly howls of
innumerable jackals feeding upon my dead pony, and
frantic prickly heat—I looked out of my tent, and saw one of
my camels lying dead, killed by the tsetse-fly.

A party of Abyssinians called whilst I was having breakfast, and then I started for the plain.   My head-shikari, as
usual, had fever and could not come out.   I hired six horsemen to look for lions, and took out a stalking camel with me.
I was followed, as usual, by a huge crowd of villagers.   We
soon found a hartebeest, which ran across the stalking camel.
Telling the man who led it to walk on, I sat down and hit
the antelope behind the shoulder, when he behaved in a

most extraordinary manner, rushing forward and jamming his head into the ground with all his force, then turning round and repeating the performance several times. At last he fell over and died. Up ran a lot of men, who were attending the Abyssinians' cattle, and between them and the villagers there wasn't much left for the jackals. After this I tried all I knew to shoot another, but do what I could I was unsuccessful, and had to come home tired and foot-sore.

CHAPTER X.

NEXT day I was followed by a perfect multitude of half-starved men, women, and infants. When an animal fell the shouts and rush towards it can be imagined. They would then form themselves into a circle round my men who were engaged in skinning the dead animal, and often became quite a nuisance by hindering their occupation, jostling the operators in their anxiety to get the meat. I was obliged to draw a line round the skinners, and make the villagers understand that I would shoot any-one who dared to cross it. This generally kept them back, as they had a wholesome dread of my rifle, with which they had seen me kill an animal stone-dead at over 200 yards. When we had taken the best of the meat for the camp-followers at home, and the head and skin, there was always a mad rush upon the carcase by the crowd.

What a sight it was! The yells, the shouts, the curses, as each man with his huge dagger sought to cut off the biggest piece for himself! How they hacked at the car-case! How they pushed and shoved each other back! Every now and then a shriek would go up louder than the rest, as a man or boy received the sharp edge of another's dagger on his knuckles, as he held a corner of the bleeding carcase. One man would seize a large piece of ribs and run away with it, when he would be tackled by others, who raced after him, reminding me of a game of 'Rugger' football, except that the players always played such a selfish game, for they never 'passed.'

Whilst the biggest of these human vultures fought for the best meat, the little ones, sometimes but eight or ten years old, would do battle among themselves for the stomach, liver, lungs, entrails, etc., with no less fury. One day I took my camera out to photograph a fight, but the men, hearing what I was up to, stopped, and laughingly said, 'Oh, no Somali fight.' I had but to sit down and patiently wait a minute or two, when they would set to

NATIVES FIGHTING FOR MEAT.

work again tooth and nail, and I got in my snapshot. At the end of a battle I always made a point of taking some of the good meat secured by the big bullies, and giving it to the tiniest mites, who had secured nothing for themselves but a few yards of entrails. The army would then dig their spears through the meat, and thus carry it over their shoulders until, perchance, another beast fell to my rifle, when down would go the little bundles of meat, another rush would be made for us, and another battle would be fought. Sometimes from eighty to one hundred men, boys,

10

and tiny children would follow me the whole day, leaving
countless flocks and herds, which they were much too
miserly to slaughter, to the tender care of the much-
despised and overworked women at home.

For about a week I enjoyed excellent sport upon this
huge open plain, over which hung a haze looking like a
large lake in the distance. Each day I sent out men on
horseback in every direction to look for lions, but not a
single one did they find whilst I was encamped at Jiggiga.
Whilst trying to kill a wounded hartebeest, I nearly blew
my hand off with my revolver, the bullet grazing the skin!
Every night hyænas and jackals came in dozens to feed on
the rotten carcases of my pony and camel, but not a single
lion put in an appearance.

One day I saw a curious sight upon the plain. I had
knocked over a hartebeest, which lay apparently dead upon
its side, but on my shikari running up to it, in spite of my
shouts of warning, it got upon its legs, and made off at an
astonishing pace, and as my shikari was, of course, in the
way, I could not again fire. We followed him until he lay
down a long way off us. Suddenly, long before we got
anywhere near him, he jumped up and began turning round
and round, and for a long time I could not make out what
on earth he was playing at. At length I perceived that a
tiny little jackal was attacking him. The plucky little
animal was trying to down the great antelope. Every time
the hartebeest tried to run away, the jackal would jump up
high on to his haunches, and compel him to turn round and
use his horns to keep the smaller animal off. Round and
round the two kept turning for several minutes, the antelope always trying to keep his head to the jackal, the jackal
trying to leap upon the antelope's back. At length I got
within range of them, and was crouching in the grass to see
what would eventually happen, when the jackal caught a
glimpse of me, and made off, so I planted another bullet
into the now tired-out hartebeest, and grassed him. He
was a very fine, fat beast, with horns 22 inches between

the tips. The little jackal sat, about 300 yards off us, bolt upright upon its haunches, intently watching us skinning our prize, which had been so nearly his. When we had taken the skin, head, and as much of the meat as we could carry, we went off, when, on turning round, I could see the little beast crawling through the grass towards the carcase, evidently smacking his lips.

I now wended my way homewards, when, on ascending a small rise, covered with loose stones and thin thorn-bushes, I came upon three Somali plateau gazelle (*Gazella spekei*), sometimes known as *Gazella nasu*, from the extraordinary flaps of skin which rise up from the front of the face above the nose in a double or treble fold. This animal must not be confused with Pelzeln's gazelle, which inhabits the maritime plain near Berbera, and which is a totally different animal altogether.

I made a lucky shot at the best male, but the ·450 bullet made sad havoc of the skin; however, as we had now plenty of meat, and I only wished to possess a head trophy, I was satisfied. These pretty little gazelle run along wagging their short tails, and are constantly on the move. When they do stand, which is but seldom, they always appear to face one, so that at over 100 yards their tiny chests offer but a small mark.

Nearing home I saw a number of large bustard, an oryx, and several herds of hartebeest, all of which game proved too wild for a shot. Passing close by the Abyssinians' zareba, I thought I would go in and say good-bye to them. Accordingly, my shikari and I passed through the gateway of the stockade, over which flew three triangular flags, two white ones with a red one in between them. We found ourselves in a large enclosure. Passing several small huts, we reached that of the headman. It was made of mud, and thatched by Somalis. We were ushered through a hole in the mud, and found ourselves in utter darkness. My shikari then said, ' Gif him hand,' but, upon my soul, I couldn't see anyone to shake hands with. However, on pushing back

10—2

the sack which did duty for a door, a stream of light was
let in, which disclosed a kind of bed raised on sticks, upon
which lay an enormous man with a most repulsive face.
Someone let the sack fall back, and we were in darkness
once more.

At last they poked up a little fire on the mud floor, and
the man lying upon the bed stretched out his hand, which I
shook.   The poor fellow was evidently very ill, and probably
dying in this mud-hole, which had no ventilation whatever.
He pointed with a long, thin finger to a corner in the hut,
and on turning round I perceived the old man who had
treated me so well.   He begged me to be seated, and, seeing
nothing to sit down upon, I sat down upon the dirty floor.

I asked my old friend how the invalid was, and he replied,
'Dying.'   I sent my shikari home for some more pills and
some mustard leaves, and sat in silence in the hut until he
returned with them.   After examining the sick man by
the feeble light of the fire, I clapped a mustard plaster
on his chest, and sat down again upon the floor.   About
ten minutes afterwards the sick man half sat up, and began
to roar and gesticulate.   'What does he say?' I asked my
shikari.   He replied : ' He wants the devil removed !'
Whether he meant me or the mustard plaster I don't
know, but after a great deal of salaaming and shaking of
hands, I shortly afterwards took the hint and bowed
myself out.

How glad I was to get out of that dark and dismal hut,
and away from that agonized face, and to once more
breathe pure air !   As I passed between the huts, all the
Abyssinian women came out to have a look at the white
man, and I must say they were a much better-looking lot
than the Somali women.

As I was walking up to my camp, a poor little chap ran
after me, saying that the others had taken from him the
tiny bits of antelope meat he had been able to snatch, and,
showing his cut hands, began to cry bitterly.   This hard
little worker (he could not have been more than seven

years old) had fought bravely with the rest, to secure a rib
or two, with a knife as big as himself. He well deserved
the huge piece of good meat I gave him when I got back
into camp.

Next morning I left Jiggiga and marched north-east,
over rocky ground, for about twelve miles, when a man on
horseback galloped up, saying that two men from a village
beyond the Abyssinian stockade had stopped three lions for
me out in the open plain.

I held a council with my headman and shikaris, thinking
that he lied, as usual. He admitted that it would take us
all our time to get there before sunset, and stuck to it that
the lions were there right enough.

Whilst everyone was talking nineteen to the dozen, a
boy, by some means or other, got hold of one of my Express
rifles, cocked it, and pulled the trigger, the bullet whizzing
past close between me and my headman, and kicking up the
dust about 2 feet to my right. There was a simultaneous
rush of my men upon the unlucky boy, who got so kicked
and battered about that I marvel how he survived it. It
was really a miracle that no one was hit, as we were all
standing close together, offering a large mark.

At length I decided to try and gallop back before sunset,
although we had but two ponies, one of which was nearly
dead-beat already with bringing the news of the lions. My
shikari and I galloped back those twelve miles as hard as
we could go.

When at last we got to the village, we were told that we
had to go five more miles before we reached the lions. We
had ridden four miles, I should think, when, to my utter
dismay, we met four horsemen slowly walking towards us,
with the news that, after standing by the lions the whole
morning, and thinking we were not coming, they had let
them run away.

There was nothing now to be done but ride those sixteen
weary miles back to camp. Riding through the darkness,
my pony nearly fell over two jackals which refused to get

out of the way. How glad I was to see the camp-fires at last, after that long day's ride and disappointment! I was hungry, too, not having tasted food for over fourteen hours. A very strong wind blew next morning, and, as we were pretty high, it was very cold. We marched north-east along the main caravan route between Berbera and 'big Harar' upon the open plain, but saw very little game. We had hardly pitched for the night, when a tremendous downpour of rain drove everyone under the camel-mats. The villagers soon rolled up, and I engaged fifteen men to scour the plain for lions next morning.

To-day I found upon the plain enormous quantities of a curious caterpillar, which fed upon grass, and made a house round its own body of dead and dry bits of grass, its head and the first few segments of its body alone protruding from the house. On being disturbed, the head and segments

of the body are quickly drawn into the grass house out of view, and nothing is then to be seen having any appearance of life.

I also noticed quantities of the dung-beetle. Two of these fat little creatures will roll along a ball of dung four times their own size an incredible distance at a very fast rate. One will pull in front, going backwards, whilst the other, standing upon its hind-legs, will push the ball along with its fore-legs. Grasshoppers were exceedingly numerous around this place, which was called Wardi.

Next morning, after seeing the fifteen lion-hunters off, I took a rest, as my feet were very sore after a week's hard walking upon the plain. During the night a daring little jackal jumped into camp, and stole a whole sheep-skin, the sentries as usual being both fast asleep. No lion was reported, so I marched at 5 a.m. the next morning through open country and plains covered with a sprinkling of trees, seeing very little game. Reaching a village towards evening, a man informed us that there were elephants very close, that he had seen them the day before, and that they frightened away the cattle from the edge of the bush every day. I accordingly pitched close to the village to 'take the news.' Some of the 'woolidgers' brought me three of the dearest, fluffiest, and fattest leopard cubs I have ever beheld. They were very savage, and barely three weeks old, and I was afraid, as they would take very little milk, I could not hope to carry them on a jolting camel all the way to the coast alive. They had large fat heads and tiny ears, with enormously long and sharp claws for their tender age. When picked up, they chirped like young birds. Their colour was a dirty yellowish-brown, with black spots covering the legs, and two black streaks running from the corners of the eyes nearest the nose to the corners of the mouth.

At noon it was so cold that I sat down to breakfast enveloped in a rug and great-coat. Soon after the temperature rose from 65° to 105°. My shikari now contracted fever at least once a week, and had to be carried on the pony.

We started off next morning for a village, to get guides to show us the reported elephants, and found it with great difficulty hidden in dense bush. Immense herds of sheep, camels, and cattle met my gaze on nearing the zareba, and in a small zareba, all to themselves, were three fine ostriches.

I sent off half a dozen men to look for elephants, and remained in camp awaiting news. They soon returned, saying they had found tracks of elephants two days old, and that some Midgans had told them that they had been driven right out of the country. They brought with them two little lion cubs which they had found in the grass. The old lion was with them, but had bolted and left the cubs to themselves. They were about two months old, and were very strong for their size. I determined to try and take them back to the coast.

In the evening I held a spear-throwing competition, two of my men throwing over 100 yards. The art of throwing a spear is only acquired after an enormous amount of practice. No great strength is required; it is simply a knack. No white man can throw a spear equal to a black; in fact, very few white men can throw one 20 yards.

The headman of a village came to me to settle a row for him. He said that the night before a man and woman had

AHEMET MEHEMET AND MURIAN BAYDIL.

gone to the well. The man descended to get water, when the woman suddenly shouted : 'Quick ! a man comes.' Up jumped the man in the well, and thrust his spear neatly through the approaching man's abdomen. He then thought it about time to ask, 'Who are you?' and the wounded man answered, 'One of your own tribe,' and immediately expired on the spot. Then there were ructions.

I told him I had enough quarrels of my own without being mixed up in his, so he retired under a tree, and deliberated whether he would kill the murderer on the spot, or take from him all his sheep and cattle. Finally the greedy man thought the last course the best, much to the disgust of my headman, who said to me :

' I am very, very sorry. I want you mek photograph man-kill.'

My lions lapped up 2 pounds of clotted blood and ate a whole leg of mutton that night—a pretty good meal for such youngsters. Round the camp came the poor old women, who greedily snatched up the stomach and entrails of the sheep to eat· at leisure. The men eat the best meat ; the women are never allowed anything better than entrails. Englishwomen who uphold women's rights would be shocked to see how low women are esteemed in Somaliland, and how patient and quiet they are under that low estimation.

There was a row at night, as usual, among my men over the sheep-skins. Daggers were drawn, and several nasty cuts given, but by gently ' coaxing 'em with my hob-nailed boots,' and hitting them on the head with the butt-end of my revolver, I eventually restored law and order.

Next day, about noon, we sighted a herd of oryx in very favourable stalking-ground, but we got almost too close, and the herd galloped off in every direction. I knocked over a fat male with very thick horns, 31½ inches long— a good head for a male. Directly after firing, and when I was in the act of reloading, an oryx rushed almost into me, and in my haste to get ready to shoot I accidentally fired the rifle before I got it up to my shoulder, the triggers cutting my fingers severely. Luckily, the oryx swerved at the report, and passed within a few feet of me, going like a racehorse.

After the mid-day rest we emerged out of the thin bush on to another large open plain, and here we found game in thousands, mostly ' owl ' and hartebeest, a few oryx running with the ' owl.' I shot a female hartebeest for its head (13¼ inches round the curve, circumference 7 inches, tip

to tip 19 inches), and missed a very big male. When we
camped, I pulled out the lions from their cage of wicker-
work, which we had constructed for them, and, tying ropes
round their necks, secured them to two tent-pegs and let
them play. It was a very pretty sight to see them clawing,
biting and rolling over each other like two young kittens.
The male measured 30 inches, and the female 29 inches,
from tip of nose to tip of tail.

Next morning I started early to look for lions reported
in the thick bush, but it was like looking for needles in a
load of hay. I returned without seeing a single track, but
I shot an 'owl' with a poor head, as it jumped across one
with a good head just as I pulled the trigger.

After breakfast, being short of meat, I went out upon the
open plain with my syce and a stalking-camel, both my
shikaris crying off on account of fever. After a grand
chase I succeeded in shooting a wounded hartebeest through
the neck with my revolver from the saddle.

The whole of the next day I spent upon the plain, where
oryx, 'owl,' and hartebeest 'jist jostled each other'; but so
wild were they that I succeeded in shooting one hartebeest
only.

In the evening I again amused myself by playing with
the lions, a rather painful amusement, I discovered, as they
bit and scratched my hands terribly. I found that their
scratch was much worse than their bite, festering, and
taking a long time to heal. The female was far more
savage than the male.

Next morning we marched off the plain into thick bush,
and pitched camp near a village, where a lion was reported.
This, for a wonder, turned out to be true, as we found a
half-eaten camel close by. The villagers reported that the
lion had killed seven camels round about in the last six
days. With walking through the long grass my legs were
infested with ticks, which had to be picked out of my flesh
every night one by one. I built two zarebas in which to
watch for the lion, but the night turned out to be one of

the most disagreeable I have ever slept out in. Terrific
thunder and lightning was accompanied by a perfect deluge
of rain. My bedding was saturated in a very few minutes,
and so for the rest of the night I was obliged to sit on the
wet ground. The dead camel, which, by-the-by, ' wasn't
no bloomin' voilets !' had been almost entirely consumed, so
we fixed up a donkey near by it.

The night was an ideal one for a lion, but not one came
near us. A curious little animal came boldly up and fed
upon the camel's carcase, close by the tail of the donkey.
I dared not shoot at it, fearing to disturb bigger game. It
was about the size of a jackal, but fatter, and I never
remember seeing anything like it before. Cold and wet, I
was glad when, at 2.30 a.m., my men came to let me out of
my prison. I found the camels already on the march.
That day we did two very heavy marches, viz., from
2.30 a.m. till noon, and from 1.30 p.m. to 5 p.m., seeing
absolutely no game during the whole day.

At 5 p.m. we reached Hargaisa again, and met with the
first signs of cultivation I had as yet seen in Somaliland.
Close to the village were huge square plots of ground, upon
which grew long stalks, at the end of which hung bunches
of seed resembling millet, and called by the natives *haroot*.
In the middle of each of these plots were erected high
platforms, on which men stood the whole day, shouting,
and continually slinging stones among the stalks to frighten
away the birds ; though why the stones didn't knock off
and destroy as much seed as the birds could eat I failed to
see.

We next saw a most unusual sight—the first house built
for a European (Lord Delamere) in Central Somaliland, or
rather, I should say, in course of building, for Mahomed
Hindi, of Berbera, who was superintending the building,
told me he could not finish it for a month. He begged of
me to enter the wooden gates in the formidable wall, some
12 feet high, and on passing through I found myself in a
large court or square. In one corner a small bungalow,

with veranda surrounding it, was in course of erection. In the court were some Arab trotting camels, which looked sleek and well cared for. Some fine wells had been dug by the 'tug,' and we stayed here the night.

Early next morning I started for a four days' tramp over a very barren wilderness to Berbera. During the preceding night my lions, after making a great noise, suddenly ceased. On jumping out of bed, and looking out of my tent into the moonlight, I discovered that they had escaped out of their cage (a lions' den with bars of string was hardly appropriate), and were careering about among the sheep and camels, the latter not taking the slightest notice of them. The sentries, of course, were fast asleep. I with difficulty managed to catch them, and tied them up again safe and sound. It was the greatest good luck I happened to be awake, otherwise I must have lost them.

The wind now blew a hurricane every day, and it was with great difficulty that my tent could be pitched. I saw no game until 4 p.m., when we sighted a herd of ten wild asses. After a long and arduous stalk after these exceptionally wary animals, I fired as they ran off, hitting two with my right and left. Both beasts were hit through the shoulder, but proved as hard to bring to earth as their near relatives the zebras. After a very long race, I overhauled and 'grassed,' or, rather, sanded, one of them (for of grass there was none). Meanwhile my syce and shikari had been following the second animal, and after a large expenditure of ·450 and revolver cartridges I bagged my 'right and left.' This large animal, which resembles the domestic ass in shape, has a beautiful French-gray ground colour, long pointed ears, and legs striped after the manner of the zebra, except that the stripes on the ass are narrower. It has no dark line along the back like the domestic ass.

Next day the heat became greater and greater as we descended. I saw two Pelzeln's gazelle, but failed to get a shot, and after passing several caravans, we pitched for the night near a dried-up 'tug.' Next day we encountered a swarm of locusts whilst going through a mountain-pass in the desert. The air was white with them. In the sun they looked like falling snow. Every bush was thick with them, and as we walked along they flew up in millions. I managed with a stick to knock over enough for the store-box and frying-pan. I had now partaken, like John the Baptist, of ' locusts and wild honey ' in the desert. The locusts literally hid the sun from view, and it took us three hours to march past the cloud.

The heat striking upon the barren rock was intense the whole day, and it was a sight to see my twenty-three followers bathing and drinking in a hollow in the rock full of water, all at the same time.

The third day was very trying to the men and animals, owing to the great heat. I got a man to walk by the side of the camel which carried the lion cubs, and dash water upon them from time to time. When we halted for the mid-day rest the cubs lay and gasped for breath ; I thought they could not live. They refused to move a muscle, except their panting tongues. I determined to march through the whole of the next night, and try to reach the coast town before the sun became strong.

Loading up at 5 p.m., we accordingly marched into the darkness. One of my camels soon fell down exhausted, and I was obliged to shoot it and march on. Two and a half miles an hour was the pace, and as the pony carried a fever-stricken man, I was obliged to tramp it on foot. Oh, the heat ! It almost suffocated me. The wind fell. It became almost unbearable owing to the dust and sand in one's mouth, nose, and eyes.

The sun at length rose, to find us still tramping over the hot rock and sand, and still a long day's march from the coast town. About ten o'clock the wind rose again with terrific violence, and at noon, when we halted for the mid-day rest, it was so strong that my tent could not be pitched, and I was obliged to sit under the very inadequate shade afforded by a single tree and barricade of store boxes. The lions seemed at their last gasp. They could eat nothing, and had hardly strength enough to lap the warm water given to them.

At three o'clock we loaded up for the last lap. After marching for an hour, several of the camels fell with the heat and exhaustion, including the camel which carried the lion cubs, their cage, which was almost in pieces, coming to the ground with a crash. Two of my men fainted, and just after we had used up our last drop of water, we crawled into the coast town of Berbera, in a terrific dust-storm, more dead than alive.

Here I pitched my tent for upwards of four days waiting for a steamer to convey me to Aden. I employed my time in packing up, selling my camels and general parapher-nalia, and paying off my men, four of whom, including my headman, I had put on the black book by the assistant resident for dishonesty and general bad conduct, so that they would never again be allowed to enter the services of a white man proceeding into the jungle. A week here in a tent and I should have been blind. Dust-storms were of daily occurrence, and the little particles of mica which blew into my eyes burnt like little sparks of fire when the sun shone upon them.

At length a tiny ship, somewhat bigger than a washing-tub, arrived in the harbour. Owing to the strong wind, and the strong whisky which the captain got on shore, the boat did not start until 6 p.m. the next day. How thankful I was to leave the odious place, with its dust-storms! On hauling up the anchor, the captain, who was so drunk that he was obliged to hold on to the bridge-rail with both hands to prevent himself from falling, shouted, 'Starbud—hic—steadee; port—hic—steadee!'

'Yes, my friend,' I thought to myself, 'you've had some-thing stronger than port to make you cry "Hic—steadee!"' In vulgar parlance he might well have been said to have fairly 'copped the brewer.'

After giving a few more incoherent orders, he utterly

subsided into a chair, where he remained until next morning. The mate informed me that this disgusting state of affairs had been going on on board this cockleshell, which carried Her Majesty's mails, for weeks, during which time he (the mate) had had the whole charge of the ship, and was nearly worn out in consequence.

During the whole voyage, a little fox-terrier dog, half the size of my lion cubs, amused itself by squeezing through the sticks of their cage, and playing with the inmates, who snarled and clawed at the black-and-white intruder with a will, much to the delight, apparently, of all parties.

Just as we reached Aden Harbour the rotten old river-tub gave a lurch that shipped an enormous quantity of water, and we finally dropped anchor opposite the rocks of this by no means heavenly hole. A more odious place than Aden can hardly be imagined. Here I was obliged to remain three weeks, as I just missed a boat, and the next was taken off. I had not been here a week before I got fever, and felt generally very ill. People affirm that there is only a bit of tissue paper between this spot and the nether regions. Although several people have no doubt fallen through the paper, we have as yet no record that they ever came back again to verify this assertion.

At Aden I designed a more substantial cage of wood, with iron bars in front, for the lions, which was very well carried out by an old Arab carpenter. At length the steamer arrived to take me home to England. That was indeed a long-looked-for and a glad day. The cubs had now grown enormously. In Aden I had bought for them two dog-collars and chains, and allowed them their liberty on the lower deck as far as the chains would permit. Nobody would pick them up but me, which I found a great nuisance, as owing to their frequent escapes, especially at night, I was continually being disturbed in my bunk. The butcher who fed them would constantly walk into my cabin at dead of night with :

' Beg pardon, sur, but the loiness 'as escape.   Please come an' cotch 'er.'

I was obliged to get up, run aft, look all over the place, and probably find her hiding under the sheep-pen, through the floor of which she would thrust her paw and pat the legs of the terrified baa-lambs above her.   Out she had to be driven with a broom-handle, whilst I used to post myself

outside the cover and pounce upon her as she bolted growling savagely.   They were always breaking their chains or slipping their collars, and I was terribly afraid I should lose them overboard, so at length I was obliged to coop them up for good in their cage.   This probably caused weakness in their legs, which grew worse and worse after I had finally housed them in a loose-box at home.   It was with the utmost difficulty I could get them still enough to be photographed. I drove them out of the loose-box into a yard, when the female, seeing the camera, made a bolt for it, dodged me, ran between the photographer's legs, and finally rushed through a door, up a steep flight of stairs into a hayloft, and sat with her back against the wall in a corner, snarling, growling and striking out at me.

I was at length obliged to don a pair of gloves and carry her bodily downstairs, lasso her with a rope, and hold her, as shown in the photograph, to be operated upon. As they both appeared to grow weaker, I deposited them in the Zoo, where they lived for only two months.

What with export duties at the Somali coast, fare to England (almost as much as the first-class fare of a passenger), dock dues, food, and tips, the importation of a couple of lions is by no means a profitable business, especially when they die a few months after landing.

11

PART II.

SECOND EXPEDITION TO SOMALILAND.

CHAPTER I.

Two years after the events related in Part I., wishing to
further my researches in the natural history of Somaliland,
and if possible to cross the Webbi Ganana and visit Lake
Rudolf, I left London, together with Mr. and Mrs. Bennett
Stanford, on May 21, and travelled overland, viâ Mont
Cenis, to Brindisi. The train, though fast, was very uncomfortable. It was almost impossible to get water and
light. The latter failed just before we entered the tunnel,
and we had to sit it out (twenty-five minutes) in pitch
darkness.

We arrived at Brindisi at 4.30 p.m. on May 23, and
found the P. and O. steamship *India* waiting for us. We
reached Port Said on the 26th, and Aden on the 30th.
Here I engaged a ' boy ' and a cook.

Before I left Aden I discovered that the stupid people on
the *India* had not put out one of my portmanteaus, and
had taken it on to Bombay. It contained *all* my boots, an
eight-bore rifle, entomological apparatus, shirts, socks, and
many other absolute necessaries. On reaching Berbera,
after a fourteen hours' passage, Stanford discovered that his
agents had stupidly not put on board his rifles and guns.

I soon discovered my headman, who had come over ten
days before, having been commissioned by my agents to buy
camels. The old misers, although they knew me perfectly
well, had waited until they had all my goods, sent by

British boat before me, safe in their ' godown ' before they had sent my headman to Berbera to buy camels; the result was, on our arrival he had bought but thirty-two, when we wanted a hundred.

The first night we all had bad sun-headaches. The heat in Berbera was very great, and the *karife*, or hot wind, had just commenced. The second day of my stay here I developed prickly heat and an awful boil on my neck, which gave me excruciating pain, and prevented me getting a wink of sleep. Finally, after pricking and poulticing it to no purpose, I was obliged to have it cut by the local black surgeon, which operation was worse than having a tooth drawn, and made a hole in my neck which will never disappear.

At last, having got together a few camels, we decided to start out of the heat of Berbera, and wait up in the hills until the remaining camels could be bought. The caravan accordingly set out on June 5, and after saying good-bye to our kind host and hostess at Berbera, and leaving our headman behind to bring on the rest of the camels, we trotted off and joined our caravan at midnight, finding camp pitched, and all in order.

Next morning we marched at 5.30 a.m., and soon encountered Pelzeln's gazelle, the animal which afforded me so many shots without effect on my entering into the jungle two years before. However, on this occasion, at the first shot with my tiny ·256 Mannlicher rifle, I killed a fine female with very good horns, a trophy I was extremely anxious to obtain, as I had during my last expedition only succeeded in collecting a male. When we pitched at 10 a.m., a gazelle offered a good chance as he stood gazing out of curiosity at us. But I dared not take it, fearing to shoot a grazing camel. We restarted at 2.30, the heat being terrific. Stanford discovered that, owing to his syce having slept, his ponies were missing, so he mounted his trotting camel, his wife seated behind him. I took it easily behind. The heat was so great that, after riding two hours, we were all obliged to dismount and sit under a very leafless tree to await sunset. I was tired out when, at 10 p.m., I turned in for the night at Hawala Tomalo.

Stanford was ill with the heat, so we made a short march next day to Deragodely. I shot a small bustard for the pot, and the ground here was covered with locusts. After going over a rocky desert, where I shot three dik-dik, we pitched at a place called Harmass for the night, all feeling very ill and knocked up with the heat. Noon next day saw us at Leferuke, and we pitched for the night at Deria

Herag, surrounded by mountains. The heat during the day was overpowering, but after my nose had bled profusely I felt it less.

Next morning we marched past Mandara, to the foot of the Girato Pass, and pitched for the mid-day rest under some fine trees by a 'tug.' Here the bird life was extremely interesting. At 2 p.m. the camels were led up the pass, and at 2.30 we followed. The path led in zigzag fashion up the steep rocky side of the mountain. From the top there was a magnificent view of the Gulis range of mountains, with Gan Libah (the Lion's Hand) in the distance, towering up over 4,000 feet. Two of our camels lay down half-way up the pass, and refused to move, so their loads were taken off and they were left to rest. We pitched camp on a high plateau at Lehello, where we intended to rest a few days. Before dark all the camels were brought up the mountain pass without mishap.

Next day I went out with my shikaris, and saw a large sounder of wart hog, the old boar of which I unfortunately missed, two herds of Speke's gazelle, and two herds of gerenook, all dreadfully wild. In the evening Stanford bagged a wart hog.

Next morning I went out to try and get some meat for the camp. I soon found a herd of gerenook, and, firing at a good buck, hit him in the horn. He ran on, and then stood looking at us through a bush, when a ·256 Mannlicher bullet caught him full in the chest. On walking up, I found that the first bullet had completely spoilt one of the horns. This was a pity, as it possessed an extra fine and massive head. After this we saw nothing but 'wifes' (females). In the afternoon I pursued a female Speke's gazelle, a specimen of which I had not as yet secured. We saw several herds, but they were fearfully wild. Whilst stalking a herd, I tripped on the stony ground, and fell very heavily on my knee-cap. This necessitated a halt for upwards of an hour. On restarting, I knocked over a female gazelle, which led us a long chase before we finally caught her.

We lost the pony now for several hours. When he arrived at last, and was having the gazelle placed upon his back, he let out and caught my shikari a nasty kick on the leg, which knocked the man clean over. After a short rest, I told him no bones were broken, and he got up and walked on as if nothing had happened. During the afternoon Mrs. Stanford shot some game birds for the pot, but shortly after got a nasty attack of fever.

Next day I went out with my gun collecting small mammals and birds, the latter of which were very numerous here, and in the afternoon employed myself skinning, rifle-mending, trap-setting, boil-dressing, and animal-doctoring. Mrs. Stanford remained in bed all day with high fever, but after a dose of quinine and champagne it had entirely vanished next morning. For several days we remained at Lehello, during which time I had splendid sport with Speke's gazelle, getting some very fine trophies of each sex. But do what I would, I could not kill a wart hog. Twice I put fine boars up almost under my feet when I was armed with a walking-stick only.

One day, whilst in camp engaged in skinning, a riderless horse was seen to be galloping towards the zareba. Fearing Stanford had met with an accident, I was in the act of saddling my pony and setting out to look for him, when I perceived the syce approaching in hot haste. He soon afterwards came into camp with the news that Stanford had killed a boar, and on attempting to put the head upon the pony's back, the animal, being a true Mohammedan, naturally expostulated, and having kicked out right and left, and got rid of its loathsome burden, it made off straight for camp at a gallop.

After following wart hog for upwards of a week without success, I shot two boars out of a sounder right and left. They were neither of them dead, and cutting their throats was by no means child's play, as they worked their heads and huge tusks about in most formidable fashion. The Somalis, being Mohammedans, would not touch them, so I was obliged to cut off their heads unaided, and sling them over the saddle, a matter of great difficulty. I have skinned every sort of head, but a wart hog's skin beats them all for sticking tight. It took me four and a half hours to take off those two skins and clean the skulls. I was utterly tired out with working at them in the sun, and my hands were covered with blisters when dinner-time arrived at six o'clock. However, these two extraordinary-looking heads well repaid me the trouble I took to obtain and preserve them.

Whilst at Lehello, I shot a large bustard with my
450 Express rifle. The large bullet (weighing 260 grains,
and propelled by 110 grains of powder) smashed up in the
interior of the body ; scarcely a feather was displaced, so
that I was enabled to skin him in almost perfect condition.
Whilst here six more camels arrived for us, and two were
reported to have died on the road. (N.B. : The Somalis
killed these two and ate them.) I tried to photograph
Mrs. Stanford's Somali maid, but she ' wasn't taking any,'
and bolted into the tent.

One evening some of our men brought in a camel, which
had strayed whilst they slept, together with a prisoner,
whom they accused of stealing it. We held a court-martial,
when it soon became evident that our men were liars, and
that the prisoner was innocent. Our men produced him
only to save themselves from being fined for losing the camel.
We gave back the prisoner his spears and shield, and turned
him out of the zareba amid a great uproar.

Stanford's guns and rifles having arrived, we left Lehello
and marched to Duldewan and Hundrugal, meeting on the
way, upon an open plain, one of the largest herds, or
collection of herds, of Speke's gazelle I had ever beheld.
There must have been upwards of one hundred of these
graceful little creatures. They were so wild, however, that
I failed to get a shot at any.

Next morning we struck camp at 5.30, marching through
a pass bordered by low barren hills. At the mid-day
rest, at a place called Arigumeret, my largest camel lay
down and promptly expired on the spot. This was a great
loss, as he carried the heaviest load of them all. It must
have been, in fact, overladen, and probably broke a blood-
vessel. I had now lost two camels in less than a fortnight.
There were some thorn-bushes out in bloom, round which
flew a great number of butterflies, so I used my net to some
advantage. We saw no game all day, and pitched under
some large trees at Odewein, close by a 'tug' (dried-up
river-bed). A little rain fell at sunset.

The morning after our arrival at Odewein, I went out north of the river on foot, and came to a large plain, upon which a number of small herds of Speke's gazelle were disporting themselves, but my shooting was erratic, and I failed to secure one. From the top of a small hill I got a magnificent view of the surrounding country—Burao Wells to the north-east Eyk and the great Toyo open plain to the south.

Along the banks of the ' tug' were a number of francolin, which afforded very good sport and capital eating. This was also the best place for moths I had ever met with in Somaliland. An enormous number of caterpillars crawled over the herbage, among which I noticed some of the hawk-moths and a curious black ' looper,' with yellow bands down the sides of its body. This caterpillar had six legs in front, six in the middle, and two at the end or tail of its body. When it moved, the loop occurred between the three fore-legs and the three middle legs, so—

The following day I had great sport upon the open plain with Speke's gazelle, and then marched for a place called Bally Maroli, where Clarke's gazelle (*Ammordorcas clarkei*) the ' dibitag' of the Somalis, was reported by my men sent out to look for game. The country now altered from stony yellow ground to red ground covered with a few low trees and bushes and huge red ant-hills.

I was the first to see a herd of dibitag antelope, and very curious they looked with their long necks and tails, the latter held up straight on end like a wart hog's. What struck me at once was their marvellous resemblance to the surrounding country and colours ; their skin, being of a purple-gray, showing up in some lights quite red, harmonized exactly with the dull purple grass and thorn-bushes, and the red sand.

We had seen no buck with the first herd, but soon after saw a second herd. After a long stalk, I got within 300 yards of a fine buck, and gave him a bullet right through the middle, followed by a second through the haunch, a third breaking his long tail. With this he lay down. I had but one cartridge left, and the pony was a mile away. I tried to stalk him, but he saw me and got up and faced me. I dared not wait, so fired my last 'cartouche' (as my shikari called it), and missed. Off he galloped, but he was badly wounded, and soon lay down again.

I sat down behind a tiny thorn-bush, and sent my shikari back for the pony and my shot-gun. The latter was forthcoming first. Cramming in a 'BB' cartridge, I stalked the antelope, which was now squatting flat on the ground, with its head closely pressed against the sand. As I crawled up to him, he jumped up and bolted ; but I fired the twelve-bore, knocking him head over heels, whilst a yell of triumph rose from me and my shikaris. He had a very good head (10¼ inches round the curve), and I was mightily pleased with him. This animal is usually very shy and difficult to bag.

I had promised my men a couple of sheep if I killed a buck, so that I was received with quite an ovation when I arrived in camp at Bally Maroli, a curious little oasis on the edge of a large plain. In the centre of this patch of trees was a small pond with enough water in it to last us a few days. The trees were covered with the nests of a lovely little gold-and-black weaver-bird. These nests, which contained little blue eggs and a few young birds, were beautifully made with a kind of tunnel-like entrance, so :

One day I was most successful with Clarke's gazelle, one

of the rarest and shyest antelopes in Africa, killing three, two of which had fine heads. One old buck, which had not seen me, stood flicking his ears, and allowed me to empty the magazine at him, when he dropped stone-dead at the last cartridge. He was a long way out, and could see no smoke, and the report was hardly audible.

After a little practice with the Mannlicher, I utterly discarded my ·450 Express for the smaller bore. I consider the Mannlicher the most accurate weapon (as sighted by Gibbs of Bristol) made. This is not an advertisement, but a fact! I shot antelopes with the ·256 Mannlicher over and over again stone-dead at distances at which I should never have even dreamed of firing with the ·450 Express.

Whilst encamped at Bally Maroli, I made an expedition to Bun Arori (the Arori Plain), which was a very long ride north-east. This plain resembled the Jiggiga, Toyo and Saylah plains I had crossed on my last expedition. From it I got a magnificent view of the Wagar Mountains in the Gulis range, over 6,000 feet high. Here we saw the usual herds of ' owl ' gazelle, and after several unsuccessful attempts I hit a fine buck, which soon lay down, but bolted again on my approach. I sent the pony after him, when they both disappeared in the haze.

After following the tracks for half an hour, I saw the pony grazing a long way off, and the syce stooping over something. So we walked up, and found him skinning the gazelle, which he said had collapsed at once on being pressed by the pony.

The enormous value of a pony for retrieving wounded game was over and over again demonstrated in my last expedition ; in fact, it would be impossible to bag half the antelope one hits at such long ranges without the aid of this useful animal.

After the skinning operation, we lighted a fire and had breakfast. After an hour's attempt at a rest under the boiling sun, I followed eight hartebeest behind the stalking camel, and shot one at 200 yards, and shortly after another

at 400 yards range.   The second ran a long way before he
lay down, and stalking up behind him, I caught him under
the eye as he rose, killing him instantaneously.

It was now 2 p.m., so that we had all our work cut out
to strip off the skins, cut off the meat, and get home before
dark.   However, at 3 p.m. I started, and arrived in camp
at dusk, the camel laden with meat arriving an hour
afterwards.   Stanford had spent the day trying to come up

SULTAN MUTHER AND ESCORT.

with ostriches, whose fresh track he had followed without
success until late in the afternoon.

Next day, Sultan Muther, head of the tribe of Habr
Yunis, came with twenty of his headmen, on horseback,
and gave us a *tomasho*, or display of horsemanship and
sham fighting.   We presented him with 20 rupees, an
umbrella, a razor, and a Jubilee medal.   It was fearfully
hot watching the *tomasho*, and the dust was almost unbearable.

After his display, we turned out all our men, and gave

him a show with blank-cartridge. In spite of a lot of drill-
ing, the men *would* jabber in the ranks. At the word
' Present !' at least three-quarters of the men fired one
after the other, and at the word ' Fire !' I usually let off my
twelve-bore gun alone. Every now and then, whilst instructions were being given them, one or two would fire a
ball cartridge instead of a blank one—just to keep up the
excitement, they said. Altogether it was the funniest
review of troops I ever beheld, and far more entertaining
than these deadly dull functions usually are.

Next morning, after filling the barrels with water, the
pond was entirely dried up ! Soon after, our headman
turned up at last with our remaining camels, and our joint
caravans now consisted of 100 camels, 80 men, 1 woman,
2 boys, 6 ponies, 2 riding camels, and a large flock of sheep
and goats. They brought with them a special message
from the Consul at Aden, forbidding us to march to the
Webbi Shebeyli. This was a terrible blow after getting so
large a caravan together.

With much regret I now sent my Berthon folding-boat
and long rope back to the coast with some bundles of skins
and boxes of skulls.

We marched next morning from Bally Maroli at 6.15 a.m.
I knocked over a gerenook, and, after a long chase, my
shikari brought him to bay with the pony. When we had
marched for four hours, we halted for the mid-day rest at
Ololdare. Here I noticed for the first time a most extraordinary lizard, with the base of the tail broadened and
flattened out in the shape of a fan. Colour of back, reddish-
brown ; tail and head ditto, covered with white spots ; legs
much lighter. Yellow round nose and eyes, under parts
light yellow ; under head and shoulders a brilliant cobalt
blue, very patchy, as if put on with a paint-brush using
water-colour. The Somalis call this creature ' asherbody,'
meaning ' baby,' as when touched it utters a cry exactly
like a little child.

We loaded up again at 1.30, and marched through

thick bush until 5.30, when we came out on an open plain
covered with long thick grass and ant-hills. Here we saw
the first spoor of a lion. It had evidently sprung upon an
oryx, the latter escaping, as we could plainly see the tracks
of each, going away in opposite directions. I measured the
distance of his spring from where he took off in the long
grass, to where he landed in the open, and it was 20 feet !
On landing he had slid along in the mud about 3 feet, the
ground having been very wet at the time. Immediately
after, on looking up, I saw a herd of ' owl ' about 150 yards
off ; and as we wanted meat, I shot one.

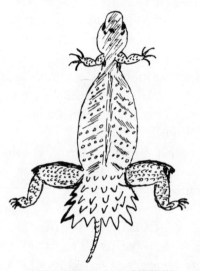

APOROSCELIS BATILLIFERUS.

There were no signs of the well yet, although Stanford's
shikari said it would take us but three hours to reach Eyk.
My headman, who was no kitten, and knew a thing or
three, estimated the distance, however, at four and a half
hours' march ; and so it turned out, for we did not reach
the well till after dark, passing on the way the ruins
of a large town built of stone by the Gallas 505 years
ago. The foundations and parts of the walls of the houses
are still visible. When the Somalis became powerful they
turned the Gallas out. Here they affirm that there is

much gold, but since the departure of the Gallas, who filled up the huge pits they had dug out in search of the precious metal before they were driven out, no Somalis have ever taken the trouble to open them up again.

Next day we went out upon the plain in search of meat. Stanford shot an 'owl' and a hartebeest, and I, after badly missing a single oryx, knocked over big 'owl' bucks right and left with my ·450 Express, to which I was giving another trial. One of the 'owl,' however, got up again, and although my shikari got fairly close up to it on the pony, he failed to spear it. He reported that the solid bullet had gone right through its neck.

Next morning, in the thick bush bordering the open plain, I saw two silver-backed jackals. On killing one, his mate at once commenced to eat him, and I knocked her over by his side. They were a pretty pair with very handsome coats. After disturbing two oryx in the thicket, we emerged into a comparatively open bit, and a single Clarke's gazelle offering its broadside got the bullet through the base of the heart, and after running 100 yards dropped dead.

As I neared home, I saw an 'owl' gazelle feeding with some others in an odd way. He appeared to have a stiff neck, as he fed moving in a straight line, never turning his head to the right or left. He carried a very fine head, and I suspected I had seen him before. After a careful stalk I shot him, and on going up found that it was the animal I had knocked over the night before. The bullet, a solid ·450 Express, had, as my shikari said, gone right through the neck below the cervical vertebræ, and both holes in the skin had almost healed up during the night. His massive horns measured 19½ inches round the curve.

In the afternoon ten horsemen turned up to pay their respects and see what they could get out of us with their 'Mot, mot, mot, io mot' (We welcome you), to which I answered 'Kool leeban' (Thanks). These *tomashos* are a perfect nuisance. One is obliged to sit in the hot sun or

dust for over an hour and look on a show of horsemanship
which never varies in the slightest detail, the prize apparently going to the man who can hit his wretched pony the
hardest. After it is over one has to fork out one's *tobes* or
rupees as presents.

When all the horsemen had gone, we went out quail-
shooting in the long grass. There were a good number
about, and they offered most sporting shots.

Next day I went along the edge of the thick bush looking
for lion or leopard tracks, but saw none, so left the bush
and walked out into the open. In the middle of this large
plain I saw a huge herd of oryx, and by crawling through
the long grass I got some 500 yards off them. As several
stood broadside on, I opened fire at them. They took little
notice of the slight noise made by the Mannlicher, and
after firing ten cartridges with the 500 yards sight up
without result, I put up the 700 yards sight and hit one
first shot. Contrary to my usual custom, I did not measure
the exact distance, but I am fully convinced it must have
been 500 yards from me ! The wounded oryx lay down,
and in spite of yells to my shikari to stop, he insisted upon
running towards it to give it a good *hallal*. The result was
as I anticipated. Up jumped the oryx, and got away at an
amazing pace, my shikari being well in the line of my fire.
Mounting the pony, I had a magnificent gallop, and at
length brought the antelope to bay, when my shikari ran
up and shot him at the third attempt. The horns measured
$30\frac{1}{2}$ inches.

After a weary tramp home, which I reached at length
very tired, I found a large crowd of men surrounding our
pond and throwing large stones into it amid a scene of
great excitement. On coming up, I found one of our
wretched camel-men with his head streaming with blood,
coming out of the water. The order had been that nobody
should bathe in our drinking water, which order had been
disobeyed by this man, who seized a spear and threatened
anyone who came near him.

When order was at length restored, two men brought in news of lions. Not believing it true, we sent two men to investigate, and waited the whole of the next day in camp for their return. Proceedings were enlivened by a fight between my shikari and a camel-man, but luckily we got them separated before any serious damage had been done.

The men sent out to get news returned at dusk reporting the lion story to be, as usual, a lie. However, excitement was caused by the men bringing in a silver-backed jackal which got caught in one of my traps. Amid howls of glee half a dozen Somalis did him to death as they thought with *hangols* (crooked sticks used in building zarebas). Five minutes after the jackal got up and ran away, and although pursued by some twenty Somalis, he evaded them all and eventually escaped!

Soon after a lion ' shouted ' about a mile off. He kept moving west, evidently following a caravan. We kept double watches that night in case he should come to our well for a drink, but, unluckily, he did not favour us with a visit. Soon after daybreak next morning two men ran in with news that the lion had 'jumped up' at their village and taken a sheep. After a hasty breakfast, we started with our shikaris, ordering four camels to follow with tents, cooking gear, and water for two days. We cantered across the plain, and arrived at the village in four hours. We then took up the lion's spoor into the dense jungle. After three hours' tracking through dangerous grass and thick thorn-bush, we unfortunately followed the track of the night before instead of the morning, with the result that we worked back to the village again instead of going away from it. When our mistake was first made we must have been very close to the lion. We pitched camp at a place called Abori.

CHAPTER II.

NEXT morning we did not go out shooting, not wishing
to disturb the lion, and at night, two zarebas having
been built, I entered one, and Mr. and Mrs. Stanford
the other. Donkeys were not procurable, so we had to be
content with tethered sheep. It was a clear, moonlight
night, and the noises in the village were kept up until a late
hour, so that I did not expect a royal visit. We had
hardly been in the zareba twenty minutes, when a hyæna
appeared, some 15 yards off the sheep, and showed up clear
in the moonlight. After staring at the sheep for a minute,
he charged it full tilt, but we kept him off at the point of
the spear. Shortly after another hyæna charged, and all
but got hold of the sheep, which jumped to and fro, and
dodged in a marvellous manner. The hyæna got the spear
well into its ribs, and then retired. The night was so hot
I could not sleep, and at 5 a.m. they let us out of the zareba.

We then marched to Edegan, our whole caravan having
arrived. Here some new wells had been dug for the first
time this year. The route lay through park-like country,
short grass, and tall thorn-trees. We saw two large
bustards, about twenty hares, and a large pack of jackals.
The hares were together, and must have been a different
kind from those generally seen, which live singly or in
pairs. I was very anxious to shoot one, but they were too

wild. I picked up the skull of an animal I had not seen before, which turned out to be that of a mature aardwolf.

On our arrival at Edegan, two men came up who had been fighting at the wells the night before. One had received a spear through his hand, and the other one clean through his arm. A third lay stretched upon the ground, with a wound from a spear, which had gone in under his left eye, and out again at the back of his head, and yet he still lived! A big fight seemed imminent, but our head-man settled their difficulties, after several hours' palavering. One of the camel-men who was with me in my former expedition came in, said 'Salaam,' and brought me a present of a fat sheep, a *harn* of camel's milk, and two skin-bottles of goat's milk. He had just returned from Abyssinia, having been with the English Mission, about which he gave me very full details.

Next morning I left Edegan to explore the Toyo plain, and after a two hours' ride I came to the edge of it, but saw nothing but ' owl ' gazelle. On the way home I shot a Speke's gazelle and saw a great number of jackal, the ground being literally honeycombed with their earths. At 2 p.m. we struck camp and marched to the edge of the ' bunker' Toyo. Here Mrs. Stanford shot an 'owl,' and did not reach camp till after dark, when we were beginning to fear she was lost.

Early the following morning I went out upon the Toyo plain after hartebeest, two of which I succeeded in bagging. I spent nine hours upon the plain, and was thoroughly tired out when I reached camp. In the evening two of my men, who were watching my camels grazing, ran in with the news that they had run to earth a couple of hyænas. After an hour's digging I left my men to go on with the work, and went home. They followed me shortly with the bodies of two aardwolves, which they had dug out, but which they had unfortunately killed. This rare animal possessed very pretty thick fur. The body is striped somewhat after the fashion of the striped hyæna, and the skin is naked round the nose.

I was too tired next day to go out upon the plain, so contented myself with shooting and skinning birds. Stanford, however, shot a hartebeest, and Mrs. Stanford two 'owl' gazelle, with a single bullet, upon the plain.

Next day I followed oryx on the plain, under a very hot sun, but was unsuccessful. In the afternoon two women came into camp complaining of some creatures in their

STRIPED HYÆNA.

throats. We gave them the strongest emetic we could think of, without any result, so we gave them another. Still no result. We gave them a feather next to tickle their throats, and asked them why 'they were not sick. They answered that they were shy before so many men. Next morning they came and said that the creatures had gone, and 'salaamed.'

After filling all my water *harns* at Edegan, I started to cross the great waterless Haud, doing a ten hours' march the first day. Mr. and Mrs. Stanford, who had a separate caravan and headman, preferred to remain a few days longer on the Toyo plain.

Next day we marched through alternate thick bush and open plain, passing Goodooby. I shot an 'owl,' a dibitag, and an oryx, the latter falling stone-dead at 250 yards (measured with my tape) with a bullet through the neck. We again marched ten hours during the day, and pitched for the night at a place called Gunder Libah. Here my men had a big fight, as usual, and were with difficulty

MR. STANFORD ON HIS RIDING CAMEL, TOYO PLAIN.

reduced to order. We made a very strong zareba at night, as we were in thick bush.

We marched at 4 a.m. next day, past huge ant-hills, some of which could not have been less than 20 feet in height. Seeing the neck and head of a dibitag 100 yards away, I fired, and caught him right through the neck, so accurately was my Mannlicher sighted. We cut old lion spoor during the day. My headman, who had charge of some hawk-moth caterpillars for me, brought them to me at night, with a sorrowful face, saying : ' All dead, sahib—all dead.' When

I looked at them I found they had all turned into chrysalides, and my headman would not believe that they were still alive. My headman was, as usual, a great scoundrel, and had to be watched. He was a great swell, having a valet in attendance on him and his pony. He donned a turban and an extremely dirty white pair of trousers, and his favourite song was ' Disy, Disy, give me yer answer dough.'

Next day we reached Allahballah, after passing through thick bush, where we saw a single ostrich and the fresh tracks of several rhinoceros. At Allahballah was a little shallow lake of rain-water, surrounded by a fringe of 20 yards of brilliant green grass. We had done the seventy miles or so of desert in three and a half days, and so well had we managed that, although we encountered not a drop of water *en route*, we still had three barrels and one *harn* full when we reached Allahballah, after watering thirty-four men, one donkey, two sheep, and one goat. Round the lake were to be seen several large storks, paddy birds, waders, snipe, wild ducks, and Egyptian geese. I spent a busy afternoon collecting and skinning. Soon after pitching, three men arrived to look for a camel which they had lost, and we had captured on the way. They brought news of plenty of lions near Gambissa, two long marches off, and rhinoceros and elephant were reported further south.

After nailing up notices upon the trees to tell Stanford where we had gone, we marched next morning through alternate bush and open plains. On one of the latter we saw two ' oysteriches,' as my shikari termed the big birds. They were off before we got within half a mile of them. At the request of the men, who wanted meat, I shot them an ' owl,' and then pitched under some curious trees, as it was too late to reach the villages that night. We built a zareba, and tethered up the donkey as bait for a lion, my men shouting, ' Hoi ! libah, hoi !' (Hi ! lion, hi !), and telling him to come quick, as there was a nice fat donkey waiting for him to eat. The row they made was more calculated to frighten him out of his wits than to attract him. The heat during the night was stifling, and I slept not a wink.

In the morning my men reported the fresh ' pugs ' of a lion, which I discovered had come within 100 yards of us, but not within sight of the donkey. There he had lain down, then got up and walked quietly away again. The ground was so hard, and the grass so thick, that after following him for two hours, during which time we advanced about half a mile, we were obliged to abandon it. I spent another sleepless night, the heat again being terrific. A lion ' shouted ' several times about a mile to the south of us, but he never put in an appearance. Every time he roared, the birds roosting in the bushes would fly up screaming, and as the beautiful sound got nearer and nearer to us, at one time it was a bit exciting.

Next day I built a zareba near one of the villages, in which I spent a third restless night. As usual, nothing came near the donkey, and I was hauled out of the zareba at 5 o'clock next morning, having been bitten by ticks and ' bugs ' of all sorts during another very hot night. Zareba work was most unpleasant here. The crickets and grass-hoppers chirped and sang the whole night. Huge beetles hummed through the air, and either settled above one's head, and fed upon the thorn-bush (which meant an everlasting shower of tiny particles of the green leaf falling upon one's face) or they settled *upon* one's face and head, when one brushed them off with a start. It was scratch, scratch, scratch all night long, as the ants and ticks crawled up one's arms and legs. The noises in the villages seldom cease before midnight. The men by your side either go to sleep and snore, or toss restlessly to and fro. The donkey makes you start up by braying now and then. The moon either persists in shining straight into your eyes, or the lightning flashes, the thunder rolls, and you are drenched to the skin with rain.

If was after just such a night as I have pictured that I

awoke to hear the news that our friend the lion had, for
the third time, come close to me, but without calling, and
had taken a goat from the next village, a few hundred
yards away. This animal appeared to be remarkably
cunning. He never visited the same zareba two nights
in succession. Sleepy and tired as I was, I was determined
to track him, and soon found the spoor.

On the way we passed a caravan which brought the
news that Mr. and Mrs. Stanford were on their way here.
The lion track was clear enough, as the feet of the goat he
carried in his mouth trailed along the ground.

Presently we came upon the contents of the stomach of
the goat, and soon after two of the feet and leg bones carefully cleaned of flesh. He then led us into most uninviting
thick bush, when it became very exciting. I was walking
close beside my shikari, when a magnificent lion with very
dark mane and skin jumped cat-like out of a thick patch of
high grass, and vanished in the bushes before I could get
the rifle up to my shoulder. He must have been within
12 or 15 yards of me, but so quickly did he vanish that I
hadn't the ghost of a chance, though I ran forward the
moment I sighted him. He did not appear to have seen us,
nor did he utter a sound. I was very dejected, but the
men all said they were very glad I had not fired, as he
would give me a better chance later on.

Well, we tracked that lion for what appeared to me to
be miles from that bush which contained the head and
neck of the goat, but at the end of an hour and a half I
found myself again at the bush, the lion having described a
large circle and come back to the goat. He had not
touched it further, however, and we now found by his
spoor that he was tracking us. However, he soon left our
spoor, and after pottering about a good deal, he must have
either heard us coming or got our wind, for his track
suddenly showed that he had begun to run. At length we
emerged from the terribly thick bush on to a grassy plain
thinly covered with small bushes. I knew then that he

had beaten us, and soon after, owing to the thick grass and hard ground, we lost the track altogether.

It was now very hot, so, after resting in the very inade-quate shade afforded by a thin thorn-bush, we wended our long, weary way home, which I reached tired and very hungry, not having tasted food for twenty hours, my last meal having been at 4 p.m. the day before ! My camp had been moved now near the villages, and on arrival my boy showed me a tiny black snake which he said he had found under the camel-mat which lay under my bed. He remarked, 'If he bite, you lif five minute—that's all !' What pleasant companions one has in one's tent in Africa !

In the evening a great crowd of men came in from the villages to see me and to show the rifles they had taken from the defeated Abyssinians. They were mostly of French 1874 and Egyptian make, but were nearly all serviceable weapons. They also had belts full of ' fire ' or ' angulation,' as my shikari called cartridge or ammunition. Later on a bevy of women, ever curious, came to look at the white man, and for a wonder allowed me to photograph them at close quarters. In all probability it was the chocolate I gave to their children which did it.

During the early morning of the following day a leopard ' jumped up ' at the village zareba, near which I was posted, over one of my sick camels. There were great cries of ' Libah ! libah !' (Lion ! lion !), but the track un-doubtedly proved it to be a leopard. In the afternoon I visited the ' wells ' at Gambissa, which presented a re-markable sight, some 5,000 camels, sheep, goats and cattle filling the lake, which was several hundred yards square and 5 feet deep. It was a long walk in the hot sun, and I came home feeling ill with a bad sun headache. I was shortly afterwards violently sick. My headman announced with a grin, on my arrival in camp, that my sick camel was dead, so I sent about twenty men to drag it to the zareba of last night, intending to sit over it that night. No lion turned up, however, and next morning Mr. and

Mrs. Stanford arrived, together with my caravan, bringing my long-lost portmanteau containing all my boots. Up to now I had been obliged to walk about in a pair of tennis-shoes, which were becoming every day more and more dilapidated. Mr. and Mrs. Stanford reported having had great sport in the Bun Toyo among the antelopes. They also brought with them two young oryx, alive. One, which they ran down on ponies, having separated it from a large herd, was about ten days old. The other was never born at all! His mother was shot, and the little one cut out of

THE WELLS OF GAMBISSA.

her alive! He was much darker than his bigger brother, which was a rich fawn colour, and totally different from the gray of the adult oryx beisa. Moses and Aaron were their names, and very appropriate ones too, as they spent their time in wandering through a wilderness. The bigger one, which had soft horns, 3 inches long, and was very timid, gave a lot of trouble, and had to have the milk poured down his throat through a funnel, the small one sucking at an improvised feeding - bottle on its own account. Between them they drank the milk of six goats daily ! When on the march they both had to be carried in hammocks by two men.

In the afternoon twenty horsemen turned up and gave us a *tomasho*. I was getting positively sick of these silly shows. Stanford brought me two fat sheep which the Sultan Muther had given him for me.

Next morning Stanford went to look for a white man, who was reported in the neighbourhood, but could not find him. Mrs. Stanford and I tracked a leopard, which had stolen a goat from one of the villages. We at length

YOUNG ORYX.

discovered that the leopard had placed the remains of the meat in a high thorn-tree. We left it until the afternoon, when, on one of the shikaris going to build a zareba under the tree, he found that the remains of the goat had gone ; no leopard track was visible, so that the meat had probably been taken away by some half-starved man or woman. Mrs. Stanford, however, sat up all night over a live goat tethered under the tree. What a surprise for the leopard on his return, to find his goat had come to life again ! However, he did not put in an appearance.

Next day we interviewed Nur Boora, King of the

Shebeyli people, who had defeated the Abyssinians in two
battles, killing a great number. They reported that the
headmen of the Abyssinians, Futto Warari and Ras
Mangashia, were dead. They took from them 600 rifles
and several thousand rounds of 'angulation.' In the
first fight they slew, with spears and arrows only, 165
Abyssinians, all armed with rifles.

At night I slept near my dead camel, which by this time
smelt horribly. Next morning we rode to the Gambissa
'wells.' The lake was now but half the size it was when I
first visited it, owing to the vast herds which had been
watered there within the last few days. I took some
photographs and shot a few birds. Here I found an
ingenious series of traps set in a long, low thorn fence, and
used for catching dik - dik antelope by the Midgans.
Nooses made of string had been arranged in little openings
all along the fence. Above the fence bits of dik-dik skin,
fastened to trees, were flapping about; these were used
as an attraction or lure. In the afternoon I dragged my
now putrid camel, all a seething mass of maggots, some
distance from the village, and built a zareba round him,
in which I made two openings, setting 'gin' traps in each
opening. They were carefully hidden in the sand. I then
warned the people in the village, and especially the children,
not to go near them, and told them if they touched the
traps it would mean instant death.

Mr. and Mrs. Stanford left me here next day, getting
news of rhinoceros further on. I discovered a fine striped
hyæna in one of my traps. After beating the brute
insensible, my men took him out of the trap, when he jumped
up, bit a man's *tobe* through and made off, but he was
saluted by my shot-gun with 'BB,' and fell stone-dead.
He had a very handsome coat, and a fine mane and bushy
tail. The ears of this animal are pointed, very narrow and
long, whilst those of its cousin, the spotted hyæna, are
rounded, very broad and short.

Not having had a shot at an antelope for upwards of ten

days, I went out north-west, through thick grass and thorn-jungle, to some open ground, some three hours' ride from camp. Here we found a small herd of oryx in very good stalking ground. As we neared them, my shikari got very excited, and whispered, 'Shoot, sahib! shoot!' but I merely shook my fist in his face, and crawled nearer the herd. Crawling to a small bush, a most painful operation owing to the thorns, I sat down and prepared to take a steady shot. The oryx had not seen me, so I waited my chance, then took a young bull which stood broadside on at 100 yards or so. With such an accurate weapon as the Mannlicher, a chance like that was 'a dead cert,' and with the second cartridge in the breech oryx No. 2 lay sprawling on the ground. Not having seen me, the remainder of the herd ran straight up to my bush, and stood within 15 yards of me, when one old bull advanced so close that, fearing mischief, I stood up and waved my hands, when they turned away right and left and bolted. After skinning the pair of oryx, the horns of one of which measured 6 inches round the base, although but 26 inches in length, we lighted a fire and cooked ourselves some steaks.

Next day I joined Mr. and Mrs. Stanford at Mirsin, passing the well at Gambissa on the way. Stanford came into camp shortly after me with a very fine female rhinoceros head and skin, and its baby (some five days old), the latter slung alive on the camel. The poor little brute, which was about 3 feet long, uttered the most piercing squeals on being released from its uncomfortable position. It was the most grotesque creature imaginable, and appeared to be blind, but butted at anyone who came near it. He was tied to a tree, and was visited by hundreds of Somali men and women during the afternoon. Stanford said that he had shot at the large rhinoceros, which immediately disappeared in the thick bushes. Then arose a series of unearthly squeals, which at length they discovered proceeded from as ugly a little brute as it has ever been my lot to see. The little fellow did not attempt to run away, but butted at the men

when they approached to secure it. They then followed
the mother's tracks, and found her under a tree, kneeling
in a most natural position, and stone-dead. Count
Wickenburg, a well-known sportsman, and a most genial
man, dined with us, and slept in camp during the night.

BABY RHINOCEROS.

Early next morning I got news of a lion, and after saying
good-bye to the Stanfords, who preferred to stay at Mirsin to
look for more 'rhino,' I marched through thick bush, passing
the wells of Ginaboo, Camiarli and Sarmon, near one of

which three female gerenook slowly walked past our track, with their long necks stretched out low in front of them. Never had I seen this usually timid animal so tame or so close (about 20 yards off) before. We camped at Seudone, where a lioness was reported with her three ' piccaninnies,' as my headman termed her cubs.

This happy family I decided to leave alone, and marched on next morning towards Garsoni, where a man-eating lion was reported. We found Elanli, and then struck out due east to Sirro and Labahgalli, where I shot the first vulturine guinea-fowl I had so far seen during this expedition. I also saw some ' gussuli' dik-dik. The following day, after passing a large lake at Abdin Libah, we reached Garsoni in time to build a zareba near a village possessing hundreds of cattle. I passed the usual sleepless night, and next morning endured agony from a stiff back through lying on the hard ground.

Next morning three men came into camp with news of a lion. One offered to show tracks ; another said a lion had killed a cow, and offered to show it us ; and a third appeared from another village, saying that a lion had carried off a girl. Each man wished us to accompany him.

We decided to follow the man-eater and build a zareba for the cattle-stealer. I rode and rode for miles until at length we reached the village. We were met by an old woman who told us that two Midgans were already tracking the lion. She showed us the place where the lion had jumped over the zareba and taken a girl fourteen years old. They had found the hands and feet of the luckless child, but nothing more. Close by was a Midgan's zareba, round which strutted a few tame ostriches, and within were to be found some dik-dik skins, together with the engines used in their capture. A huge lion-skin lay against a hut, and several tiny mangy dogs growled at me savagely when I approached.

After resting here a couple of hours, I went on to another village where a lion was reported, but finding it to

13

be a lie, I returned home very tired and went to bed. I
had not slept long before I was awakened by cries of
' Shebel! shebel !' (Leopard! leopard !). Seizing my gun and
some ' BB ' shot cartridges, I rushed out of my tent, and
saw a crowd of men in the direction of the traps I had set.

Running up, I saw an animal in one of the traps, which
my men assured me was a leopard and begged me to shoot ;
but as I was equally positive it was a spotted hyæna, and
not wishing to disturb lion by firing my gun, I ordered
them to hit it on the head. In the general excitement
which then ensued, my headman picked up a *hangol*, and,
swinging it round to strike the beast, hit me full across
the face, knocking me down and cutting my nose and cheek
badly. For several seconds I could see nothing but stars
and blood, but after bathing my face and ascertaining that
my nose was not broken, but that the hyæna's back was, I
turned in again. This spotted hyæna was a three-quarters-
grown male with very good mane and tawny yellow skin.
I consider hyænas, and especially the striped variety, by no
means a trophy to be despised, as in Somaliland they seem
to have unusually fine skins free from mange.

Next morning an old man came into camp offering to
show us a village round which the man-eating lion
prowled every night. I was getting perfectly sick of this
lion-hunting game, but as there was absolutely nothing
else to be done, I consented at last to follow him, after
making him swear that what he said was true. Accordingly, after a very long march we reached a village called
Gorly, taking with us three camels and a few men. The
headman of the village, who was an old man with one eye
and a gray beard, met me on arrival and behaved in a
very friendly way. He showed me where the lion had
squatted the night before in an empty zareba by the side
of one full of sheep, and when the noises in the village had
ceased, he had jumped over the fence and stolen a fat sheep.
We built a zareba, and he gave me a sheep to tie up outside. Nothing but hyænas, however, broke the silence of

the night. Two of these voracious animals charged the
sheep together. However, my shikari kept awake, for a
wonder, and stabbed one with his spear, and prevented the
other one getting a proper hold of the sheep.

When I had stayed there another night with no better
result, two of my men galloped into my camp from my
main body in a state of great excitement. They brought
the news that the man-eater, who evidently was having
a game of hide-and-seek with me, had taken a sixteen-year-
old boy from the village close to my main camp, and had
made off with him into the jungle. Swallowing a cup of
chocolate, I was soon in the saddle, and galloped hard
the ten miles which separated us from the main caravan.
After going about eight miles, my second shikari's pony fell
heavily, and man and rifle felt the sand, but luckily neither
was hurt. On arrival in camp, my headman showed me
where the cheeky lion had actually slept *inside* the little
zareba I had built and slept in myself a few nights before.
When all was quiet, he had crawled out and through the
village zareba (his hair being plainly visible on a sharp
stick in it), taken up the boy, and vanished into the jungle.
We at once took up the spoor, which led into the very
worst thorn and grass jungle imaginable. There were a
few spots of blood along the track, but as hyænas were
following him, we found no remains of the boy. After
passing over some stony ground, where the track became
almost invisible, we tracked him into an impenetrable
jungle, out of which he did not appear to have moved.
I and my shikaris took up our places to windward of this
spot, some hundred yards square, whilst my gunbearers fired
the grass. After a long pause, a dense cloud of smoke
became visible, and soon after the roar of the flames could
be heard, as they leaped over the branches of thorn-bush
and high, dense grass. On and on came the fire, fanned by
a strong wind. The smuts filled my eyes, and the volumes
of smoke darkened even the sun. The roar of the flames
became louder, and the heat almost unbearable. A hare,

with a coat which looked like that of a klipspringer, rushed
panic-stricken almost into me. I instinctively raised my
rifle, my nerves being strung to the utmost.

At length I could bear the heat no longer : the gigantic
tongues of flame were almost upon me, the roar of the fire
had become deafening. Just as I made one wild rush to
avoid it, I heard shouts to my right of ' Libah ! libah !' (Lion !
lion !). Running fast round the flames, I discovered that
the lion had broken covert close to three of my men, but
he had either been too quick for them, or they were too
frightened to fire. We literally raced on the spoor. All
at once my shikari shouted excitedly : ' Kill him ! kill him !'
' By all means,' I replied, ' but let me see him first ;' for I
saw only a tiny dik-dik antelope dash through the grass.

Soon after this excitement we fired the grass again, but
the lion dodged us a second time, and began to run, and
eventually we lost the track in utterly impossible jungle.
I went home dead tired, as I had not tasted food for
upwards of twenty hours. Determined to try my utmost
to bag the man-eater, I built zarebas near four different
villages, tied up baits outside each, and posted men inside
them. But the lion beat us even then, as he stole a small
camel in broad daylight, and retired with it into the jungle.

Whilst pottering about the villages, I met an eye-witness
of the death of Prince Ruspoli, who was killed by an
elephant south of the Webbi Shebeyli, after having behaved
extremely badly to the natives about the river. He said
that he had joined the Prince's caravan very reluctantly, well
knowing that the Prince was utterly mad. One day the
Prince, seeing a large elephant in the track, laid his rifle on
the ground, saying, ' I have killed three elephants ; see me
catch this one !' A minute afterwards, the narrator told
me, he was flying up skyward, and on coming down was
soon trodden into a jelly by the infuriated monster. All
this time I had been waiting for the Stanfords, to fetch
whom I had sent my guide.

CHAPTER III.

Fever—A big fight—A daring lion—Charged by a lion—Death of a leopard—Three lions reported—Troublesome natives.

NEXT morning a man came running in to say a large snake lay coiled up asleep in a high tree. I could not see his head, so when a large crowd of villagers had collected, I fired at its body, when two large pieces came wriggling down to the ground, amidst the applause of the astonished natives. It measured $5\frac{1}{2}$ feet in length, and was an African cobra. My boy and my cook further enlivened the morning by falling out with each other. They were careful, however, first to hide their knives, and preferred to fight with words only. ' You're a liar !' shouted my boy. ' You're a d—— liar !' hissed my cook. ' You sell the master's coffee !' roared my boy. ' You sleep all day, and steal his stores at night,' retorted the cook. ' You think of nothing but your billy ' (belly), sneered the boy. ' And you helped to eat your mother,' answered the cook, when he could think of nothing better to say. The noise became deafening, some of the men taking the boy's part, and others the cook's. Seizing a saucepan full of boiling water, I threw the lot, pan and all, right into the middle of the crowd, which in consequence quickly dispersed.

Early next morning I went with two men to a lake called Abdin Libah. Seeing a lot of duck upon it, I hid in some reeds on the bank whilst the men drove them over me. They came over me three or four times before they finally left the lake, offering very sporting shots. I made one of two 'gallery' shots, the crowd of natives which had come to water their cattle shouting out with astonishment when the ducks doubled up in the air and fell.

Going home my men said they knew a short-cut to camp; so, leaving the cattle track, we entered thick bush, and were soon afterwards utterly lost. I began to get very thirsty, foolishly omitting to drink at the lake, and not having my water-bottle with me. For several hours we wandered about in the dense jungle hopelessly lost. We fired our rifles and got up into trees, but all to no purpose. We tried to find the lake again, and then the cattle track. My throat became parched and very sore, and I began to cough. Just when I had had quite enough of it, we fell in with a boy tending some cattle, who put us on a cattle track and we finally reached camp in time. There was still no news of Stanford, and as I could find no guide to take me back to him, I could do nothing.

Next morning I was seized with fever, sore throat, and swollen glands. A man brought me in a present of a young bull, which immediately proved most refractory. First it charged the men, who leapt over the zareba like toreadors out of a bull-ring. Then it charged the camels, causing a general stampede. Next, after trampling over some hyæna-skins which were drying in the sun, it took it into its head to charge me or my tent, but got entangled in the tent-ropes just when I was about to put a ·450 solid into its head. We eventually secured it and tethered it to a tree.

That night the lion passed one of my zarebas, and, jumping into a village, killed an old man and dragged him out into the jungle. I was so bad with fever that I utterly refused to follow him, but sent some of my men, who followed the track, and found the remains of the man, but did not come across the lion. In the afternoon the same lion killed a large cow and dragged it close past my tent into the thick bush. This I thought might drive my fever away, so I started tracking. We soon found the half-eaten cow hidden in a frightful maze of thorn-bush. I crept in on hands and knees, expecting the lion to charge me every moment, but with a snarling cough he bounded out on the far side of the thicket, and I was too ill to follow him further.

We built a zareba by the dead cow, and I very foolishly slept in it that night. Next morning my fever was worse, I having passed a most miserable night. I joined my caravan at Abdin Libah, as I was determined to get away to a change of air.

Two days before I had sent two men to look for Stanford, but they now returned saying they could neither find the way alone nor get a guide to show it them; and as Stanford did not send any answer to the message I had sent a fort- night before by my former guide, I never expected to see him again.

In the afternoon one of my camels refused to move, so I was obliged to shoot it. Sultan Abdi turned up and did his level best to detain me at Abdin Libah; but I was firm, knowing that unless I got out of this fever district at once I might die.

Next day we marched through miserable, dried-up country, with not a bit of green to be seen. I felt so ill and weak that I could not sit in the saddle, and finally had to be supported on either side by two men. We camped at night at a place called Well Wall.

Next day I was worse, for I had now contracted a bad quinsy in my throat, so that I could with difficulty swallow. I was again supported on my pony. At length we reached an open plain, about half a mile square, dotted over with large green trees, the first I had seen since leaving Abdin Libah. Under each green tree was a well, some of which reached a depth of 14 fathoms. The name of this place was Wardare. Here I was lifted off my pony and deposited under a tree until my tent was pitched. I then gave orders to my shikari to shoot dik-dik to make soup, feeling as I did so like Isaac when he told Esau to ' go out to the field and take me some venison, and make me some savoury meat

such as I love, and bring it to me that I may eat . . .
before I die.' I don't know what happened after this until
I found myself in bed in my tent, when my boy remarked,
'At last you wake up, when alsame dead.' I drank some
soup, dosed myself with quinine, and made myself dead
drunk with champagne.

On waking next morning, I found, much to my surprise,
that my quinsy was better, and, lo and behold! my fever
had vanished entirely. I could eat; in fact, I felt a
different person. I began once more to look about me
with interest, and to examine the two new dik-dik skulls
and skins my shikari had shot for me. I remained in bed
all day, and although very weak ate ravenously. Luckily
it was a comparatively cool day.

In the evening a caravan arrived, and begged and prayed
me to wait another day, as they wished for the protection
of my armed escort to pass through a hostile tribe. When
I consented, they all came and clasped my hand, touched
their foreheads, and said, 'Salaam, sahib, salaam.' I spent
a sleepless night, tormented by thousands of mosquitoes
(the first I had met with since leaving Berbera), the cries
of dozens of hyænas, which howled quite close round the
camp, and the chattering and croaking of guinea-fowls,
crickets and lizards. I rested long in bed, still feeling very
weak, but was at length aroused by shouts outside the
zareba, followed by a bustle on the part of my men in camp.
Peeping through the window of my tent, I saw my men
buckling on their cartridge-belts, seizing their rifles, and
rushing out of the zareba. I blew my whistle and inquired,
'War wassidy?' (What's up?) My boy replied, 'Somali
only tarking (talking) bunterbust (business).' Something
more exciting than 'bunterbust,' I thought to myself, as I
fell back again in bed, and went fast asleep.

I did not wake again till the sun's rays forced me out of
bed. A large crowd of men instantly surrounded me.
I was given a long account of how one of my men had
attempted to get water at the well, but a young man had

come up and said that the wells had been dug by his fore-
fathers, and that none but his tribe should drink therefrom.
He then proceeded to hit my man a severe blow across the
cheek with his spear, to which my man responded with
excellent judgment, for he threw down his loaded rifle, and,
giving his assailant two smart blows above and below the
eye with a thick stick, knocked him head over heels to the
ground. A big fight followed, and I was called upon to
patch up the wounded, some of whom showed very nasty
deep stabs and gaping gashes. When they saw I was a
' medicine man,' they all ran off to their villages and brought
their halt and maimed and blind for me to cure. Amongst
this ghastly array was a child with the most hideous disease
I have ever beheld (probably lupus). I will not defile
these pages with a description of this loathsome object which
was presented before me. I could only shudder, and refer
the patient to the doctor at Berbera. Poor child! it would
have been really merciful to have put a bullet through the
piece of matter which was supposed to be its head, for it
suffered agonies. It would have been a priceless treasure
in pickle in some medical museum in England.

I sent my shikari out shooting, being too weak to walk
myself, bought some milch goats, mended *harns*, and prepared for a long, waterless march across the Marehan desert
on the morrow. My shikari was very busy with the gun
(rather too busy, considering the number of cartridges he
exploded), but he brought home half a dozen guinea-fowl
(vulturine), some guyu, and some ' gussuli ' dik-dik antelopes. I tried to buy or hire extra camels and water *harns*
to carry us across the desert, but failed, and decided to
trust to what we had. I dosed myself again heavily with
quinine and champagne, and, remembering the night before,
rigged up the mosquito-curtain.

At 5 o'clock next morning I started to cross the great
Marehan waterless desert in a south-easterly direction
in quest of elephants. Soon after it became light I sighted
an antelope, and seized the first weapon that came to hand,

which happened to be my shot-gun. Aiming for the
animal's neck, I fired. Result : a fine male dibitag stone-
dead 30 yards off. I bore my first day's march after my
fever fairly well. At the mid-day rest we watered all the
horses, and sent back all the empty *harns* and barrels to be
refilled, the men having instructions to march until they
caught us up again, which they did shortly after midnight.

Next day we passed some real hills (the Gabo range of
mountains), and camped at Isor, upon a large open plain at
the foot of the mountains. Here we tracked, unsuccessfully, a leopard which was dragging a dik-dik along the
ground.

Next morning we marched at 3.30. I was so sleepy
that I twice fell asleep in the saddle, and woke up to find
the reins hanging loose upon my pony's neck. Passing
Berisodare, where I caught a glimpse of a cheetah or
hunting leopard ; Jade, where there were shallow dried-up
wells ; and Gorishor, where we passed hundreds upon
hundreds of camels, sheep and goats, we at length
reached a place called Habr Heshi, in the heart of
the Marehan country, having been on the march for five
and a half days without encountering a drop of water *en
route*. At this place there had evidently been a large lake,
but it was now all but dried up, a few shallow wells dug
out by the natives holding the last few *harns* full. All
round the lake were to be seen the fresh ' pugs ' of a large
lion, so we built two zarebas for him on arrival. Thousands
of pigeons were here to be seen drinking. Brown birds flew
about in coveys, and looked when on the wing not unlike
partridges. These birds turned out to be sand-grouse.
The natives seemed a bit troublesome, and twice we were
obliged to seize the spears, shields, and knobkerries of men
who threatened to kill some of my escort.

At sunset, taking the donkey with me, I selected the
zareba furthest away from the main camp and the noise of
my caravan, and also because it was the larger of the two
and would accommodate my bedding with more comfort.

It also, from a lion's point of view, afforded a better sight of the donkey, which could be seen by him a long way off. I put my shikari in the other zareba outside which my young bull was tethered, the main camp being between us, some 200 yards from me.

Directly the sun set I foresaw that it would be a very dark night, as the sky became overcast with heavy rain-clouds and a strong wind was blowing. It must have been ten o'clock and pitch dark, when suddenly we heard a tremendous commotion in camp on the other side of the dried-up lake. Men shouted and hooted, and this was followed by a perfect babel of talking. Then all was quiet for about five minutes, when another uproar arose, hisses, hoots and yells, again followed by absolute silence. I sat and marvelled. About three minutes after the second uproar, a shot was fired by my shikari in the second zareba. This was quickly followed by a second, and shortly after by a third. Nothing further occurred to disturb my night's rest, and I awoke about 3 a.m. to find it intensely cold. I wrapped myself up as well as I could, but stop shivering I could not, and I knew that my fever was coming on again.

About 3.30, when the moon came up, a caravan approached the wells to drink, singing loudly. Just before sunrise I was let out of the zareba, feeling very feverish and miserably cold. Whilst walking across the dried-up lake, close past a lot of wild geese and guinea-fowl, as tame as sparrows, I was met by one of my men, saying that the lion had sprung right over the zareba round my camp, run between a boy and a man who lay asleep a couple of feet apart, almost touching them, and killed my best milch goat, which was tethered to a stake in the very centre of the herd of camels. The sentry, who for a wonder was not asleep, seeing my pony prick his ears, and hearing him snort, suddenly caught sight of the lion close to him, and shouted to the men to be on their guard. All the men jumped up, yelled, hissed and hooted. The lion got bewildered, dropped the goat, and jumped out.

Two minutes after the lion actually jumped in again, and was once more driven out by my men, who had been given strict orders by me not to fire at him unless absolutely necessary in order to save life. The lion then walked round the zareba towards the water, where he fell in with the bull tethered up outside my shikari's small zareba.

The story was now taken up by my shikari himself, who, to say the least of it, looked very glum. He said that after the noise in camp had ceased for the second time, the lion came and contemplated the bull, when he (my shikari) fired at the lion, and killed my bull. The lion still looked on in wonderment, with his head carried low, some 10 yards from the dead bull. My shikari took a long aim and hit the bull again. The lion didn't seem to care a button, but only moved a little closer, when my shikari fired a third time, right in his face, and, according to his account, hit him, for he bolted. Small wonder! When it was light enough to see, I examined the bull, and found the two bullet-holes in his neck.

After a cup of coffee I started tracking the lion. Now, tracking a lion, especially if you think he may be a wounded lion, is not exactly child's play, but in order to be successful in this exciting sport one must throw one's fears to the winds. I carried my favourite ·450 rifle and revolver, whilst my shikaris attended with my eight-bore and another ·450. About 100 yards behind us came some of the camel-men leading ponies. We had not proceeded through the bushes more than a quarter of a mile, when I saw the lion trotting, or rather ambling, along, with his head carried, as usual, very low, and apparently going at a great pace several hundred yards ahead of us. I could not get in a shot, he was too quick. We now shouted back for the ponies, as the bush here was not so thick. Five minutes after I again saw the lion ambling along in front of me. I fired, and hit him somewhere behind. He gave a low growl and disappeared. We were following his spoor very fast, when suddenly from a thick bush came a terrible snarling and growling. I peered into the bush, but saw nothing. My second shikari, who stood on my left, however, called to me that he could see the lion, so I stumbled over a small bush to get near him. At last I caught a glimpse of his tail lashing his sides violently, the growling continuing. I could see nothing definite to fire at, when all at once the growl turned into a terrific roar, there was a great scuffling sound in the bush, and a lion's head appeared in an opening in the bush. There was no mistake about it, he was coming. In less time than it takes to say ' knife,' he was clear of the bush and coming straight at me. With a coughing roar, with his tail working up and down stiff as a poker, his ears well back, and his huge teeth showing, he looked the very picture of rage and agony. I didn't let him come far, I can tell you, and taking as careful aim as I could at his head, I put a bullet in exactly between his eyes when he was within 15 yards of me. He doubled up and fell, but as he still moved, I put another ball into his head to make sure of him.

Then I sent up a yell of triumph that would have frightened the bravest lion out of its wits. It was well echoed by my men, who came racing down upon me, firing their rifles in the air, and tumbling over each other in a mad race to shake me by the hand. The ponies galloped up, followed by a huge crowd of men, women and children, who shrieked and yelled and careered about as if they were all stark staring mad. Bullets whizzed through the air, till I marvelled nobody was shot. The excitement had entirely driven away my fever. Four men lifted up the huge frame of the lion and bore it to camp, and my headman—nearly weeping for joy as he thought of the fat sheep I should have to buy to do honour to the occasion—took me by the hand and led me back to camp, muttering, ' It is goot—it is *very* goot.'

All the morning I busied myself measuring, photographing and superintending the skinning of the lion, which, although possessing a poor mane, was in point of size a magnificent fellow. Length from tip of nose to end of tail *before* skinning, 9 feet 3 inches; *after* skinning, 11 feet; girth behind shoulder, 43 inches *before* skinning; length of tail, 33¾ inches; girth of fore-paw, 12¾ inches; breadth of ear 6 inches; weight, 402 pounds. I could not very well measure the skull, as the brain pan was smashed up entirely. His teeth were much worn at the tips, showing that he was a very old fellow. In fact, an old man who saw him, recognised him at once, and said that he had drunk at these

DEAD LION AND GUNBEARERS.

wells for the last twenty years. Three things struck me as he lay stretched out dead before me : first, the enormous breadth of the ear ; secondly, the quantity of ticks which infested every portion of his body, and especially the mane ; and thirdly, the quantity of particles of wood and thorns which had gone in at the foot and worked their way right up the legs between the flesh and the skin, some having reached the armpits, causing the poor animal a good deal of pain, I should imagine.

At night I tied up my goat, which had been killed by the lion, and also a live kid, and slept, or rather lay awake, in the zareba by them. I also set the traps, hoping for a leopard. Remembering the night before, I took extra thick clothing with me, and in consequence it was a very hot clear night. I could not sleep a wink, owing to the bleating of the kid and the noise made by a caravan taking water at the wells all night. A lion roared to the north of us about midnight, but he did not put in an appearance. Soon after something crawled round the zareba and pounced upon the kid, which never uttered a cry, and directly afterwards there was a great crunching of bones and scratching of flesh. I was up in a second, and, peering through the loophole, could see the goat and kid, but absolutely nothing else. The men close by the wells were making a great noise, but the scratching and crunching continued. One of my men now looked through the hole, and immediately whispered excitedly, 'Shebel! shebel!' (Leopard! leopard!). I gazed through the hole again, and strained my eyes to their utmost. I saw nothing. I cracked a twig, hoping the animal would put up its head. Not a bit of it. I held a loud whispering conversation with the man, who begged me to ' Shoot! shoot!' But I was determined not to be in any hurry, and so perhaps imitate my shikari and the bull episode. I pushed my rifle through the loophole and stared hard. I suppose my eyes got accustomed at last to the darkness, for all at once I made out a dark object lying very flat on its stomach facing me, and, as far as I could make out, endeavouring to pull the goat away, whilst the crunching and scratching still continued. I pointed my rifle at the object—to take aim was impossible, as, on putting the rifle up to my shoulder, I could not even see the hammers, much less the sights—and fired. Then I listened. I heard two gurgling sobs, and then all was still. Leopard or hyæna, I knew I had killed him. I made out a dark form lying beyond the goat, but although we could just touch him with the *hangol*, we could not drag him nearer. My man was positive it was a leopard, and so, as we could not possibly get out of the zareba alone, we shouted to the men in camp to bring a lantern. After a great deal of talking in camp, and an interval of what seemed to me an age, some men were heard approaching bearing a lantern. I grew quite excited. Would it turn out to be a leopard or merely a spotted hyæna? The light arrived at last; I saw the beautiful spots at once. Hurrah! I had killed a leopard. They bore him to camp, whilst I took a drink of water, for the night was very hot.

When the men had, as I thought, all but reached camp, two rifle-shots were fired in quick succession. At first I thought it must be my shikari again firing at the bull. My men, however, assured me the sound came from the direction of the traps. Nothing further occurred, and I got out of the zareba at daybreak.

On reaching camp, my first inquiry was into the firing we had heard. I was told that the men who were bearing back my leopard to camp thought they might as well have a look at the traps on the way. On reaching one of the little zarebas, out jumped a leopard, and they had both fired, the bullets striking the ground between my boy and a camel-man, who were lying in the middle of my camp. ' I go very near to dead,' said my boy to me, with a piteous grimace. The camel-man echoed his sentiments. In one of the traps we found a little animal of the ferret tribe, with long black and yellowish-white hair and bushy tail, which I was very pleased to get. I now examined my leopard. The bullet had gone through his left eye. He was small, but possessed a beautiful skin. He measured 5 feet 4 inches from tip of nose to tip of tail before skinning. And the pegged skin measured 6 feet 10 inches. A lion and a leopard in two nights! Come, things were improving.

During the day one of my men had a fight with a stranger at the well, the stranger getting off second best. He came up to me for money, but I told him I did not give presents for fighting. I offered to bandage up all the cuts he had received on his face, but he said, No ; he wanted backsheesh, so I bundled him out of camp. These petty fights were getting serious, as they might lead to some big row in which the rifles would have to be used.

I again sat in my zareba over the dead goat and kid ; the former by this time was ' not all lavender ' to the olfactory nerves. During the night a striped hyæna came along and began eating the carcases. I let him have it in the face, and after running after his own tail for a minute, he collapsed and expired. He had a fine skin.

After breakfast I made a thorough examination of all my skins, and found that the well-known larvæ of the black beetle with white shoulders had been playing sad havoc with some of them. I anointed them freely with turpentine, the stock of which I was sorry to find was rapidly vanishing.

At 2 p.m. we marched from Habr Heshi, and encountered a number of ' gussuli ' dik-dik. I stalked, I ran, I crawled, I crouched, but I could get nowhere near the tantalizing little antelopes, which run in triplets as a rule, unlike ' guyu ' and ' golass ' dik-diks, which run in pairs. After a mile we saw absolutely no game, and no wonder ! for a more parched, burnt-up country I never saw, not a green leaf nor a green blade of grass to be seen. Certainly a most unpromising country to find elephants in. We camped at Godargal as the sun set.

About 9.30 next morning we reached a shallow lake called El Deneli. Here I found a huge flock of vulturine guinea-fowl with brilliant blue and white feathers on their breasts. After a careful stalk I managed to bag three. These fowl are excellent eating.

Some men reported three lions about some villages two hours' march off, so directly my men had finished their rice I sent them off there to build a zareba for me. Here I discovered that the ears of my lion were beginning to ' smile ' (smell), which caused the hair outside to ' slip '—*i.e.*,

14

come off. The ears of a lion are very thick, and contain a
good deal of flesh. They should by rights be skinned right
out, which, by-the-by, must be done with great care. By
rubbing alum and saltpetre well into the inside of the ear
the hair on the outside will be preserved.

After marching west for two and a half hours, passing
immense herds of camels, cattle, sheep and goats, we
reached a place called Harari Wana. Here were two or
three villages situated some 100 yards apart. I was glad
to find that the report of lions was true, for a wonder, as I
saw the well-known appliances hung up round the village
zareba to frighten away the lions : bits of *tobe* tied to poles
and stuck up like flags ; ropes with bits of tin attached,
which banged against the zareba, making a clanking noise.
But little does a hungry lion care for such trifles. Most of
the people here had never seen a white man before, and the
men looked upon me with suspicious and scowling looks at
first, whilst the women grinned and leered. For two nights
I sat in a small zareba between the villages, but no lion
put in an appearance. Singing and prayer-chanting was
kept up till a very late hour at night, and began again
early in the morning. Crowds of children surrounded their
elders, who gabbled off texts from the Koran, which were
written upon long wooden tablets in Arabic.

I marched back to the lake at El Deneli, and from there
to Gerigeree, where there was the same monotonous lake.
Everything is the same in this beastly country. One sees
the same trees, the same thorn-bushes, the same rising and
falling ground, the same red sand for miles and miles and
miles.

At Gerigeree we fell in with a great crowd of people,
some Marehan, some Ogaden, and some Haweea. I went
out in the morning to look for small koodoo, which were
reported, but saw nothing but cattle. Hearing firing going
on in camp, I hastily returned, when my headman told me
that the natives were ' saucy,' and that my men had been
obliged to fire blank-cartridge over their heads, when they

all 'ran away like birds.' We found it very difficult to trade with these people, who swarmed into the zareba like bees, and had to be quietly, but firmly, ejected by my sentries. In the evening they started a dance, the men throwing themselves about, tying their legs into knots, and behaving like raving madmen.

CHAPTER IV.

NEXT day I followed some dibitag in thick bush, and,
peeping under a thicket, saw a fine buck staring at me.
I had just time to put up my rifle and 'snap' at him,
hitting him right in the chest; he took an enormous bound
and fell dead. The bush was full of 'gussuli' dik-dik, but
I failed to get within gunshot of these wary little antelopes.

Coming home, I found natives assembled in hundreds
round my camp, and my headman assured me they meant
to fight, as they spoke of looting my camels. In the
afternoon more people arrived, and at 3.30 I left the
zareba to witness their dancing. The ladies of the party
were at first very shy, and hid in the bushes close by;
but hearing the clapping of hands and stamping of feet,
they could resist it no longer, and came forth to join
in the dance. It was not exactly a drawing-room enter-
tainment, and if the Licensing Committee of the London
County Council had been present, and the song had been
translated to them, I think they would have been carried
out on stretchers. It was with the greatest difficulty
that the crowd could be kept back so that I could see, and
I could not help laughing when one of my men fired a
blank-cartridge in the air, for at least ten men would fall
flat on their faces to the earth in terror, on hearing the
report. During the dance I had extra men on sentry,
watching the grazing camels about half a mile away; and

it was well I did so, as natives were stalking them the whole time. After the people had danced themselves into a perfect frenzy—some of the young men falling down as if in a fit, their arms dropping helplessly to their sides when lifted up—I thought it was time to stop, so entered the zareba to fetch them out a present. My headman walked out with a bundle of *tobes* under his arm. Then commenced such a hubbub as I had never before heard in Somaliland. Before my headman could give the *tobes* to the head dancing man, there was a general rush made for him by the crowd, the *tobes* he carried were snatched out of his arms, and he himself was sent backwards rolling upon the ground. The thieves then made off at best pace through the bushes. It was now all I could do to prevent my men from firing at the runaways. Half a dozen of my men rushed madly after them, when two of the thieves dropped their spoil, whilst the others disappeared in the bush with four *tobes*. Now, my headman, although a great villain, was a shrewd man, and the moment he picked himself up he whispered something in my ear, and, beckoning to four of my men, calmly walked up to a pony which was tied up to a bush, undid the halter, took up the saddle and bridle, and trotted him into camp, with two men with loaded rifles in front and two behind. After them came a huge crowd of natives, shouting, jeering, shaking and poising their spears. By this time I had upwards of fifteen men with loaded rifles all ready for action, and as the pony was ' run in ' to camp, I gave the order to each to cover a man with his rifle and fire the instant the first spear was thrown. As the crowd neared the camp, the elder men stopped, and the younger men stooped and ran off sideways when they saw the rifles levelled at their heads. We then held a palaver with the headmen, telling them that they would receive their pony back when they returned our *tobes* to us. The dancing-men were of course furious at losing their present, and at once sent off after the thieves, and in a very short time we heard a song of welcome and the well-known ' Mot, mot,

mot, io mot !' (Hail, all hail !), as two horsemen galloped up, followed by a crowd bearing the looted goods. A pair of sandals which had also been looted were not to be found, so one of the men took his own off his feet and gave them to me. The pony was immediately given back to them and peace restored. Great praise was due to my men for keeping so calm and reserving their fire, for at one moment, had they used their rifles, we should most assuredly have been in for a big fight, the crowd being of course far superior to us in point of numbers.

Next day, in the presence of an enormous crowd, we marched for Sinnadogho, where elephants were reported. I started off with my shikaris a little in advance of the main body, but was not destined to go far, as shortly afterwards one of my men rushed after me with glaring eyes and intensely excited, and began, ' Five hundred men——'

' Great Scot !' thought I to myself, 'has the whole caravan been annihilated, or what ?'

He went on to say that a great crowd of natives had entered the zareba just as the last two or three camels were being loaded up, and had looted some of my rifles. My headman had then harangued the crowd, telling them that, as the sahib was not there, he should do nothing until he had seen him, and that unless the rifles were forthcoming on the morrow at the ' well ' at a certain time, further steps would be taken against them.

On hearing the news I pitched camp, intending to take an armed escort against the village on the morrow, and drive off some cattle or camels from them in the event of my rifles not being returned to me. These steps had to be taken, as the news spreads so quickly in this country. Otherwise every tribe in the Marehan country, on hearing that we had been looted would have at once come down upon us to see what they could do in the same direction.

At daybreak next morning I set out at the head of my little army of twenty men (leaving the rest on guard in camp) to do battle if needs must with the ' five hundred men,' and retrieve my stolen rifles. My men had twenty-five rounds of 'angulation' each, and I took my ·256 Mannlicher and revolver.

We marched without incident to the 'well' at Gerigeree and along the shore of the shallow lake, past crowds of natives watering their flocks and herds, to a shady tree, where we quietly halted. We then sent our guideman, who belonged to the same tribe as the thieves, to the village to ascertain if they intended to give up the rifles. We awaited events for several hours. I was beginning to get very tired of sitting under the very inadequate shade afforded by the tree, when in the distance we saw our guide walking alone, bearing in triumph my looted rifles. I must own I was perhaps a little bit disappointed at the tame ending of hostilities, as I should dearly have loved to have given those villagers a good thrashing.

When our guide came up, we all turned and marched back to camp, where we found the Sultan of the Marehan country, who had come to pay his respects to me. He told me he had seen but one white man before me. He begged food, as he said his men had come a long distance. It sounded rather odd that a Sultan should have to beg for food, but so it was. I gave him a sheep and a red *tobe*, and he promised to keep his people from molesting me further.

During the night a lion walked all round our camp, but luckily did not jump in. The caravan which had joined us at Wardair gave us this information when they came up to us at the mid-day halt at Alanli. It was then too late to go back and attempt to track the lion. Here the caravan, which had marched with us for over 100 miles, left us. I had not encountered a single head of game throughout the day.

Next morning, after killing a fine male Clarke's gazelle, we left the red-sand country and encountered uneven ground covered with horrid white loose stones, like the ground in the Boorgha country in the west. These stones

are fearfully tiring to walk upon, and my pony stumbled
about on them in such a slip-shod manner that I expected
every moment to feel how hard they were.

For the last few days the heat was very great, and it
was piteous to see how the animals suffered from thirst, the
goats becoming so tame that they actually came into my
tent and drank the water in my bath as I sat in it pouring
the precious fluid over myself with a sponge.

The whole of the next morning we marched over the
horrible stones, seeing a great number of ' gussuli ' antelope,

HALT FOR THE MID-DAY REST.

four of which I shot for the pot. Two of the males had
very good heads. The nose of this extraordinary-looking
animal is shaped like a miniature tapir's snout.

At noon we emerged into an open stony plain, in the
middle of which was a deep well, the water bubbling up
through the rock. Here were half a dozen Midgans, who
on seeing our approach began to fix their poisoned arrows
in their bows, but on our firing a couple of shots in the air
they dropped them and sat down. They told us there were
a great number of elephants in the neighbourhood, that

they had seen five that very morning, and that if we encamped here (a place called El Dara) we were sure to find them.

Giving them some dik-dik meat, we sent them off in search of elephants, and camped on the stony plain. I tried to enjoy the luxury of a bath with plenty of water, but the bees swarmed into my tent, and after they had stung me three or four times in the bath, I swore vengeance on them, and sent out two of my men to look for honey. They returned in a very short time bearing a quantity of most delicious honey which they had found in the rotten trunk of a tree.

We had now passed the regions of clouds, and must have been some six or eight days' march from the east coast. The heat during the day was very great. In the evening one of the Midgans returned saying he had tracked a big male elephant on its way to drink at Sinnadogho, but as it did not stop moving, he did not come and tell us of it before. He reported plenty of koodoo three marches west, at a place called Gaboon.

I sent off four men to examine the wells at Sinnadogho, and prepared to set out on an elephant hunt on the morrow. We started out at daybreak after elephant, going east. We found nothing but old tracks, and the heat during the day was terrific. I drank all the water in my bottle, and half of the men's, and then wanted more! We took two Midgans with us, but the hunt was an utter failure, as most elephant hunts are nowadays, for the common reason that there are no elephants to hunt. The loose stony ground, the great heat, and fearful thirst all helped to tire one, and I reached camp that night utterly worn out. On entering my tent, I threw myself on my bed, hoping to find rest at last, only to be stung in the back by a bee. Then I tried to have a bath. Not a bit of it! Twice was I stung in the head by bees which had settled in my damp sponge, and three times I picked out the stings from my body. After this I ran amuck, threw

bath, water, pails and towels in every direction and fled, all
naked as I was, out of the zareba.

Next morning we marched at daybreak, and for a wonder
had nice fine weather; that is to say, the sky was covered
with dense black clouds, and it was quite cold. Bright sun
all day is called very bad weather in this country.

At 8.30 a.m. we camped, and as I was lying resting on
my bed I heard yells of ' Bundook! bundook!' and a sound
of men rushing in every direction to find their rifles.
Seizing my revolver and rushing out, I shouted : ' Wa
wassidi ?' (What is it ?) to my headman ; he answered that
as he saw all the men were asleep without their rifles near
them, he thought it best to give them all a scare.

At 3.30 we reached Sinnadogho, a lake of comparatively
clear spring water, 100 yards square in the solid white
rock. Its rippling surface was covered with a flock of
upwards of 200 wild geese, several dabchicks, and a
few duck, whilst some ' waders ' stalked about its edge.
My men were most of them expert swimmers and divers.
They would swim under water for upwards of 50 yards,
when a wild goose would suddenly disappear below the
surface of the water, and up would come a man with it in
his hand, having taken it by the leg from under the water
and dragged it down. Several were caught in this way
and allowed to escape, until they became too wily, and flew
when on the point of being grabbed. We found the tracks
and dung of elephants about three days old round the
edges of the lake.

A Doolbahanta man came up with his wife and said
' Salaam ' on our arrival. His wife was the prettiest—in fact,
I may say the only pretty—woman I ever saw in Somaliland.
Tall, and with a very good figure, she had a beautiful face,
with long aquiline nose, snow-white teeth, and lovely
languid-looking eyes.

On camp being pitched some 200 yards from the lake, I
was horrified to see that the thorn-bushes had wrought
great havoc amongst my dried skins ; some of the noses and

ears of the antelopes were literally torn to shreds. I had a most enjoyable swim in the cold water. It was the first really clean-water bath I had enjoyed since leaving Berbera.

Whilst I was dressing next morning in my tent, my headman rushed in shouting, ' Bundook, sahib, quick !' Seizing my Mannlicher and dashing out, I beheld between sixty and seventy wild dogs quietly making off on the opposite side of the lake. I followed them into the bushes, but owing to the stony nature of the ground it was utterly impossible to track them, and I looked for them in vain. I was much disappointed, having always wished to collect a specimen of this comparatively rare animal.

During the morning a prisoner was brought into camp. He had stalked one of my men at the well, and was on the point of stabbing him from behind with his spear, when another of my men, seeing him, knocked him head over heels, took his spears and shield, and brought him into camp. We tied his arms behind his back and attached him to a tree. All my men wanted me to shoot him, but I laughed at them, telling them I had come here to shoot elephants, not men. This man of the tribe of the Goom Adla was only acting after the manner of his tribe, trying to kill a man in order that he might be able to wear an ostrich feather in his hair, and then marry. We kept him in camp the whole day and night, in spite of his friends' prayers that he might be given up. But I was determined to frighten them, and stop this dangerous game of theirs once and for all. I told them to fetch all their headmen to apologize for him, and told them I was going to take him to Berbera to be judged. This produced a great impression upon his friends, who at once sent off to his village for the headmen, and then started one of their dances, which was even more abandoned than those of the people at Gerigeree.

Next day about 100 men turned up at the well, determined to rescue the prisoner if possible. When they

were well in sight, I made a great show of preparing for
a fight ; made a big barricade of store boxes and rice-bags,
reviewed the men, their rifles and cartridge-belts, and
opened fresh boxes of cartridges.

For upwards of two hours we sat awaiting results, the
enemy watching our movements with great interest. At
length one man advanced and asked for the release of the
prisoner, but I sent him back to confer with the old headmen. After half an hour they all turned up and came into
my tent, and then began such a long harangue between
them and my interpreters that I all but fell asleep in my
chair. The result of it was that they all agreed to tell their
tribesmen not to molest my men in any way. They gave
me a fat sheep and a shield as a peace-offering, and promised
good behaviour in future. I gave up the prisoner's spears,
shield, and tomahawk, to the headman, and let loose the
captive. Then followed the usual *tomasho* and dancing.
Several women, and very ugly ones, too, took part in the
dance, which was kept up for upwards of two hours. The
women stood on one side, the men on the other. A man
advances clapping his hands, singing, and stamping first
one foot upon the ground, and then the other, in the usual
African fashion. A woman then advances from the opposite
side in a shuffling sort of way, her hands clasped as though
in prayer, her eyes on the ground, and emitting a curious
hissing noise through her teeth. The rest of the dance
is best left unexplained. This dance went on for fully a
couple of hours, some of the young men working themselves up into a perfect frenzy. As I wished to put the
people in a good humour, I sat it out, though I wished all
the dancers at the devil. At last they stopped, and after
giving the headman of the dance a present, I showed the
whole gang out of the place, and right glad I was to be
quit of them. When they had all gone, I threw myself on
my bed, for I was tired out with the long anxious day, the
dust, and the heat.

I spent four more days at the lake at Sinnadogho,

searching in vain for elephants. I held swimming races, some of which were most exciting, and a shooting competition, giving money prizes to the winners. The heat during the time I was there was very great.

Early one morning my headman rushed into my tent and woke me with the pleasing news that ' A force comes.' I then heard the well-known ' Ou, ou, ou, ou, ou !' shouted by men when on the war-path, and hastened to get at my rifle and cartridges ; but it proved to be a false alarm, the noise being occasioned by a crowd of men and boys pursuing a hyæna which had run off with a sheep.

From Sinnadogho I had my best pony looted by natives, whilst my syce, who was supposed to be looking after it, was asleep. I at once sent out men in every direction to get news of it. Some of the men came reporting fresh elephant tracks, so I went after them with seven camels and ten men, with four days' rations. The track turned out to be at least a day old, and after walking for six hours without a halt, we camped for the mid-day rest.

On the way we stalked two Midgans (low-caste Somalis), and when they were in the act of putting poisoned arrows into their bows, we put up our hands, and they sat down. They were seeking gum, and had seen no elephants.

Soon after restarting, two men we had sent some days ago to a well far off, in search of elephants, came racing after us with the news that elephants were to be seen in plenty at a place called Joh, two days' march from Sinnadogho. I asked them if they had seen the elephants, and they replied :

' No ; but we hear him drink and shout at the well.'

As there was absolutely no hope of ever coming up with the elephants we were following, I turned round and made back again for Sinnadogho, where I had left the main camp. On the way we discovered an ant-hill some 12 feet high, in and out of the top of which flew bees by the thousand. We held a council of war. I was for making a huge fire, but my men pooh-poohed the idea. No, they would knock off the top of the ant-hill with stones, and then abstract the honey. No sooner said than done. We stormed the stronghold with stones, a breach was made in the fortress, when out issued thousands upon thousands of the enemy. My men fell backwards into the bushes, and were covered with the enemy's poisoned arrows. Those who had not fallen rushed pell-mell through the bushes, swinging their arms about in every direction, and tearing bits off their *tobes* as they dashed panic-stricken through the thorns.

I stood still and shrieked with laughter, but directly I moved away I was followed by the enemy, who wounded me in the head in several places. At last I gathered together my scattered forces. Oh, how I laughed at the swollen faces of the men, although I could hardly see out of one eye myself! When I caught sight of my head-shikari's swollen pouting under lip, I laughed as I had never laughed before in this most distressful country. Nearly all were stung about the head, and the groans and ' Allahs !' that were emitted on every side betokened our utter defeat.

We next set to work to collect wood, and soon had an enormous fire burning close to the stronghold. When the heat became great, I attached a rope to the tall ant-hill, and pulled a portion of it down ; then, as the enemy became suffocated with the smoke, we attacked the walls with axes, and at last took the stronghold and its spoil. We filled two buckets full of honeycomb, the ant-hill being full from top to bottom. Soon after this battle we pitched for the night. I laughed afresh at the sorry-looking objects of men as I doled out ammonia and applied it to their poisoned wounds.

Next morning, as soon as it was light enough to see, we marched back to Sinnadogho, arriving there about 10 a.m. The whole caravan packed up at 2 p.m. *en route* for Joh. Two hours south of Sinnadogho we passed a small shallow lake, called Leberdooli, after which we went up and down over hilly and stony ground, the worst possible going for camels, horses, and men.

Next day we passed a lot of men, quarrelling, as usual, at a deep well in the solid rock, called Goohedli. One man said he must water his flocks first, another man said he must, and I expected every moment that spears would be used in the arguments, when up came my cook, with a rifle in one hand and a stick in the other, and jabbering fifteen to the dozen. Presently off went his rifle, bang! when all the men fell flat with their faces to the earth, whilst the cook calmly went on jawing. We gave the poor ponies drink, and then left the noisy, snarling people.

Soon after we descended into a flat, sandy plateau, with open bush, and here and there a plain. Not a sign of animal life was to be seen. We camped at Hengoodah in great heat on a dry, grassy, open space, the first grass I had seen for weeks. Passing a village, where we bought some ghee at an exorbitant price, we camped at sunset at Gelgoodlah. The day was brought to a close with a fight in camp between two of my men, which ended in their precious ghee being spilt in the sand, at which I was much pleased.

Next day we reached Joh, where there were two wells of spring water coming out of the rock. At night the camels kept starting up, and at last we caught sight of some natives in the bushes. My guideman went out of the zareba, and addressed a long speech to the bushes. He said that we were not an ordinary caravan, but an expedition to shoot elephants, and that if they tried to steal anything from us, we should get out our elephant-killing engines and blow them all into a thousand pieces. After this address the night passed in peace.

Next morning I sent men in every direction to look for fresh elephant spoor. We were now in the heart of the Haweea country, having left the Marehan country far behind. The natives reported that we were within six days' march of the east coast. I doubled the night-watches, and put extra day-sentries over the camels and ponies, as the people seemed so troublesome. I had men continually out, looking for, and taking news of, my looted pony, and discovered that some people of the Marehan tribe had stolen it. In the afternoon I photographed my men and shot some 'gussuli' dik-dik, one of which possessed extremely good horns, $3\frac{1}{4}$ inches long (the longest recorded being $3\frac{1}{2}$ inches). I was in the act of stalking a flock of the beautiful vulturine guinea-fowl, when one of my men ran up, saying he had received news of fresh elephant spoor. It was too late to march that night, so we made

PART OF THE AUTHOR'S ESCORT AT JOH.

preparations to leave Joh, the furthest place south-east I was destined to reach, on the morrow. We were now running short of food for the men, which caused me a good deal of anxiety, as it was impossible to procure rice so far inland.

Next day we left Joh, to spend a day or two in the dense jungle, far away from villages, in the midst of elephant spoor. We stopped for the morning rest near a dried-up well, which literally swarmed with ants and bees.

It was most difficult to eat, as the insects crawled into my tent, over my meat and into my coffee by the thousand. At night we stopped at Muganguno. Here the swarms of bees and other insects in my tent became unbearable. I was again driven out, could not have a bath, and employed my evening picking out the stings and applying ammonia, as I snarled to myself:

> Never more, never more,
> Will I be seen on this hateful shore,
> Eaten by ants and stung by bees;
> Next time I'll shoot at home, if you please!

The next day was destined to be one of the most miserable I spent in this most miserable country. From the very moment the sun peeped up over the horizon until it set at night, an enormous army of bees pestered and annoyed me. I could neither eat, drink, sleep, sit, stand, nor walk, but the pests must needs crawl over me and sting me. It was all very fine to say, ' Don't touch them, and they won't sting you.' But the plagues tickled me so dreadfully as they crawled up my breeches, down my socks, into my shoes, round my head, and over my whole body, that it was impossible to help brushing them away. I was stung almost everywhere. I was driven from my tent into a Somali ' tent ' under a tree, and from the tree back again to the tent. At length, in despair I sat in the heat of a roaring fire. The scorching rays of the sun, the burning warmth of the fire, and the poisoning heat of my numerous bee-stings, nearly drove me into a frenzy.

If Somaliland, which certainly 'flows with milk and honey,' in any way resembles the Promised Land, I think the children of Israel during their wanderings in the desert were well out of it. And if the Garden of Eden was planted in this country, as some ridiculous person tried to make out, I don't wonder that Adam and Eve fell! Somaliland is about as far removed from a Promised Land and a Garden of Eden, in my estimation, as hell is from heaven!

15

The. curious part of these swarms of bees was that they always attacked me and my ' boy,' and left the other men in comparative peace. Poor Deria stamped and jumped, and cursed and swore in Somali, but, then, Deria was always in hot water. If a man threw a stone, it was always Deria's head on which it would alight. On the march, if a branch stuck out beyond the rest, Deria's face would feel its thorns. If a camel fell down, and boxes flew in every direction, on picking up the pieces, who but Deria was ever to be found underneath? Poor Deria! No wonder he wore such a disagreeable expression.

Added to all these discomforts was the cruel disappointment, when all the men returned at night, that we could not find elephants, having wasted so much time and come so many hundred miles out of the way on a useless search through a country utterly destitute of all game.

I had now barely ten days' rations for the men. It became absolutely necessary to race out of this hateful country, where there were plenty of sheep, but where none could be bought.

Next morning I was awakened by the noise of the camels being loaded up, to find myself stiff and sore all over from bee-stings. Whilst on the march, we passed the fresh carcase of a gerenook killed that morning by a pack of wild dogs, the tracks of which we saw in the sand. At 10 a.m., after our guide had lost his way more than half a dozen times, we camped on a grassy bit of open plain devoid of the horrid stones. Here, instead of bees, hundreds of ' gingerbread ' ticks swarmed over me. A nice change! It was very hot as usual, so that, on the caravan marching at 2 p.m., I rested under the shade, and watched my shikaris making fire with the twirling-rod. Two men sat opposite each other. One held a piece of thorn-bush stick (having a small indentation in the middle) firm against the ground, whilst the other man placed another rod with a blunt point into the indentation and twirled it round and round as fast as he could, holding it between the palms of his hands.

When tired, he seized the stationary stick, whilst the other man took his turn twirling. The first or stationary stick was of a soft and very dry wood, the twirling-stick of a hard wood. After twirling for a very short time, the wood began to smoke, and in another second the 'tinder' made by the constant twirling of the hard upon the soft wood was seen to produce a spark, and then to glow. This glowing tinder was carefully collected in a piece of *tobe*, some dry grass dust was put upon it, and the sparks blown upon, when, lo and behold, real fire!

CHAPTER V.

Crowd of threatening natives—Across the waterless desert—We lose the road—A race against death—Saved in the nick of time—We run short of provisions—Lesser koodoo.

NEXT morning we reached El Dara again, where, it will be remembered, I looked for elephants a fortnight before. Now some of the thorn-bushes were beginning to show a little green. Spring was appearing again, the wretched winter, with its scorching heat, being now at an end. On nearing the deep well, I perceived upwards of a hundred and fifty vulturine guinea-fowl together; but they would not allow of my near approach, and the whole army flew up together. A grand sight, reminding me of an enormous 'bouquet' of pheasants! I then marched to Kadea, passing elephant spoor two days old. Here I camped to await news of two of my men who had gone to Gaboon, further west, in search of my looted pony. The whole of the day I waited for them to return, sending out men in every direction to look for elephants. The bees were more troublesome than ever, and at night the men came back saying they had seen no real fresh elephant tracks.

> O elephants, you are unkind,
> When I have so made up my mind
> That if but one of you I shoot,
> No more I'll hunt you, monstrous brute!
> No more I'll follow on your track,
> Expecting soon to see your back;
> No hand of mine shall hunt you more:
> In peace I'll leave you on this shore.
>
> So run, you little elephant,
> And go and tell your pa,

If he but sacrifice himself,
He'll save both you and ma ;
He'll save his brothers, sisters, aunts,
His cousins and his wives.
Surely it is his duty
To save so many lives.
O elephants, you are unkind,
When I have so made up my mind !

Next day my men at last arrived from Gaboon, but without my pony. We made a long march to the wells of Kadea, and seeing a couple of ponies on the way, I looted one of them which belonged to a Marehan man. This caused a great influx of people to the well, and a great deal of talking was done by them to try to induce me to wait until they fetched my property. I said I would wait until ten o'clock next day, and then march. I sent out some men to try and buy some sheep, but at midnight they had not returned.

During the night we all watched, expecting every moment to be attacked. Next morning, which I expected would prove the most exciting day of my life, and perhaps the last day of it, the men sent ou tfor sheep returned at 9 o'clock not having been able to purchase a single one. There was now an enormous crowd of natives round my zareba, and the headmen were running about in a great state of excitement. Four of my men guarded the ponies as they grazed outside, and a number of men looked after the camels. Several attempts were made to stalk and steal a camel, but my men fired repeatedly over the heads of the thieves, and kept the people off.

At ten o'clock I gave orders to load up the camels, and my men ran off to drive them in. Then commenced a tremendous jabbering and commotion on the part of the crowd of natives. Young men danced and shouted, and I thought the moment had arrived to act, when an old man came up and claimed an audience. He said that the pony we had taken belonged to a young man who was poor, and he added that he would put us on to the big road to War-dare if we would wait half a day upon the road. He would send for his own ponies, and let me have the pick of them, if I would give him the one I had looted in exchange.

As he seemed to be the most influential man in the place, I consented, taking him and our looted pony with me. Before I left I tried my level best to engage a guide to take me to Wardare, but nobody would come. I gave the word to start, and we slowly marched out of a country I never wish to set eyes upon again. No one knows how things will turn out ! Those three hundred loafers stood still and watched their pony taken from them without one moving !

We had a very trying march over rough stones, and several of the camels fell down. I had a racking headache, and the heat was very great ; but a clouded sky probably saved my life that day, for had it been a really piping hot sky, I think I must have 'knocked under.' The old man was as good as his word. He showed us the big road which led to Wardare, and about four o'clock two men on horseback were seen approaching at a gallop a long distance off, for we were encamped upon an open, stony plain.

On their near approach, they pulled up their horses dead, and shouted 'Mot, mot, mot, io mot.' One animal was very fast and strong-looking, and I chose him at once. He was quite frisky, or, as my headman said, ' very hart ' (hot), and two men had to hold him to allow a third to mount. We filled up all the *harns* and barrels at the well close by, preparatory to marching across the big waterless desert ahead of us, *en route* to Wardare. There is one occasion, and only one, when Somalis are willing and anxious to march fast, and that is when no water is to be encountered on the way.

I loaded up at 4 o'clock next morning, shook the dust off my feet on this detestable country and its inhospitable people, and marched in the pitch darkness through thin bush and stony level ground. When the sun rose and the chill of morning passed, I rode my new pony, and found he went well over the stones.

There was absolutely no game to be seen, but I shot one

of the most beautiful sun-birds I have ever seen. Its
brilliant red breast attracted my notice when it was flying
fully 50 yards off, although it was smaller than a sparrow.
The exquisite beauty of this perfect little gem baffles any
description I can give—a dark olive-green back and wings,
the 'shoulders' of the latter and the rump being of a
metallic green. The upper part of the breast was a bright
vermilion, surrounded by a thin fringe of metallic blue.
The base of these red feathers of the breast had a thin
band of copper, showing in some lights green, in others
yellow. The lower part of the breast and the throat were
a rich black. It had a long, curved black beak, black legs,
and a brown eye.

In the afternoon we left the stones behind, and encountered similar low thorn-bushes to those seen on the
maritime plain near Berbera. Tall trees were to be seen
every half-mile or so. As I was resting under the shade of
one of the latter, I caught sight of a plover squatting on
the sand, and thinking it was wounded, I walked slowly
up to it, when it jumped up, disclosing three pretty little
nestlings. I retired hastily to the tree again, some 5 yards
off, when the mother came running back, and, without
taking the slightest notice of me, sat down again upon the
youngsters. Presently up ran the cock bird with a fat
slug, which he deposited before his spouse, who promptly
swallowed it, and off her husband ran again to find another.
The whole performance was enacted within a few feet of
me. so tame are the birds in Somaliland.

Next morning we were going at 3 o'clock, and the thorn-
bushes, some 3 feet high, scratched my legs so fearfully that,
in spite of the intense cold, I was obliged to ride the pony,
upon which I fell fast asleep twice, and all but fell out
of the saddle. We camped at Goorasafsaf at 10 a.m., after
passing several huge plains without seeing a sign of animal
life. The wilderness here was devoid of trees, so that one
could see for miles around. ·On camping, I lay on my bed
and went fast asleep, and was with difficulty roused for

breakfast, after which repast I went fast asleep again until we restarted at 1. About 4 p.m., as I was riding the pony, a fine leopard jumped out of a bush under the horse's hoofs, and made off through the bushes at a great pace. I was out of the saddle in an instant, and my shikari in. Seizing my rifle, I fired, and missed him. Off galloped my shikari after him, and soon brought him to bay in a small thorn-bush, where he lay flat against the ground, showing his teeth and uttering low growls. As I ran up, the pony, which was very frightened, reared and backed, and the leopard turned his head from me to look at him. I took a careful aim, and put a bullet in at the back of his neck, killing him instantaneously. He was a large leopard for Somaliland, and had a handsome skin. On getting back to, or rather coming up with, the caravan, we camped. I climbed a large tree, and could see in the distance the same range of hills we had passed on our left when marching into the Marehan country.

Next morning we approached the range of hills, and camped close by the side of a small one, which stood out alone on our right. In the evening we were passing the big range on our left. We found an empty well, round which were numerous old elephant and rhinoceros tracks. We passed the Bur Gabo range of hills at about four miles distance. Between us and the hills there was thick thorn-bush with big trees, the former all burnt up with the heat, and not in leaf. The trees reached right to the top of the hills. In the bushes I saw two lots of dibitag and one herd of gerenook, all of which proved frightfully wild. I also saw fresh lesser koodoo tracks, and a lion's spoor two days old. Two of my men were sick and had to be carried on camels, and one of my goats was so 'pumped' with the long marches that it had to be killed.

Next morning we started at 3.30, and the thorn-bushes tore my hands all to pieces again. How I longed for the sun to rise! When at length dawn appeared, we discovered that the old caravan tracks we had been follow-

ing for the last three days had suddenly disappeared, or
rain had obliterated them. Perhaps we had taken the
wrong road. I pictured to myself the whole caravan
dropping down and dying slowly of thirst, one by one,
as we struggled on, not knowing when we might find the
precious fluid. I sent my shikari galloping back to the
place where we had last seen the tracks, to look all along
the route for another road, whilst I sat down, a prey to
a thousand fears. We were leaving the hills, to my mind,
far too much to the west. The road we were following
bore north-east by east, instead of north-west by west.
In about an hour my shikari returned, saying that he
could not make out another road, so we were obliged to
follow our present one. The bush was so dense that it
would have been utterly impossible to reach Wardare by
striking out a line through it with the aid of the compass.

My headman now came up, saying that two of the camels
could not go a step farther, so I ordered a halt, it being
about 8 a.m. I saw a small herd of dibitag, the first
antelope I had seen for weeks, and after a very long and
hot chase I succeeded in shooting one. My headman next
announced that all the food was finished. What was to be
done ? I gave them some of my biscuits and the whole of
the little antelope. What would happen on the morrow I
could not foresee, but 'sufficient unto the day is the evil
thereof.'

On restarting, one of the camels fell with four water-
vessels containing the last drops of our precious fluid, all of
which was spilt in the sand. The camel refused to get up,
so I was obliged to shoot him and march on.

About 4 p.m. there was a slight shower of rain, but not
enough to allow us to collect any water. It became very
cold, and I was obliged to walk. The wet leafless thorn-
branches gave out delicious scents of spice, especially the
smell of cinnamon and white pepper. ' Ceylon's spicy
breezes ' weren't in it with these ; in fact, the only smell
which was wafted on the breeze to my nose on entering

Colombo was a decided sniff of drains! So much for poetry and the ideal!

At night the men had no food and no water. I had a few pints locked up in a barrel, but I dared not eat much. I offered the men some of my food, but they refused it.

At 2.30 next morning we restarted, when one of the camels could not walk. I had the poor creature shot, and then we trudged on in the darkness. Just when it was beginning to get light another camel fell, and could not be induced to rise. My headman rode after me and asked for orders. It was a race for water, we could not stop; I said, 'Shoot him.' The rifle rang out its death-knell a few moments after. There was next to no water in its stomach; the poor exhausted beast, having had no fresh grass, had used up its supply. The men seemed to think it rather a joke, and shouted after my headman, ' If any camel fall down, shoot him, and if any man fall down, shoot him, shoot him !'

As the men had no food to-day, I was determined to try my best to shoot them some meat. We passed some magnificent open *buns* covered with long, dried-up grass, without seeing an oryx. At length we found fresh tracks, which I followed. Unfortunately, the oryx took the direction of the caravan, and I knew then they would get the better of us. We followed in silence, and I knew we must be close to them, when all at once I heard them lumbering along back again towards us, having seen the caravan; but they passed too far out for us to shoot, and although I ran as hard as I could to try and cut them off, they beat me, and I had the mortification of seeing all that good meat (there were upwards of twenty oryx) sail right away. I followed for about a mile, but they did not stop, so I returned dejected to the caravan.

No food and no water! I tried to think of more pleasant subjects. But my thoughts would always revert to the dreadful fact that we had no water. I tried to sing comic songs : 'At Trinity Church I met my Doom ' was too dismal ; 'A Lot of Wet' was singularly inappropriate to present circumstances ; and after ' We drew his Club Money this Morning,' I stopped.   I could not help noticing some graves, surrounded by the usual piles of wood, and, further on, bones lying bleaching in the sun, and wondered if mine would lie in the same manner later on.   When the sun set we camped.   I noticed the men spat a good deal, and my headman's eyes glared and his hand shook.   At night I dared not eat, as I had nothing to drink.   And so passed the fifth day we had been on the march.

Next morning I was awakened by the men loading up the camels at 1 o'clock.   None of the men spoke.   I said to my headman, 'Well, shall we reach water ?'   He pointed to the sky, and answered, ' Allah knows.'   On and on we marched in the darkness.   I kept imagining the dreadful scenes ahead of us.   The men falling down maddened by thirst—perhaps mutiny and murder !   My thoughts made me begin to swallow, for already I fancied I wanted water, although I knew if it was an overclouded day I should in all probability last till nearly sunset.

At last up came the big red globe which was to kill us with its heat.   I saw we were going to have a piping hot day.   I now spat a little blood.   I felt, I suppose, as a condemned man feels the day before his execution, hoping for a reprieve.   The sun's rays shot down upon our heads with blinding, withering heat.   Crash ! crash !   Two more camels down.   Sometimes we could get them up by kicking them, but not often.   As each succumbed, its burden was added to that already carried by another.   Still we raced on.

Curiously enough, I remember that those among my men who had been the most talkative were the very first to show signs of extreme distress.   The silent, morose fellows who had spared their throats and scarcely uttered a word seemed to bear their sufferings best.

In another hour my pony, which was foaming at the mouth, fell, and I was obliged to walk.   The men them-

selves began to drop by the wayside, with their heads
between their knees, determined not to go on, and preferring
to die where they sat.   I was obliged to kick them up,
and set them going again, coughing and spitting blood
as they went!   The silence was only broken by the coughing and an occasional crash, as another camel fell by the
way.

I knew we could not last much longer, and the wells
might be three days away.   I felt myself collapsing.   My
throat felt as if it would burst.   It was, I think, as though
I had poured a stream of scalding spirit down it.   My
vision was blurred and hazily red, so that I could no longer
tell a man from a tree, and could not walk alone.   I had
to be held up on each side by a giant Somali.   Still the
sun blazed down with choking, killing heat.   Everywhere,
as far as I could see, stretched the dreary expanse of rock
and scrub, for the ground had become more open, with
never a tree, and scarcely a green thing.   I knew if I fell
I should never rise again, and yet the temptation to give
way became stronger and stronger, until at last I was on
the very verge of unconsciousness.   I spat a great deal of
blood, and whenever I tried to gulp or swallow I suffered
the greatest agony in my throat.

I roused myself for a last effort.   Calling to me a
couple of the strongest and most reliable men, I whispered
to them to go forward before us along the track to see if
they could find water or see any human beings who could
help us in our last extremities.   These men shot on ahead,
and we, too, kept going.   After their departure, I noticed
a dove fly past.   I welcomed that bird as Noah must have
welcomed the dove which returned with the leaf to the
ark.   Shortly after I noticed a great excitement among
the men.   I was nearly unconscious, and could see nothing.
They told me that my scouts were running back towards
us.   Long before we could make out their expressions we
shouted, 'Bier? Bier?' (Water? Water?); and the answer
came back, ' Wa badunti !' (Plenty !).

'Saved! Saved in the nick of time!' I shouted, though my throat was as parched and dry as tinder.

The moment the Somalis heard this cry they shook off their death-like lethargy and sent up a hoarse shout such as is rarely heard in Africa. They seemed to be going mad in their frenzied excitement; they gesticulated like maniacs, and began shooting off their rifles in the air as a thanksgiving to Allah. It was a miracle no one was killed. Discipline was at an end. We all raced forward up a slight ascent.

At length, as we stood upon the brow of the hill, we looked down upon a scene which will never fade from my memory. Below us in the valley was what looked exactly like an English park—beautiful green grass, big trees, and a luxuriant vegetation! This oasis was somewhat over a mile square. Dotted all over the oasis were a number of ancient wells, hewn in the solid rock by Gallas centuries ago. We made a desperate rush forward, but, to our dismay, we found the water was 20 feet below the tops of the wells! Immediately, however, we lowered drinking-vessels into the depths, but these at first brought up nothing but a disgusting mass of yellow putrid matter. This filth, it seemed, formed a kind of crust on the 'water.' The water itself was virtually stinking yellow sewage. At one time, perhaps, it had been clean water, but the millions of birds which visited the place—— I need not say any more.

We could not wait to boil the stuff. Each of us got a vessel full of it and gulped it down in quarts. It did not cool my throat; in fact, after drinking the stuff I felt rather worse than I had done before. I was taken to my tent and put to bed after giving orders to kill a camel as meat for the men. In a short time I began to get delirious, and realizing my danger, I handed my revolver to my headman, fearing I might do myself some injury. Then came pains in the head and high fever.

Next day I was better, and able to look around me.

Upon the plain were several large trees, having a huge
dark-green leaf, which was very broad. This tree, which
the natives call 'boor,' bore a small round fruit, the size
of a cherry, green when unripe, and afterwards turning to
a brilliant orange colour. The branches hung down in
festoons interlaced and plaited together, some reaching the
ground. My men supposed this place to be Galadi, which
they said was some three days' march east of Wardare,
where we should have arrived if we had followed the right
path. I saw some francolin on the plain, and shot one for
dinner. I saw also a small herd of gerenook feeding at the
edge of the bush, but felt too weak and ill to pursue them.
During the night the sentry had to fire at some hyænas
which were stalking the ponies, and the shot frightened
away twenty men—probably robbers—who had rested by
a well about half a mile off us, as we discovered by the
tracks next morning.

I stayed in the camp all the morning, being too weak
and ill to go out. I sent men after the tracks of the
supposed robbers, but the latter got right away. However,
during the morning two men of the tribe of Goom Adlah
turned up to drink. We stalked, surrounded and captured
them. I offered them a *tobe* to show us the road and guide
us to Well Wall or Wardare, which they agreed to do.
After having watered all the camels, ponies and donkeys
again, and filled all the *harns*, barrels and our stomachs
with reeking water—which gave me violent diarrhœa—we
marched at 2 p.m. due west, passing fresh rhinoceros tracks
all the way. I shot a 'guyu' dik-dik, and saw a large
bird, which proved to be an owl, sitting among some rocks.
Unfortunately, he flew before I fired, and getting behind a
bush, the latter got all the shot. Leaving the white
rocky ground, so hateful to walk upon, we traversed the
usual red sand, covered with low thorn-scrub, without a
bit of green to be seen.

Next day we passed through the same sort of country,
seeing a few fairly fresh rhinoceros tracks. About

ten o'clock the sky became overclouded and a little
rain fell. It was so cold that I had my tent pitched
when we camped for the mid-day rest, and sat in it
enveloped in a sweater and rug. An hour afterwards the
sun came out, and it was so hot I thought I should die. In
the afternoon I saw an animal which was new to me. It was
the shape of a ground-squirrel, but about three times the
size. I saw two pairs of them, and they appeared to be of
a brown or rabbit colour. This animal made its burrow in
ant-hills. It was extremely annoying not to have got hold
of the gun in time to have collected what might have been
a most interesting, and perhaps unknown, animal. There
was a magnificent sunset, the sky being streaked with
gorgeous blood red and orange. At night the guides
wanted to go back, but I told them they must show us
the road until dawn on the morrow, when they could then
leave us if they could swear we should find no difficulty in
tracing it to Well Wall.

In the morning, unless I shot something, the men would
have nothing to eat. I careered in vain after a herd of
dibitag. I had not fired my rifle for weeks in this miserable game-forsaken country. Just before we were about to
camp for the rest, a single oryx trotted across the camel
track in front of us. I jumped out of the saddle and seized
my rifle, hoping he would stand to have a last look at us.
Sure enough, when he had got about 150 yards off he stopped
dead, turned broadside, and stared hard at us. My hand
shook, as I knew if I hit it meant breakfast for thirty-four
hungry men. Bang went the rifle! I made a clean miss.
I could hardly believe it. Away and away galloped the
huge antelope. In sheer desperation I pulled the trigger
on him as he was disappearing in the bushes, now fully 300
yards away. Providence directed the bullet—luck, fluke,
call it what you will. Down came the oryx to the ground
with a crash, and lay with its legs kicking in the air. My
shikari gave a shout of joy, and rushed towards him, in
spite of my yells to him to stop. The antelope jumped up

and disappeared at a great pace into the bushes. To see
our breakfast, which was, I thought, as good as in our
mouths, vanish like a dream, was a little too much. I
yelled for the pony, but the bushes were so thick it was
impossible to see the oryx. We had to track him on foot.
There was a little blood, but the track showed that the
animal was getting away at a great pace without falling.

After going about a mile, the track suddenly disappeared.
I turned my head, and there, in the middle of a huge
thick bush, was the oryx squatting a few yards from me.

I put a bullet through his neck to put him out of his misery,
and dragged out the good meat which had so nearly escaped
us. I ' did a smile' to see the men making a hearty breakfast upon him soon afterwards. But what was one oryx
among so many hungry mouths ? Every scrap was eaten
ere we marched again. In the afternoon the heat was
intense.

We marched all day from spring into winter, and from
winter into spring ; that is to say, every two or three miles
there had been rain, and here were to be found green
bushes, trees, and grass, some of the bushes being of the

most magnificent emerald-green hue. Dozens of extra-ordinarily-shaped ant-hills were visible here on every side, some of gigantic proportions. In them I pictured several Salisbury Cathedral spires, a Tower of London, two or three Towers of Pisa, and a Magdalen College, Oxford, all appearing to be in a more or less advanced state of drunkenness.

We had been marching through winter, *i.e.*, burnt-up scrub and dried-up yellow grass, where the bushes were not in leaf, and of a grayish-brown colour, for some time, when about 4.30 my shikari, who was in front of the pony, stood suddenly stock-still. Seizing the rifle from him, I peered round a bush. What a picture presented itself before my astonished eyes! Here was an oasis in the desert indeed! A small open space covered with long, brilliant green grass, surrounded with thick bushes and trees, all clothed in emerald, and in the midst of the picture stood, staring intently upon us, one of the most beautiful creatures in Somaliland—a lesser koodoo (*Stripsiceros imberbis*), carrying a magnificent pair of horns. Instantly the tableau reminded me of J. G. Millais's beautiful picture of a big koodoo in ' A Breath from the Veldt.' I put the rifle to my shoulder (the distance was but 50 yards), took a long, careful aim, and pressed the trigger. At the same instant the antelope bounded away. I had made a clean miss! At first I almost tore my hair, until I reflected that, at any rate, I had not spoilt that beautiful picture. We followed the spoor for a long way, and then gave it up.

Immediately after I caught sight of a second lesser koodoo. But it disappeared behind a bush. My shikari got into a wild state of excitement. ' Shoot, shoot!' he cried. I could see nothing. He pointed, and implored me to fire. The setting sun was in my eyes; I saw nothing but a bush. I thought my shikari would have gone mad. He wrung his hands, stamped his feet, pointed, and gesticulated. The koodoo heard the noise, bounded from the bush, and dashed away. I saw him then at once, fired, and made

16

another clean miss. Two good chances at this rare and
beautiful animal missed in an hour! Oh, the cruel dis-
appointments of big-game shooting!

Soon after we camped, and heavy clouds gathering in the
west betokened rain, which soon after came down in
torrents. Oh, how hateful the rain is when living in a
tent! My dinner consisted of dry biscuits and water, whilst
my men went tired, supperless, and drenched to the skin
to bed. About 10 p.m., when it was still pouring with
rain, my sentry made a very clever capture of two would-
be thieves, who were caught red-handed in the act of
stalking one of my donkeys. We got all the news from
them, and kept them prisoners until morning.

CHAPTER VI.

Effects of rain—Death of a lesser koodoo—Jungle folk—News from the coast—The Dumberelli Plain—Waller's gazelle shot—Across the waterless Haud—Gazelle—Death of a leopard.

WHEN morning broke, it was apparent that no marching could be done, as the camel-mats were soaked through and through, and, if placed upon the camels, would have given them all terribly sore backs. So I determined to spend a long day after lesser koodoo. I sent the camels to the little oasis, which would now hold water after the heavy rain, and started in pursuit of the pretty animals I had missed the day before.

The day was intensely hot, and after going for a couple of hours, I turned round to look for my water-bottle, when I discovered that both shikaris had forgotten it. Ever since that long thirsty march I imagined I wanted water at least every two hours, and if I did not get it, I began to cough and feel uncomfortably nervous. But if I had a full water-bottle with me, I would go the whole morning without touching a drop. I sent one of my shikaris racing home for it, and went on.

We cut the spoor of oryx which appeared to have passed but a few minutes ago, so I thought I would follow them until I saw koodoo on their fresh tracks. Walk, walk, walk, through thin bush, through thick bush, over open grassy plains and stony ground. Those oryx did not stop for a minute, but they led us to some holes in the rock which contained rain-water. I put my head into a hole and lapped the precious fluid like a dog until I choked, so

16—2

eager was I to get it down my throat. I wished I could fill my pockets with it. I had a good wash, and went on after the oryx, until soon after I spied a koodoo dash across the track in front of us. After it we raced along. I saw it in the distance several times. It doubled back a dozen times, went round and round bushes, and tried all sorts of tricks to put us off the track. At length I got a good sight of it in the bushes, but what a disappointment—it was only a female !

My man turned up with the water-bottle, and I felt more comfortable. I thought we must now be a long way from camp, but my men assured me we were quite close, so I determined to go back, have a rest and some breakfast, and then try again in the afternoon. As we walked along, I nearly trod on a huge leopard which was lying in a very thin open bush. This demonstrates how wonderfully like the jungle this apparently brilliantly marked animal is. I did not see him until he was well out on the other side, and before I could grasp my rifle he was into some long grass and out of sight in an instant. But he had not seen us, and just as a lion did, as before related, he made a circle and came back to our tracks to see what had disturbed him. He tracked us for about 100 yards, when he must have caught sight of us, as he made off at a fast pace.

I looked up now and saw my camels grazing about a quarter of a mile off, so sent my shikari racing off to fetch the only goat kid which had survived the long thirsty march. When it arrived, we tethered it to a tree, and hid close to it behind a thick thorn-bush. When we had disappeared from view the goat at once began to bleat, and in less than a minute after the leopard charged it full tilt. I waited until he lay still on the top of the kid, then took careful aim at his head (for I was but a few yards off him) and fired. The bullet caught him right in the centre of the forehead, making a tiny little hole, and killing the leopard stone-dead. I seemed to have extraordinary luck with this dangerous animal.

When we got to camp I drank a few more gallons of water, had some breakfast, and rested an hour. As the men complained that they were very hungry, I was obliged to kill another of my camels for them.

In the afternoon I wended my way to the little oasis. About 3 o'clock a hyæna ' shouted ' close to us. This was the first time I had heard a hyæna in brilliant sunshine. Soon after I saw a grand lesser koodoo, all unconscious of our presence, feeding on a green bush which has an oval leaf, apparently much sought after by these antelopes. Bang! went the rifle, and the grand beast gave a leap

LESSER KOODOO AND GUNBEARER.

into the air and then rolled over dead. What a beauty he was, and what a fine head ! Twenty-two inches his horns measured in a straight line, and 28 inches round the curve.

I went once more to the pretty little spot in the desert, took off my clothes, and, sitting in the cool rain-water, splashed it over and over my heated body. I lay at full length and wallowed in the muddy water. I had not had such an enjoyable bath since leaving the lake in the rock at Sinnadogho. Hyænas prowled round the camp all night after the remains of the dead camel, and a sharp look-out had to be kept to prevent them stealing the good meat.

Next morning we marched in dull, close weather. We had now reached a game country at last, as was apparent by the frequent fresh tracks of oryx, dibitag, koodoo, and rhinoceros. I had been going about two hours, when I perceived three male dibitag about to cross the camel track. I slipped out of the saddle, unseen by them, and ran hard to cut them off. They walked slowly behind a large bush. I sat down, and made up my mind I would do my best to bag the three, as I was getting rather tired of killing my camels for meat for the men. What an age they seemed to be behind that bush! Would they never appear? At last one slowly emerged from the bushes, and quietly walked broadside to me. I let him walk on till I saw No. 2 appear, and then took a careful aim at No. 1. Bang! and No. 1 ran a few yards and dropped on to his knees. Bang! and No. 2 fell with his heels in the air.

The Mannlicher was working well, and the cartridges did not stick. Taking a cool aim, I let the third dibitag have it as he galloped away, but hit him too far back. He fell, but picked himself up in an instant, and made off at a great rate. I raced after him, when the first one shot picked himself up, and also disappeared into the bushes. Two wounded and one dead! I yelled to my shikaris to follow one, whilst I went after the other.

The syce had, as usual, utterly disappeared with my water-bottle, sun-helmet, and pony. I soon found my beast going very slowly before me, but could not make my syce hear, and so I lost the chance of running it down at the very start. I had been tracking for about ten minutes, when I heard my second shikari shoot, and soon afterwards I heard a second shot followed by shouts of joy. So I knew that No. 2 was in the larder. On and on I went after my beast, which doubled, turned, and jumped in a most extraordinary manner, and was followed for a long way by a leopard. We described several large circles, but I never saw the animal again ; and as the sun came out strong, and I had nothing on my head, I was forced to let it go. When I got back to camp I felt a bit sick, and had a bad headache, owing to the terrific heat striking upon my exposed head. All the afternoon there was not a breath of air.

We had now made seven marches, or three and a half days, without seeing a sign of Wardare or Well Wall. Our guides told us it was five marches to Well Wall. ' All men are liars,' I know, but all Somalis are d——d liars ! I was just thinking I dared not have a bath, owing to the scarcity of water, when down came the rain. I tried to collect some in buckets, waterproof ground-sheets, bath, pans, and cooking-pots, but the net result watered one pony only. I retired that night into a damp bed, feeling very miserable.

Next morning we had to wait till 8 o'clock, as the camel-mats were soaked through. At 11 we camped, as we heard sheep in the distance, the first we had heard for upwards of ten days. At 4.30 we reached a village and camped. An enormous crowd of people collected, and examined everything. The day had been so close that I think I must have got a slight sunstroke, as it was with difficulty I could keep conscious, my head feeling very bad, my eyes swimming, and my feet and hands losing their feeling. Next day my head was very bad, and I dared not stir out of the shade of my tent.

The people here proved, as usual, great liars. They had promised the day before to bring a large flock of sheep to sell, but the whole day produced but three sheep and two wretched camels. They were regular jungle folk, and had never seen matches nor money, and went into fits of laughter and jabbered nineteen to the dozen at some pictures of Somalis I showed them. Some of the young men were very insolent, and had to be forcibly ejected from the zareba.

Next morning we marched to Well Wall, where I had

been two months ago.   By going out of our road at Galadi
we had wasted nine days !   The place was so altered I did
not know it.   I remembered it as a barren plain, with
several deep wells in the centre.   Now all the bushes and
trees were of every possible shade of brilliant green.   On
arrival here, I procured a guide, killed one of the camels
I had bought for the men, filled all the water-pots with
water, mended all my torn clothes, washed my dirty ones,
overhauled my collections of beasts, birds, butterflies, and
beetles, doctored the men and animals, and prepared to
march northwards to Berbera, which I hoped to reach in a
fortnight or a little over.

Everything went well with these preparations, until at
1 p.m. one of the camels was found to be missing, so I sent
men in every direction to look for it, suspecting it had been
looted.   During the day I shot a marabou stork, the first I
had seen during this expedition, though I often saw them
in my last in the Boorgha country.   This specimen was by
far the largest I have ever seen, and measured no less than
6 feet 1½ inches from tip of beak to tip of toe, and 9 feet
from tip to tip of wings !   I saw several other birds here,
such as the red-vented thrush, the superb glossy starling,
and the hoopoe.   About midnight two of my men came in
with the lost camel, saying they had found it sitting in a
thick bush.

Next morning we marched at 3.30.   Thunder and
lightning were heard and seen round us all the morning,
but not a drop of rain fell upon us.   After passing through
burnt-up country, we reached at daybreak green trees and
bushes with the rain of the night before still wet upon
the leaves.

It was all a toss-up how much water we found until
reaching Edegan Wells, which are distant from Well Wall
about nine days.   So that, unless there had been plenty of
rain further north, I feared we might again experience a
march like the one across the Marehan desert.

I had tried hard at Well Wall to hire some camels and

water *harns*. Five men said they would come with us with five camels, but of course they did not turn up. I could now carry five days' water-supply for the whole caravan, but not a drop more. I had obtained with great difficulty, however, a guide to take us as far as Hodayu, three days' march from Well Wall. From Well Wall we took a straight road to Sirro, leaving my former route to Wardare far to the east.

On reaching Sirro again, I could hardly recognise the place in its spring dress. Now the burnt-up plain had been transformed into a garden, covered with a mantle of brilliant green, to the great joy of the camels, sheep, and donkeys. There was very little water, but enough to fill up the empty *harns*.

When watering the animals, one of the camels fell into a hole, and had to be hauled out with ropes by twenty of my men ! Here we found a man who had just returned from Berbera, and we at once besieged him with a thousand questions as to which route we should take in order to find water. We were told to go east of Farfanya. He told me that Mr. and Mrs. Stanford had reached the coast more than a month ago, and that the poor little rhinoceros they captured had died, and gave us a host of interesting news from the coast. He seemed so well informed. I almost asked him how the Queen's Jubilee procession went off!

Next day, after losing our way, and having to march through frightful bush, we reached a place called Mus Arra, which resembled Sirro exactly. We passed on the way several fresh rhinoceros tracks and a lion's spoor of the night before, but saw no game. In the evening I shot five guinea-fowl at a single discharge, which formed a most welcome addition to the larder.

Next morning my Marehan pony was so fresh with the green grass he had eaten all night, that he broke the rope with which he was hobbled, and galloped away, eluding all our efforts to catch him. The caravan moved on and the pony followed, but he was not finally captured until we had proceeded several miles, and some hours after sunrise. Soon after we came upon another hollow full of rain-water. The ground about here was so wet and slippery that the camels had the greatest difficulty in standing up. One after the other fell, their burdens coming to the ground with a crash, and scattering in every direction. There was now too much water, a curious contrast to the Marehan desert. It was a curious sight to see the legs of a camel slide as it were from under him, and the boxes rolling next moment over and over.

'Oh, Lord, this is ridiculous!' as the man said when he prayed for rain, and it came and washed his house away!

We encountered fresh rhinoceros tracks, so, taking my eight-bore, I went after him, but in half an hour we came upon his dung, which was evidently a day old.

At the mid-day rest my shikari produced a tiny thorn-tree with a thick red root, which he proceeded to scrape, disclosing a pure white root, which he gave me to suck. I bit it, when a quantity of very sweet water oozed out of it, which was most refreshing. One of the camel-men caught a young dik-dik antelope alive, but the poor little thing soon died of fright. Its legs were quite as long as those of a full-grown one, but its body but half the size.

We reached Hodayu at night, and luckily found enough water to fill up for our second great waterless march across the Haud to Edegan. Here I found the shell of a water-tortoise. These reptiles are rare in the east, but very plentiful at the bottom of wells in the west of Somaliland. At night I killed another camel for the men.

Next morning was spent in repairing the *harns* and filling up with water. We started on our last great water-less march at mid-day. I killed some more guinea-fowl here for the pot. They literally swarmed in the brilliantly green grass.

At the mid-day rest one of the men was detected stealing the water, and a free fight ensued. At the finish I expected there would be fewer mouths to water! However, after cutting each other across the knuckles with their knives, they threw them away, and, grappling with each other, fell backwards into the bushes, where they lay until hauled apart.

Next day, as usual, we started about three hours before dawn, and a leopard 'coughed' quite close to us in the bushes as we silently marched on. I had never heard the sound so near before in the jungle ; the animal must have been within a few yards of me.

At dawn we followed very fresh lesser koodoo tracks. They led into the densest bit of jungle I had ever been in ; the brilliant greens and the sweet scents of this jungle were most remarkable. Passing a large ant-hill, upon which we saw the marks of his horns, we walked on tip-toe, when behind a bush, some four yards ahead of us, we heard the alarm bark of the koodoo, and then he crashed through the bushes and away. It was far too dense to follow now, so we returned to the caravan, which we found pitched close to fresh rhinoceros tracks. We followed these for some way, but the animal got our wind, and went sailing through the bushes like a steam-roller, unseen by us in the dense thicket. We emerged from this thick jungle upon the Dumberelli Plain, a large open *bun* covered with long green grass and tiny bushes. We immediately sighted an enormous herd of oryx, which, however, would not allow us to approach within a thousand yards. Soon after we saw another huge herd of upwards of a hundred, and after creeping, crawling, bending and crouching, we were left far behind. We next followed some lots of 'owl' gazelle, the plain literally crawling with game. After several attempts to get near them I fired in sheer desperation at a fine buck a prodigious way off, and knocked him down with a bullet through his heart. He had a very fine head indeed and was very fat. Here the Somalis did a grin. We then camped in a magnificent sunset, after having been on the march twelve hours during the day.

Early next day it was bitterly cold on the open plain,

and my teeth chattered as I walked along. About 8 a.m.
we reached Gunder Libah, and soon after joined my old
route to Allahballah.   On a patch of burnt ground, upon
which grew some emerald-green grass, we spied a small
herd of oryx feeding.   I fired at the one with the largest
horns, and she fell with a loud bellow to the ground.   Her
horns measured 31 inches in length, and she produced an
almost incredible amount of milk (about as much as a
small cow) which was most delicious after the hot tramp in
the sun.

We then 'made the tanks,' as my boy called pitching the

DEAD ORYX.

tent.   At 3 we encountered a man, and took the news.
He told a lie, as usual.   He said we should find plenty of
water at Edegan, which was then 'tidings of comfort and
joy' to me.   Shortly after a silver-backed jackal all but
ran right into us, so noiselessly did we march.   He was so
close that I shot over him with the gun.   I tried my old
pony for the first time for two months.   He walked all on
one side, and gave me a 'crick' in the side, which was most
uncomfortable.   When I dismounted, I put him up for
auction, but as none of my men would bid more than a
sovereign, I bought him in.   At night there was the usual
row about the water allowance.   I asked my boy what was

the matter, and he answered with the greatest scorn,
' These bleck peoples no good,' as if he himself was as white
as a blooming sepulchre !

Next day the heat, as usual, was very great. We
passed two caravans of gum-pickers. One said there was
plenty of water at Edegan ; the other said there was none.
They both lied.

Next morning I seemed to have slept but half an hour,
when I was awakened by the camels roaring as they were
loaded up. It must have been 2 o'clock when we started.
I fell asleep in the saddle, and got so cold that I was obliged
to dismount and walk. On and on we marched in the
moonlight through open grassy country thinly covered with
trees. On dawn appearing I shot a Waller's gazelle, the
first I had seen for months. When struck by the bullet
he jumped a great height into the air, and then fell dead.
Soon after we passed dozens of villages, and hundreds of
sheep, goats, camels, and people. I shot a silver-backed
jackal a great distance off me, and camped at 9 a.m.

I had my breakfast in an ideal lion's lair—a bower of
grass some 7 feet high ! A man brought me in a present
of two sheep, and shortly after five more were forthcoming.
It would have taken a month to have procured so many in
the Haweea and Marehan countries. The natives reported
very little water at Edegan, half a day's march off. It
was being closely guarded, they said. The men complained
of being very hungry, but I could not allow them to cook
sheep now, as our water-supply was all but exhausted. In
spite of its being cooler, I felt very unwell all day. The
caravan moved on in front of me at 2 p.m., whilst I followed slowly on the pony.

As we reached some villages, a francolin ran into a bush
round which a crowd of men and women were sitting.
Now was a chance of showing off before all these people.
It was an anxious moment as I approached that bush. Up
and away flew the bird at a tremendous pace. I fired, and
he came down plump, and never moved another feather.

Shouts of amazement were heard on all sides, and cries of
' Allah ! Allah !' I felt more pleased over that shot than
over many at bigger game. Soon after the bush still
further opened as we neared the edge of the Toyo Plain on
our left hand. Here extensive grass-burning was being
carried on, and the smoke in the distance, rising in clouds
at small intervals, quite reminded me of Manchester.

At sunset we had not reached Edegan and the water.
On and on we marched in the darkness. At length, about
8 p.m., we saw the lights of the people watching over the
precious fluid in the distance, and soon after arrived at the
first well, which was being watched by a woman and a boy.
The woman, getting frightened on our telling her we must
have water, and would pay for it, yelled out lustily, when
a man ran up with a spear. After begging, beseeching,
and threatening, we at last received two bucketfuls for the
pony, but not a drop more would he give us.

At the next well we found nobody in possession, so sent
a boy down to get up some water, when up ran two men,
who most assuredly would have speared us had we not
snatched their weapons from them. Then began such a
quarrelling and shouting between my men and the natives.
I was obliged to drag my head shikari away by main force,
as he was drawing his knife and shouting, ' I swear I will
kill you !'

By this time, luckily, my main caravan arrived, and we
pitched camp to consider what was to be done. After a
long palaver, I eventually bought with the greatest difficulty enough water to fill two barrels, for which I had to
pay an enormous price. I knew that my donkey and old
pony would die next day unless they got water, so I did
my utmost to buy some more. I got half a bucketful, which
I gave to the wreck of a pony, and the wretched donkey
went without !

Next morning we started to do the two marches to
Odewein. It was a long distance to the main caravan track,
over rough grass, and it took it out of the camels consider-

ably. This was a bad start for the long day before us.
Soon after reaching the caravan track, one of the camels
fell down. Its load was taken off and transferred to another
animal, when it got up and walked another mile or so, and
then fell down again and utterly refused to get up. I shot
the poor, worn-out beast and marched on. Ten camels
dead since leaving Berbera ! We had not proceeded much
further when we came to a sharp rise in the ground, covered
with loose stones. Here the donkey lay down, and could
not be persuaded to get up again. I put the merciful
bullet, which ends all pain and trouble, into the poor
brute's brain ! What that animal had suffered since leaving
the Marehan country no one could tell. On and on we
marched, until we at length reached some green grass,
where we camped. A native came up and said, in perfect
English :

' Do you wish to buy some sheep ?'

At last we had come among a comparatively civilized
people. I told him I had just bought twenty sheep at
Edegan.

At 2 p.m. we started on our eleventh and last march
across the waterless Haud, and a very long march it proved
to be. On the way we passed many villages, people and
flocks, and encountered Sultan Nur, who promised we
should water all our camels and fill up the vessels before
anyone else. This was indeed lucky, as we found a great
deal of quarrelling going on at the well, as usual, later on.
A nice cool wind blew from the Gulis Range across this
plain, but, as we neared the *tug* (river bed), the dust got
thicker and thicker, until it became almost unbearable.

At sunset we had not reached water, and my herd of
sheep were now miles behind the caravan. It was lucky
such a well-defined track had been made to the 'tug,' otherwise we must have lost our way in the utter darkness. At
last we saw fires ahead, and going down a bank, we reached
water. We crossed the *tug*. In the centre two or three
wells had been dug, round which a number of natives were

quarrelling violently. We pitched camp under some big trees. All night long the quarrelling went on, after we had taken what water we wanted.

After my supper, the amusing and lazy fat man who had

MRS. STANFORD IN SHOOTING KIT.

been with the Stanfords came in, shook hands, and patted me on the back. He told me all the news, and made me laugh, in spite of his familiarity and unbounded cheek. He recounted everything that had happened since I lost the Stanfords in a voice which could have been heard a mile off, interrupted with broad hints that he wanted a big present. As he shouted out his news he emphasized it by patting me violently on the back and digging me in the ribs. I heard from him that Mr. and Mrs. Stanford had left months ago; that Stanford had killed a lioness, and that Mrs. Stanford had killed rhinoceros and leopard with her own rifle; that one of the young oryx they had captured had died, and the other, together with four young leopards, had been safely placed on board ship. I gave the funny man a *tobe*, and, thanking him for his amusing discourse, turned in for the night.

I spent the next day resting in camp, watching the

camels being watered, and examining my heads and skins. Some beautiful fat ponies came to be watered during the day. Night was again rendered hideous by the incessant quarrelling.

We started in the morning for Upper Sheik, in the Gulis Range, which we hoped to reach in three days. We crossed the big stony plain upon which I had killed Speke's gazelle more than four months before, and saw several lots of these beautiful creatures, but they were too shy to allow me to get in a shot. All day we were mounting upwards from the Toyo Plain, which I could see far behind me. As I had now for myself but one sheep and a ' goat bullet,' as my boy called my billy goat, to eat between here and Berbera, I did my level best to bag a gazelle. Passing over the plain we encountered rough, stony ground, and went over small ravines, an ideal place for gerenook, I thought. Some of these wily antelopes we saw soon afterwards. At last I got within shooting distance of gazelle, but unfortunately put up the wrong sight, and the bullet went high over it. However, there were plenty more about in this thin bush, and a nice male, standing broadside on at 250 yards, gave me a chance I couldn't miss with such an accurate weapon. We found a little green tree and grass at Cabook, and camped. On restarting, gazelle were tamer, and feeding with sheep and goats, making it too dangerous to shoot. I spotted one alone, however, which fell to my shot, but he proved to be what my boy called ' a small big one,' i.e., a small male. After this I passed by scores of gazelle which were very tame, but I had now enough meat, or I could easily have shot half a dozen. We camped at Reget.

Just as the sun rose next morning we came to the top of the rising ground, and beheld the Gulis Range in the distance bathed in the red glow. Seeing a male gerenook in an unapproachable place, I thought I would try a long shot, as I had been shooting so accurately of late. I sat down and fired as he stood broadside. The early

17

morning light was bad, and I could hardly see him at
the distance, but I knew I hit him and sent the pony
after him. He fell dead, however, before the pony reached
him. This proved the longest shot I ever made, and
measured with the tape the distance was 704 yards.
We next raced after an oryx, which had got the wind
of the caravan, but he dodged us. Soon after we
saw two oryx together. Sitting down I hit them both.
The distance, however, was so great it was impossible to
make sure of getting them in the right place and they
both made off. I looked round for the pony, but, as usual
my syce was nowhere to be seen, so I was obliged to run
after the antelopes on foot, and a long chase I had, to be sure.
Over the roughest stony ground imaginable I careered,
downhill, uphill, over river-beds and through thick bushes.
I was determined to bag them, and, in spite of my shikari's
entreaties to give it up, I kept up a repeated fire whenever
they stood for a moment at about 500 yards. Down fell
one at last, and the other disappeared over a stony ridge.
I was so blown when I reached the top of the ridge I could
not shoot straight at the antelope slowly descending below
me, but I managed to give him one bullet, after firing a
whole magazine at him without effect. He squatted, and
keeping well away from his formidable horns, I put him out
of his misery ; and a beautiful animal he was, the finest
bull oryx I have ever killed. His size may be gathered
by those who have shot this large antelope when I say
that his fore-hoof measured 3¼ inches in breadth. His
horns measured 31½ inches, an unusual size for a male, the
females nearly always furnishing the best heads.

My shikari now left me to try to find the pony and
syce, and show him the first oryx killed. I waited and
waited, but he did not return. What an age he seemed to
be away ! ' On your lonesome ' in the desert is not particu-
larly pleasant. Not a sound was to be heard. The sun
came out strongly. I had no hat and no water-bottle.
I shouted and then listened. Only the moan of a jackal

answered me. I waited another half-hour, then walked to the top of the rise. What a scene of desolation ! Not a bit of green to be seen ; nothing but sand, stones, and burnt-up scrub. I fired my rifle at intervals, but had no response. Just when I thought they had utterly lost me, I heard a shout, and soon after three men and a pony came over the sky-line. After loading up the pony with the best of the meat, the skull and skin, we followed a river-bed for several miles, until we reached the camels' spoor. My best pony now showed an inclination to lie down. We took off the meat and rested him. Poor beast, when he was given me in the Marehan country he was fat and frisky. Now I could count nearly every bone in his body, and his spirit had fled.

On and on we marched in the deep sand, the wind throwing up the dust and nearly blinding me. Oh, intending colonist, be warned in time, and leave this country well alone : a country full of bad people, no water, and little green grass. The wilderness of Canada is bad enough, but quite a paradise after Somaliland. Presently a shot was heard far to the north of us. Two hours after we reached camp, pitched by the side of a stony *tug*. I examined the neck of the bull oryx, and the skin measured here half an inch thick. From the neck of the oryx the best shields are made, costing from 6 to 10 rupees in Berbera. The skin over the shoulders furnishes a second quality shield, not so thick, costing 3 or 4 rupees.

In the afternoon we marched through aloe and euphorbia jungle, passing many villages. A man came up and said that a leopard had killed nine sheep in his village the night before, but had taken none away. This is a common practice among lions and leopards in Africa. I felt too ill to hunt, in spite of the promising-looking jungle, and we camped early, building a fence, outside which we tied up another ' goat bullet,' which I bought on the way. At 8 p.m. the sentry fired at an animal which charged the goat, but nothing resulted. About 11.30 p.m. a man crawled into my tent and awoke me, saying that a leopard was eating the goat. I jumped up and crept to the fence, which was but a few feet off. I peered through the loop-hole, and there, sure enough, was the dim form of a leopard crouching over the goat. I fired at what I imagined would be his head, and he rolled over on his side without a sigh. We hauled him inside the zareba, and I found I had put the bullet through his eye, so that when skinned no bullet-hole could be seen anywhere. The skull was smashed into a thousand pieces. This leopard measured 5 feet before skinning, and 6 feet 4 inches when pegged out.

CHAPTER VII.

NEXT morning we marched up a gradually ascending slope, and across several deep ravines, where the going was very hard for the camels. After trying in vain to stalk two herds of gerenook, and missing a fine boar wart hog, we camped at Upper Sheik, half a mile south of the Sheik Argudub's tomb, a dome-shaped structure, which, on account of its whiteness, could be seen miles away. This place was one of the few picturesque spots I had seen in Somaliland, the Gulis range of hills to the east and west of us being exceedingly grand. Here I proposed to stay a couple of days to rest the camels, preparatory to the difficult descent of the Sheik mountain-pass to the north of us.

I started early next morning for the tops of the hills to the east, taking a guide with me. The mountain track led us through a maze of ravines. Up and up we went, the view becoming grander as we ascended. This was an ideal spot for elephants, and to think that but ten years ago they roamed over these hills in numbers! But so destructive had been the hands of so-called sportsmen, who slaughtered male and female alike, that to-day there was not a single one left, and never would be again. Never more would these countless ravines echo with the majestic roar of the lion or the weird trumpet of the elephant. They were both as extinct here as the dodo. At length we reached the top. What a magnificent view met my

eyes ! Turning to the north, I could see far below me the
maritime plain, and thirty-three miles off the sea. In the
west, as far as the eye could see, the huge barren range
stretched away into the morning mist Turning about,
the panorama was even grander still. Valley and ravine,
mountain and river-bed receded, until the whole was backed
by the great Mount Wagar, 6,800 feet high, the grandest
mountain in the Gulis Range. The whole scene reminded
me of the view from Lady Horton's walk near Kandy,
Ceylon, without the latter's magnificent wealth of foliage.
I sat and gazed and gazed upon the scene, and seemed to
be in fairyland. There was not a sound to be heard. The
silence of morning lent an additional charm and inspiration
of awe to the scene. I took my telescope and surveyed
the yawning precipices, but could see no sign of life. At
last I tore myself away, for the sun was becoming powerful,
and I had a long day of hard climbing before me.

Descending to the southern slopes, that I might not be
accused of shooting in the reserved area, I wended my way
down the rocky elephant paths. As I descended I found
many villages, some of which were perched right on the
tops of the peaks. I was obliged to descend further south,
where I was told I might shoot.

I had walked for several miles without seeing a sign of
animal life, when, after passing over a plain to some hills
to the south of the main Gulis Range, two pretty little
klipspringers jumped up in front of us, and disappeared
with huge leaps over a precipice. I ran to the edge and
there, far below me, beheld one of the rock-jumpers standing upon a huge boulder. I took a steady aim, and put
the bullet in the centre of his back, rolling him over and
over down the steep rocky mountain-side. It was a pretty
sight to see the other bounding away from rock to rock.

It was with no little difficulty that we reached the dead
one. A beautiful little antelope he was, with his peculiar
rounded and hollow hoofs, and rough, olive coat. After
carefully skinning him, I wended my way further south,

through a maze of hill and valley, until at last, when I was beginning to think that the aforesaid ' sportsmen ' had also exterminated the koodoo, I caught sight of a female watching me intently. I dared not move a finger. But she had made us out; it was too late, and, followed by several others, she crossed a bit of open, and disappeared from view.

We ran hard to our right to cut them off, and beheld seven females appear over the sky-line and make towards us, and a moment later one of the grandest sights which a sportsman can conceive slowly and majestically appeared over the line—a huge bull koodoo, with a fine pair of horns. But alas ! the wily cows had not advanced more than twenty yards towards us when there was a loud bark, which echoed far up the valley, and the whole herd slowly turned round and walked back again.

When they had slowly disappeared over the sky-line, I ran as fast as the rough, rocky ground would allow me, and cautiously peeped over the top. The herd had raced downhill, and were now across the valley, standing watching us from half-way up the next hill. I crouched down and watched them, when my eye caught sight of another cow some way to the right of them ; a moment later there was a rumble of stones, and five more females appeared, again followed by a huge bull. These two herds kept apart, so I followed the last, as they had not yet seen us. Up and down the hills we careered after them for miles. A herd of three cows, and soon after another herd of three cows and two young bulls, with poor horns, joined them.

The country was literally alive with koodoo. But as fast as I got to the top of every hill, there was the herd half-way up the next, standing staring at us, and then slowly walking up to the top to run hard down on the other side. It was most tantalizing, and at length, having left the man with the water-bottle far behind, I had to give it up, and after a long tramp returned to camp. 1

had had a most enjoyable day, and was well-pleased to see
so many koodoos in such a short space of time.   Long may
they live there to afford the hardest and the grandest
stalking in the world !

On the way home we disturbed a huge leopard, which
was lying up among some rocks.   In fact, she was so big
that we all shouted ' Libah ' (lion) on first sighting her.
She was off among the thick bushes without giving me a
ghost of a chance, and, of course, in such uneven country
it was utterly impossible to track her.   I was very tired
when I reached camp, and spent the rest of the day taking
photographs close at home.

Next morning I went out before the sun peeped over
the hills, and spent the whole morning looking for koodoo
south of our camp.   At length we found fresh tracks, but
on my gun-bearer loosening some stones and making a
noise, two females jumped up, with two calves running at
their heels.   As we went further on, village upon village
appeared, perched upon the tops of the hills.   How on
earth the camels and cattle got up and down the mountain
passes without breaking their legs goodness only knows !

I returned to camp at 12, and rested.   About 2 p.m. I
was roused by cries of ' Dofar, dofar !' (wart hog).   Seizing
my glass, I discovered there were two sows with litters of
five and eight squeakers.   However, I put on my boots, and
went out in search of a good pair of tusks.   But there was
nothing to be seen upon the plain but villages.   At length
we heard a man shouting ' Dofar,' and on running up beheld
the pigs feeding amongst the sheep.   I took out my glass
and saw there was one boar with good tusks.   Two others
had poor weapons.   Run, run, run—they would not stop.
At length, taking advantage of some thick bushes, I got
within 150 yards of the hindermost, and fired.   I knew my
rifle too well by this time to miss.   However, the wart hog
ran on, and disappeared in the bushes.   I raced after him,
and almost stumbled over his body as he lay behind a bush
at the last gasp.   I could easily have shot both the others

now as they stood watching me, but I had already enough
of these peculiar trophies, and let them run away. The
Somalis, of course, would not touch him, so I was obliged to
cut his throat and decapitate him unaided.

In the evening one of my men brought me in a live
animal I had not seen before in Somaliland. It was a
young caracal. It had a dirty reddish-yellow coat of
coarse hair, a cat's face and skull, long pointed ears, black
behind, with long black tufts protruding from the tips of
each. A short tail was the same colour as the body.
The natives called it *gododema*, and said that it grew
nearly as large as a hyæna. I made a cage for it out of an
empty store-box. It was a savage little beast, but ate raw
meat ravenously.

Next morning I sent the whole caravan down the Sheik
Pass, a matter of no small difficulty. At the bottom was
a real running rivulet, the first running water I had seen
during the whole of my expedition. Off came all my
clothes, and I wallowed in it like a wart hog.

After drinking till I nearly burst, I wended my way
towards camp, turning back to have a look up at the
precipice I had just come down. The pass now looked
utterly impossible. On reaching camp, I was surprised to
hear that not one of the camels had perished on the difficult
descent. I reckoned that four at least would never reach
the bottom. I found that my letters had been brought me
from Berbera. What a various lot they were! Stamps
from Europe, Asia, Africa, and America. There was one
from Hong Kong, whose barren rocks reminded me somewhat of these ; one from Ceylon, with its beautiful foliage
unrivalled in the world ; some from England, telling me I
was reported in the London papers massacred in Somaliland ;
one from New York and another from Bombay, saying the
same thing ; one from America's greatest waterfall, Niagara,
grand to all except the Irishman. When his guide was
cracking up the fall, remarking : ' Look, gentlemen, at
the vast volume of water rushing madly down the preci-

pice,' Pat interrupted him with, 'Sure, and whhat's to hinder it?'

Next morning we loaded up before it was light, and on peering into the box in which I had placed the little caracal, I discovered that the animal had made good his escape, thanks to the carelessness of the man I had told off to look after it. He had not tied up the lid of the box tight enough. I was much annoyed at losing so rare an animal. I left three men behind to wait till dawn and hunt for it, but they followed some hours after, saying that the jungle was so thick it was impossible to find it.

After leaving the pass through the great mountains the going improved somewhat, and on reaching some big trees we camped. Looking back, the view of the great barrier of mountains was very imposing. The heat at twelve was very great. My camels had been going very badly all the morning, not having as yet recovered from their descent of Sheik Pass. About half of them walked bow-legged and very slowly. I saw that it would be impossible to get them all to Berbera in three more marches. So, as I wished to try and catch the steamer, which was expected in a day or two, I decided to take six of the best camels on with me, and leave my headman to bring on the halt as fast as he could. Accordingly, I started with my little caravan over some very rough ground under the broiling sun, with not a blade of green grass to be seen. We reached at last an oasis, a pool of water surrounded by magnificent green grass. I dismounted and let the pony feed, whilst I bathed my hot head.

After a rest we reached a huge gorge, at the bottom of which our road lay along a 'tug.' Water was flowing in a tiny stream a foot wide, and every now and then as we marched it would disappear below the surface, to reappear further on. We passed some tall reeds in which lions used, once upon a time, to sleep. But, alas! they were now asleep for ever. This country is called Guban (the hot country), a most appropriate name. When the sun set we were still in the valley of rocks. Huge boulders towered up above us, making me almost shudder to look up. Then the rock would come straight down as though it had been cut with a huge knife. Not a sign of animal life was to be seen in this desert. First the valley ran east, then west, then north. All the afternoon we zigzagged along at the bottom of the rocky gorge. Before the sun rose next morning we were on the move, and at daybreak we left the gorge and emerged on an open plain. Here I witnessed a most extraordinary and beautiful effect. The mountains, all bathed in red, appeared to be floating in the air!

Soon after I saw a herd of Pelzeln's gazelle, which appeared to be tamer than those close by the sea. I killed a male, and shortly after saw another with a very good head. After a tiring stalk I shot him. This I decided should be my last shot in Somaliland. Soon after we passed a number of caravans with the news that the steamer had gone the night before! We camped at the foot of a steep, rocky hill for the mid-day rest. In the extreme heat I ascended the hill with difficulty, and from the summit caught sight of Berbera, some nine miles to the north. My head was very bad all day, and I was as weak and thin as a kitten. Eventually we loaded up for the last lap, and slowly wended our way into Berbera, as the sun set on my second expedition into Somaliland.

CHAPTER VIII.

Trapping and collecting in Somaliland.

'TRAPPING ! How very unsportsmanlike !' I fancy I can hear someone say. I hope, however, that every true sportsman is a bit of a naturalist, and will collect for the advancement of science as well as shoot for the advancement of perhaps nothing but a private collection of game trophies.

Do not go into the country with the sole idea of lion or elephant hunting only; you will probably be miserably disappointed. Do not take a shikari who says he cares for nothing but lions; he will turn up his nose at the idea of an oryx, almost have a fit if you fire at a bird, and promptly expire if you bring out a butterfly net ! If you take out a man like this your expedition will be an utter waste of time and money. It will be a useless expedition.

Without traps it is almost impossible to collect certain of the animals of the country. They cannot be shot, because they are either seen only at night, or they are too small and would be spoilt with a charge of shot at close quarters. Amongst the animals to be trapped, which can seldom be shot, may be mentioned the wild dog.

In a three months' expedition it is about twenty to one against getting a shot in the daytime at a spotted hyæna, and about one hundred to one against seeing a striped hyæna, much less shooting one either by day or by night ! But both these animals can, with care, be trapped. The striped hyæna (which is comparatively rare, and possesses,

to my thinking, a beautiful coat, making a very handsome
trophy) appears to be trapped much more easily than his
cousin, the spotted hyæna (*Hyæna crocuta*). Next, let us
take jackals, which are very numerous in this country, and
many of which are little known. These animals cannot
well be shot. In the first place, one can never get near
enough to them to shoot them with the gun, and if one
fires a rifle at them, the skin is in nine cases out of ten
utterly ruined. They must be trapped. Let it be remembered that when I advocate trapping I am addressing true
sportsmen, *i.e.*, those who wish merely to collect specimens
for public or private museums, not the professional skin-
hunter. May the latter pest be for ever excluded from
Somaliland !

After the jackals, in order of size, come innumerable small
animals—many of which are, no doubt, totally unknown to
science—such as badgers, otters (look for a light-coloured
one at the Webbi Shebeyli ; he must be there, although he
has never been seen), porcupines, stoats, weasels, ratels,
mungooses, rock rabbits, ground squirrels, gerbils, bats,
rats, and mice, all of which cannot easily be collected with
gun or rifle. It may encourage others to hear that during
my last expedition I discovered no less than three animals
new to science. Birds are, to my thinking, best collected
with a small-bore gun and dust shot, as they are apt to
knock themselves about in traps, so I will dismiss the idea
of setting traps for them. The birds of Somaliland are far
better known than the animals, especially the small animals,
every one of which collected should be carefully preserved.

But first catch your hare. I have tried a good number
of traps at home and abroad, and have come to the conclu-
sion that there are but three worth a trial. These three
are the oldest, and perhaps the best known of any—namely,
the ordinary ' gin ' trap, the common mouse-trap, and the
well-known poacher's twisted wire noose and pegs. The
two most useful sizes in ' gin ' traps (*i.e.*, the ordinary iron
or steel rat-trap acting with a spring) are those with 4-inch

jaws, of a pattern known as the ' Dorset,' for animals the
size of jackal, and those with 6-inch jaws, known as
' badger ' traps, for leopard and hyæna. They should have
a loop of iron at the end of the spring, to which may be
attached a chain or stout rope. Ordinary ' catch 'em alive
oh ' mouse-traps may be of all sizes, from 2 feet to a few
inches in length.

Any old poacher—I beg his pardon, I mean gamekeeper
(same thing !)—will show you twisted brass wire nooses,
and how to cut the pegs and set the snare. Having procured your traps, the next thing is to know how and
where to set them.

Now, we will suppose that you have some black-backed
jackals prowling about the camp in the day-time, but which
would not allow your near approach with the gun, or you
have listened when in bed to the weird, unearthly howls of
hyænas. The first thing to be done is to procure some
meat—some with a good deal of ' whiff' about it for choice ;
the stomach and intestines of a freshly killed sheep or
antelope will fetch them from an incredible distance,
especially when a strong wind is blowing. Remember that
putrid meat is better for trapping purposes than fresh
meat, always excepting smoking-fresh entrails, which are
best of all.

The next thing to be done is to build, in a quiet, lonely
spot, a small circular zareba, or fence of thorn bushes,
having one narrow opening. This zareba need not be
more than 4 feet high (except for leopard), but must be
thick enough to prevent the animals crawling through, and
so avoiding the traps, which are to be set in the entrance.
You will probably remark, ' But the hyæna or jackal will
jump over the zareba,' to which I answer : ' When *you*
encounter a small bush in your path, do *you* jump over it ?
No, never. You always walk round it !' I don't wish to
infer that you are lazy, but that it is natural to take things
as easily as you can find them.

Having built your tiny zareba, with a space of, say, 5 or

6 feet diameter inside, take two of your 4-inch or 6-inch 'gin'-traps, and place them in the entrance—neither inside nor outside, but *in the entrance*—of the zareba. Knock a strong peg through the iron loop of the trap, and well into the ground. Tie a strong rope to the loop, which must be secured to a tree-trunk, stump, or thorn-bush which forms the zareba. Always tie a rope to the trap, as, if simply pegged down, a hyæna will pull it up in no time. Having now all in readiness, wait until the sheep and goats, and, more important still, the men have returned to their villages, and just at sunset sally forth with your reeking sheep's entrails, which deposit plump in the middle of your zareba, so that an animal's paw thrust through the zareba cannot well reach it, and then proceed to set your trap.

This latter operation you *must* do entirely by yourself. Natives will never take enough trouble to set them properly, and nearly always end by trapping themselves. Scrape a hollow in the ground, set out the jaws of the trap, and place it in the hollow so that the plate of the trap is on a level with the surrounding ground. Now sprinkle sand over plate, jaws and spring, and the whole is entirely hidden from view. Don't be afraid of putting too much sand on, as the animal is sure to spring it if it be a strong, well-made trap. When the trap is set in the entrance of the zareba, cut some small bushes, and fill up any gap that may appear over the spring of the trap, so that the animal must walk over the jaws of the trap, and not over the *spring* of the trap.

Now take a *hangol* (crooked stick) and restore the ground around to its usual appearance. This will efface your foot-marks, and help to take away your smell. It is perhaps better, for the large animals, to set two traps in the one entrance, as the entrance can then be made wider to allow them to pass in and prevent them jumping over the fence. On the next page is a bird's-eye view of the zareba, with traps set, before the latter are covered over with sand.

Twisted wire snares must be laid in the runs of the

animals, which can be discovered in the grass and bushes. Mouse-traps may be set anywhere where the animals are suspected, either by their footmarks in the sand, their droppings, or holes in the earth.

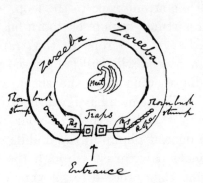

The Natural History Museum, South Kensington, supply full directions for preparing small mammal skins, which should be carefully studied, and a mouse or two should be skinned by the would-be collector according to these instructions before he leaves England.

CHAPTER IX.

Glossary of useful Somali words and phrases.

Tamboo -	- tent.
Soccer hi -	- go fetch.
Halcar -	- over there ; in that direction.
Waraba -	- hyæna.
Ferol -	- zebra.
Chebelle -	- leopard.
Beit - -	- oryx.
Libah -	- lion.
Marodi -	- elephant.
Gael - -	- camel.
Ardi - -	- sheep.
Damarah -	- donkey.
Urgi - -	- kid.
Lor - -	- lot of cow.
Sar - -	- one cow.
Sakaro -	- a ' dik-dik ' antelope.
Kodur -	- koodoo.
Dofar -	- wart hog.
Feruska -	- pony.
Mus - -	- small white snake.
Averso -	- big blue snake.
Gelbis -	- black snake.
Munso -	- very large snake.
Gorango -	- small ant.
Gemer -	- large ant.
Debro low -	- scorpion.
Shindy -	- bee.
Ko - -	- one.
Luber -	- two.
Sudder -	- three.
Affer - -	- four.
Shan - -	- five.
Lier - -	- six.
Todubber -	- seven.
Sedate -	- eight.
Sagale -	- nine.
Duban -	- ten.
Kobeatuban -	- eleven.

Lubeatuban	- twelve.
Labarten -	- twenty.
Kobealabarten	- twenty-one.
Sudun -	- thirty.
Affertun -	- forty.
Kuntun -	- fifty.
Bogol -	- one hundred.
Wahlii, belihi, terlii suder wa-hind -	- I swear truly.
War kumah ?	- who is there ?
Hangol ki me ?	- where is the hangol ?
Warrior ! -	- I say ! hallo there !
La karli -	- bring here.
War wassidi ?	- what's up ?
Kubidi -	- look out.
Muddu -	- black.
Assan -	- red.
Addan -	- white.
Bundoo -	- rifle.
Daghar -	- stone.
Ait, amoot -	- sand.
Gate - -	- tree.
Sudier -	- thorn bush.
Sorbishice -	- cook.
Rob - -	- rain.
Dagal -	- to fight.
War - -	- I
Ardeggar -	- you
Hagar kartemi ?	- where do you come from ?
Tubmati -	- what tribe are you ?
Kubber -	- sandal.
Ushara murro arro gurdo skutter -	take your stick and clothes and be off.
Warmoor -	- spear.
Garshen -	- shield.
Garasor e guboe	- bow and arrows.

18

E - - - and.
Canna donisar? - which one will you
have?
Hagar kosorta? - where are you going?
Sonorgor - - come back.
Nimad, or ninki
ferungi - - white man.
Sharbo dare - long moustache.
Horyu - - mother.
Arbe - - - father.
Warl - - - brother or sister.
Wafuckti - - too far.
Deggar - - what's up? here, in
this place; hallo!
or almost any-
thing you like.
Armuss - - shut up.
Megardi mete-) are you going to the
gisan? -) coast town?
Toomar? - - which one?
Gurra - - breakfast.
Asho - - - dinner.
Arri - - - tooth-brush.
El - - - well, as El Dara.
Bally - - rain - water, lake,
tank, as Bally Ma-
roli.
Bun - - - plain; open country,
as Bun Saylah.
Bier - - - water.
Dareter - - big trees.
Girdir - - long grass.
Webbi - - river.
Tug - - - dried-up river-bed.
Gabbow - - thunder.
Shorrah - - sun.
Diah - - - cloud.
Ici - - - I want.
Donici - - he wants.
Dat car donien - those people, or they,
want.
Wab boocordi - I feel sick.
Nincasi wab booci he feels sick.
Dat car order wab
boocorden - they feel sick.
Daggah - - stone.
Wir iari - - I grumble.
Wir iaren - - he grumbles.
Beloweh - - Somali dagger.
Wasoo - - Somali drinking-
bottle.

Barki - - pillow.
Cori - - - saddle.
Hackomi - - bridle.
Gorful - - hobbles.
Googul - - bed.
Argul - - Somali tent.
Bur - - - big hill, as Bur Dap.
Guff-guff - - stony ground.
Bunun - - flat ground covered
with trees.
Url - - - well.
Assho - - supper.
Subback - - ghee.
Berrice - - rice.
Heelif - - meat.
Hide - - - fat.
Timer - - dates.
Mihi - - - what do you say?
Mudda - - no.
Hah - - - yes.
Wurrer anonesha headache.
Aloche anonesha - stomach-ache.
Anow - - tsetse fly.
Dowar - - a frying-pan.
Ourara - - camel-driver.
Dicksi - - huge cooking-pot.
Herrer - - head.
Fundah - - spoon.
Mindi - - knife.
Modar - - fork.
Usboh - - salt.
Fil-fil - - pepper.
Hurick - - rope.
Haro - - - zareba.
Gudamoo - - native axe.
Hangol - - wooden crook.
Nin - - - one man.
Rug - - - 'bunch' of men.
Nagot - - married woman.
Gobot - - girl.
Aror - - - child.
Kordass - - leather chaplets
worn round the
head or neck, and
containing texts
from the Koran.
Tushba - - ebony praying beads.
Coogeri - - inside.
Scudie - - leave it alone.
Deel - - - native vessel for
holding milk.

CHAPTER X.

The spoor of big game.

THE white man can never hope to compete successfully with the black man in following the spoor of big game. One would imagine that an animal possessing the weight of a rhinoceros would leave such an imprint upon the ground that it would be impossible to lose it. But wait till the rhinoceros walks over stony ground, and you will be nonplussed in less than five minutes; your shikari, however, will follow almost at a run, pointing with his finger at the track among the stones, which, stare as you will, you cannot make out. The track of an elephant is much more easy to follow over rocky ground, owing to the havoc wrought on the trees and thorn-bushes by his trunk on either side of his path, which is strewn with half-chewed branches and leaves. The rhinoceros, on the other hand, when on the march, does not appear to feed as he goes, but waits until he reaches his favourite feeding-ground. An ostrich is a tiresome bird to track. He walks and runs in large circles.

When a lion has discovered he is being tracked, he will often make a circle, and, reaching his own track again, will follow it up till he sees you, when he will make off at a run. You will easily see when he begins to run by his spoor. The claw-marks will show in the sand, and the sand will be thrown back a little by the pad of the foot. A leopard will follow you round like a lion, and often see you home, as he knows that where men live, there will in

18—2

all probability be sheep and goats also. Half the reported
leopards round villages turn out to be hyænas.

It is of no use to send a man to look at the spoor, you
must go yourself and examine it. The leopard is a cat,
and when walking and undisturbed, its nails, which are
retractile, do not show in the sand. The hyæna is a dog,
and has non-retractile claws which always show in the
sand ; besides, the formation of pad and toes is totally
different. The spoor of the leopard is like that of the
lion, but smaller, measuring 3 inches long and 4½ inches
broad. It is almost impossible to distinguish between the
spoor of a koodoo and that of a young bull or heifer. As
a rule, however, cattle are found in much larger herds and
frequent much more level ground, except in the Gulis
Range. The spoor of the oryx bull is short and broad in
the fore-foot, but the hind-foot leaves a long and narrow
spoor. That of the hartebeest, which resembles the koodoo
somewhat, is short and rounded at the toe. The spoor of
the hippopotamus is like that of a camel with four toes.

The imprint in the sand of a crocodile is like a glove
with four fingers, and gives you quite a shock when you
come out of a river, after a nice quiet bathe, and behold
it fresh in front of you.

The rough sketches of spoor have all been drawn and
carefully measured by me from imprints found in the sand
in Somaliland. The measurements, of course, vary according as the ground is hard or soft, loose or firm.

RHINOCEROS.   ELEPHANT.   HIPPOPOTAMUS.

9½ in. long.   16 in. long.   9 in. long.
8½ in. broad.   17 in. broad.   10 in. broad.

LION QUIESCENT.

5 in. long.
7 in. broad.
1 in. toes.

LION RUNNING.

LEOPARD.

3 in. long.
4½ in. broad.

HYÆNA.

3½ in. long.
2¾ in. broad.

HARTEBEEST.

4½ in. long.
4 in. broad.

OSTRICH.

7 in. long.
4 in. broad.

CROCODILE.

3½ in. long.
2 in. broad.

WALLER'S GAZELLI

2½ in. long.
1¾ in. broad.

ORYX (FORE-FOOT).

4 in. long.
4½ in. broad.

ORYX (HIND-FOOT).

KOODOO.

4½ in. long.
4 in. broad.

LESSER KOODOC

3¼ in. long.
2 in. broad.

APPENDIX.

APPENDIX.

MAMMALS.

PRIMATES (Apes, Monkeys and Lemurs).

The Guereza (*Colobus guereza*).
To be looked for along the Abyssinian and Shoan boundaries. Skins are sometimes on sale in Aden, brought over by Somalis. Gallaland and the dense forests bordering the Webbi Shebeyli.

This strikingly handsome monkey has the head and body a beautiful black; long white hair on the sides of the body; neck, chin, and line above eyes white; a long tail with a white tuft.

The Grivet Monkey (*Cercopithecus griseoviridis*).
To be sought for among the hills on the Abyssinian and Shoan boundaries, and in dense forests bordering the Webbi Shebeyli.

Sides of face, belly and chin white; body dark green; root of tail gray; a broad white band above the eyes.

The Nisnas Monkey (*Cercopithecus pyrrhonotus*).
Harrar highlands.

Body red; belly and sides of face white.

The Arabian Baboon (*Cynocephalus hamadryus*).
Among the rocks in Guban; Issutugan River.

Size of collie dog; colour gray; males have a large mane; face and ears pink; face very long and dog-like.

Maneless Baboon (*Cynocephalus   ?*).
Banks of the Webbi Shebeyli.

Same colour as the Arabian baboon, but males have no mane on neck and shoulders.

African Lemur (*Galago galago*).
Colour of back ash; belly white; legs lightly tinged with yellow; top of nose and brows dirty white; sides of nose and temples dark ash colour; eyes very dark black; tail at root same colour as body, then gradually darker; the greater part tinged with black spots. Head and body 190 millimetres; tail 260; ear 24; hind-foot 64.

CHIROPTERA (Bats).

Among the bats tne following are to be found :

The Horseshoe Bat (*Rhinolophus antinorii*).

Tail long; four incisors below, and two very small ones above; the membranes of the nose present the figure of a horseshoe.

(*Hipposiderus euryale.*)

Nose-leaf False Vampire (*Megadema frons*).

Known by the great height of the nasal leaf, which is oval, and nearly as large as the head, and the length of the tragus of the ear.

(*Coleura afra.*)

(*Scotophilus nigrita.*)

Schreiber's Bat (*Miniopterus schreibersi*).

This bat has the crown of the head above the face greatly elevated, and is distinguished by the presence of a gap in the middle line between the first pair of incisor teeth, and by a second gap between the second incisor and the tusk (LYDEKKER).

(*Vesperugo minutus.*)

The Egyptian Nycteris (*Nycteris thebaica*).

Ears large ; nostrils simple ; forehead furrowed by a longitudinal groove ; four incisors above, and six below.

(*Nychrinomus pumilus.*)

INSECTIVORA (The Insect-eaters).

Jumping Shrew.

Revoil's Jumping Shrew (*Macroscelides revoilii*).

Collected at Lehello (4,500 feet), sixty-five miles south of Berbera, and seen at Sinnadogho, Marehan country, south-east.

Fur gray ; belly white ; fairly long pointed snout.

The specimen I collected at Lehello was not fully adult (1¼ inches long), having the milk-teeth still in place.

Musk Shrews.

Musk Shrew (*Crocidura nana*).

Collected at Eik (4,500 feet), July 4.

The Thick-tailed Musk Shrew (*Crocidura crassicauda*).

Colour entirely ash gray, slightly washed with drab ; beneath, silver gray ; tail very thick at base ; head and body (c.) 140 ; tail (c.) 70 ; hind-foot (c.) 20.

Somali Musk Shrew (*Crocidura somalica*).

Webbi Shebeyli.

General colour above slaty gray, more or less variegated with brown ; belly clear gray ; chin white; ears whitish-gray, finely haired ; hands and feet white ; tail fairly long, slender and not markedly incrassated, but yet thicker at its base, whence it evenly tapers to the tip ; pale brown above, white below, the bristles white ; head and body (c.) 55 ; tail 39; hind-foot 11·2 (THOMAS).

CARNIVORA OF SOMALILAND.

CARNIVORA (The Flesh-eaters).

The Lion (*Felis leo*).

Owing to the ruthless slaughter of females by so-called sportsmen, the lion is becoming extremely scarce within 150 miles of the coast. During two expeditions I saw none north of the waterless Haud. They are totally extinct in the Gulis Range, where but ten years ago they made the valleys re-echo again with their magnificent music. North of the Gulis Range in Guban there is not a single lion track to be seen among the reed-beds, where they were once so numerous. With the exception of a few, perhaps, in the Gadabursi country, I think I may say that the lion is practically extinct north of the Haud. For obvious reasons I will not mention localities for lions in Somaliland to-day.

Lions differ greatly in colour, from a dark tawny-yellow brown to a light yellow. As a rule, the Somali lion is very light coloured, and is often very beautifully spotted on the belly and legs with a darker shade of yellow. The mane is usually very poor, and a long dark mane very rare. A fine male shot by me at Habr Heshi, Marehan country, measured:

From tip of nose to end of tail	9 feet 3 inches.
Girth behind shoulders	43 ,,
Length of tail	33¾ ,,
Girth of fore-paw	12¾ ,,
Breadth of ear	6 ,,
Weight	402 pounds.
Length after skinning, from tip of nose to end of tail	11 feet.

Lengths of lion-skins obtained from natives:

Male	8 feet 10 inches (dressed).
,,	8 ,, 9 ,, ,,
Female	8 ,, 5 ,, ,,
,,	8 ,, 2 ,, ,,

Skull of old lion (teeth much worn) picked up by me:

Length from back to front	13¾ inches.
Width across zygomatic arch	9¼ ,,

The Leopard (*Felis pardus*).

Found nearly all over Somaliland. Common a few miles south of the Gulis Range, and in all waterless desert country, where they feed upon dik-dik antelope. Half the reported leopards round villages turn out to be hyænas.

The leopard's coat varies in colour and texture as much as that of the lion. In the hills and high ground the fur is, of course, thicker and more handsome than that of those killed on the hot, low plains. I have four distinct shades of ground colour, varying from dark yellow to almost white.

Measurements:

Large male: before skinning	7 feet 1½ inches.
after skinning	7 ,, 6 ,,
,, ,, before skinning	7 ,, 0 ,,
after skinning	7 ,, 6 ,,

Other skins (dressed) measured respectively, 6 feet 4½ inches, 6 feet 4 inches, 6 feet 2 inches, and 5 feet 5 inches.

Egyptian Cat (*Felis maniculata*).

Common in Berbera, running about the houses, and stealing anything they
can pick up at night. Never seen in the daytime.

Colour grayish-yellow spotted with black; body marked with faint pale
stripes; legs striped with a darker hue; two black streaks across each
cheek; ears short; size a little larger than our domestic cat; long tail
with dark rings to the tip, which is black.

The Jungle Cat (*Felis chaus*).

Found in long grass on the borders of thick jungle, and upon open plains.

About the same size as the Egyptian cat—average 3 feet; ears furnished
with a few long hairs at the tips, and have two black bars behind; colour
dirty grayish-yellow; tail short, ringed and with a black tip.

The Caracal (*Felis caracal*).

Caught alive by my men in the Gulis Range near Upper Sheik.

Colour dirty reddish-fawn; two black marks above the eyes; length about
3 feet; a cat's face and skull; long pointed ears, black behind, and
having long black tufts protruding from the tips of each; a short tail the
same colour as the body; native name ' gododema'; a rare and beautiful
creature.

The Hunting Leopard (*Cynælurus jubatis*).

Localities for the hunting leopard are the Marehan waterless desert, Gaboon
in the Marehan country, in the Boorgha country, and on the Shoan
boundaries.

The hunting leopard is easily distinguished from the panther by its non-
retractile claws, differing from it in this respect as a dog from a cat. The
face of the hunting leopard is smaller and far rounder, the legs and tail
longer and more slender. The spots are dotted unevenly over the body,
and there are no rosettes of spots as in the panther's skin.

Colour a dirty fawn, lighter on the chin, chest, and belly.

> Length of one killed in the Boorgha country:
> from tip of nose to end of tail (dressed
> skin) ...   .   6 feet 1½ inches.
> Length of one killed in the Marehan
> country (dressed) ...   .   6 feet.

Caffre Mungoose (*Herpestes caffer*).

I saw this animal east of Wardare, in the Marehan country.

Colour gray-brown; hairs ringed with black and white. Length from tip
of nose to end of tail, 40 inches.

The Yellow Mungoose (*Herpestes ochraceus*).

Collected at Abori (5,000 feet), July 7.

Mr. W. E. de Winton says of this specimen: ' Mr. O. Thomas in a re-
vision of this group' (*P. Z. S.*, 1882, p. 69) 'makes of this form his
" variety *d*. " of *H. gracilis ;* but with further material and entire skulls
instead of the mutilated specimens then in the museum, it is now shown
to be a distinct species. Size smaller than *H. gracilis.* Colour ochraceous
red or bright rusty on the dorsal surface, paler on the sides; fur less
annulated with blackish. It is also smaller than *H. grantii* from
Zanzibar, but has rather more annulation on the fur. The size of the

teeth and the much shorter and more rounded skull distinguish it from either of the above species.

'Head and body (c.) 290 millimetres; tail (c.) 245; hind-foot 52; skull: greatest length 57, breadth 31, brain-case 25·5, breadth outside teeth 20·3, length of carnassial tooth (outer side) 5·5, breadth of first molar 6·2, breadth of second molar 4·4, mandible length (bone only) to condyle 37, to angle 37·1. The most marked differences in the skull compared with *H. gracilis* are its shortness, the less developed occipital and sagittal crests, the post-orbital processes not joining, the shorter tooth-row (measurement of entire tooth-row about equalling that from the front of the canine in *H. gracilis*), teeth individually smaller (especially the carnassial and first molar), last molar longer in proportion to the first, and the greater vertical depth of the auditory bullæ; in the mandible the most striking difference is the much shorter angular process, the measurements from the front of the jaw to the condyle and to the angle being practically equal.'

The White-tailed Mungoose (*H. albicauda*).
Abyssinian boundaries.

Lydekker says of this animal: 'This is the largest of the African species. Length of head and body from 22 to 26 inches. This species is distinguished from all the above by the under surface of the ankle being hairy instead of nearly or quite naked, and also by its bushy tail. The general colour is blackish-gray, the longer hairs being ringed with black and white, and having the tip black.'

The fur of the tail varies in a remarkable manner, appearing sometimes to be black, and sometimes white (THOMAS).

Atkinson's Mungoose (*Helogale atkinsoni*).
Found at Hargaisa.

Colour dark grizzled gray; chest and belly brown; muzzle blackish-brown. Head and body 192 millimetres; tail 153; hind-foot 41; ear 17.

The Zebra Mungoose (*Crossarchus zebra*).
To be looked for on the Abyssinian boundaries.

Distinguished by the rufous colour of the under parts (LYDEKKER).

The Somali Mungoose (*Crossarchus somalicus*).
Webbi Shebeyli.

Colour grizzled ashy gray on head and fore-quarters; long hairs of back indistinctly blackish and dull yellowish-white, so that the transverse dorsal bands are almost imperceptible, although they are distinctly present; under surfaces very sparsely haired, grizzled gray without any mixture of rufous, except just on the chin; limbs coloured like body; tail has *no* black tip. Head and body 400; tail 250; hind-foot, 75.

The Aardwolf (*Proteles cristatus*).
Two young ones caught alive, and an adult skull picked up at Edegan, near the Toyo Plain.

This remarkable animal is smaller than the hyænas. It has a dirty yellow skin striped sparingly with dark brown. It possesses a long crest or mane down the centre of the back, the hairs of which are tipped with black. Long bushy tail; upper part yellow, lower part black. Length of two immature ones caught by me, 29 inches. This animal differs from the hyænas in that it has *five* toes on the fore-feet and four on the hind-feet, and in its small teeth.

The Striped Hyæna (*Hyæna striata*).

Gunder Libah; district of Farfanyer, south of waterless Haud; Garsoni Ogaden.

Quite one of the handsomest trophies to be obtained in Somaliland. Ground colour yellow-gray; beautiful mane of long gray hairs, tipped with black; large bushy gray tail; broad black stripes run down the shoulders, hind-quarters, and across the legs; muzzle black; ears pointed; long black whiskers; under chin and neck a beautiful velvety black.

Measurements of two fine males:

Length from tip of nose to end of tail ...	$\begin{cases} 4 \text{ feet } 10\frac{1}{2} \text{ inches.} \\ 4 \text{ ,, } 10 \text{ ,,} \end{cases}$
Girth	$\begin{cases} 1 \text{ foot } 7\frac{1}{2} \text{ ,,} \\ 1 \text{ ,, } 10\frac{1}{2} \text{ ,,} \end{cases}$
Length of whiskers	5 ,,
Length of ear	5 ,,
Length of hair on mane...	$7\frac{1}{2}$,,

The Spotted Hyæna (*Hyæna crocuta*).

Found nearly all over Somaliland, but especially round villages.

Colour of adult: dirty yellow-gray; faint black spots; enormous strength of teeth and jaws; ears rounded at tips; width of jaw 6 inches. Colour of young: dirty yellow ground colour; bright yellow mane; black near tail; covered with large black spots; beyond shoulders covered with small spots; muzzle black; black tip to hairy tail.

Measurements:

Very large male shot by me.

Length	5 feet 5 inches (dressed).
Girth	2 ,, 6 ,, ,,

Young male.

Length	4 feet (dressed).
Girth	1 foot 10$\frac{1}{2}$ inches (dressed).

The Yellow Jackal (*Canis aureus*).

I saw a large pack of these animals at Odewein, Central Somaliland.

Length from tip of nose to end of tail, 40 inches. Colour light rufous; ears long; sides of body grayish.

(*Canis lupaster.*)

Collected at Edegan (5,000 feet), 130 miles south of Berbera, June 20. Other localities are: Jiggiga Plain, Saylah Plain.

Colour: dirty reddish-yellow. Lengths of two dressed skins from tip of nose to end of tail, 3 feet 11 inches and 3 feet 5 inches respectively.

The Black-backed Jackal (*Canis mesomelas*).

Found in Guban, at Eik, and over the waterless Haud.

Black back with silver-gray hairs; sides a brilliant yellow, with black stripe running down centre, and black tip. A very handsome skin. Lengths: 4 feet, 3 feet 7$\frac{1}{2}$ inches, 3 feet 7 inches, 3 feet 6 inches, 3 feet 4 inches, and 3 feet 4 inches.

Domestic Dogs.

Kept by the Midgans (low-caste Somalis) to hunt the oryx and antelope, from which the Somali shields are taken.

Colour yellow as a rule ; very savage.

Abyssinian dogs seen at Jiggiga ; size of large collie.

Colour red and white. They resembled Chinese ' chow-chow ' dogs, with long bushy tails curled over their backs.

The Pale Fox (*Canis pallidus*).

Collected near Hargaisa.

Colour pale yellow ; black tip to tail; long ears; smaller than the common fox.

The Cape Hunting Dog (*Lycaon pictus*).

Seen several times at Sinnadogho, Marehan country, in huge packs.

Colour varies considerably; ground colour yellowish-gray, blotched with black and spotted with white ; tail yellow, with a white tip. Can run very fast. It has four toes only on each foot. Length 4 feet ; height at shoulder, 1 foot 10 inches.

The Long-eared or Laland's Dog (*Octocyon megalotis*).

Collected at Lehello, June 10.

Colour brownish-gray or dirty dark yellow ; black tip to tail, which is very bushy ; belly dirty white ; head gray ; muzzle dark brown. This animal possesses enormous and very beautifully-shaped ears. The jaw is furnished with more teeth than any other member of the family.

N.E. African Zorilla (*Ictonyx erythrea*), *sp. n.*

-- Collected at Habr Heshi (4,000 feet), in the Marehan country, South-East Somaliland, August 24.

Fur black with long white bushy tail, four yellowish-white streaks running down body lengthways; black head.

' Measurements taken from dried skin : Head and body (c.) 335 milli-metres ; tail (c.) 255 ; hind-foot (c.) 46 ; skull: greatest length 55·5, greatest breadth 33·5, brain-case 28·9, intertemporal constriction 14·5, basal length 51, length of entire tooth-row 21·5, 'greatest breadth outside teeth 20, length of carnassial (outside) 6, breadth of molar 6, mandible length (bone only) to condyle 34·5, to angle 33·2. Shape of skull generally as in *I. zorilla*, differing only in size. The front of the palate is scooped out, forming a shallow sinus, in which the incisive foramina are placed. The carnassial tooth is shorter in proportion, and the molar narrower, especially internally. The specific name chosen is intended to express some idea of the range of this species.'—W. E. DE WINTON.

The Cape Ratel (*Mellivora ratel*).

Shot in the Boorgha country.

This honey-badger has the back a slaty gray ; upon the sides of the body is a white line followed by black; belly black; lower part of head black; long black claws on fore-feet. Length of ' green ' skin, 2 feet 11 inches ; length of claws on fore-feet, 1¾ inches.

Otter.

Look carefully for an otter at the Webbi Shebeyli. He will have a light-coloured coat.

19

UNGULATES (Hoofed Mammals).

Galla Bull.

These humped cattle are bred extensively by the Somalis, and are most
numerous on the Shoan and Galla boundaries, where they fall into the
hands of the Abyssinians in great numbers.
All colours.   The horns of this humped bull are very large and thick.

African Buffalo (*Bos caffer*).

Tracks seen by Major Swayne at Sen Morettu, in the forests on the banks
of the Webbi Shebeyli.   Said to be plentiful on the Webbi Web, a
tributary of the Ganana, four days' march from Karanleh (Major
H. SWAYNE).

Colour black; black fringes to ears; massive horns.   Considered to be the
most formidable of big game to approach when wounded.

Black-headed Sheep (*Ovisaries streatopyza*).

Found all over Somaliland.

Body white; hair short; enormous flaps of fat on either side of tail, which
expand or contract according to the feed; head and neck black; no
horns.

Sudan Goat.

Found all over Somaliland.
Generally white; male has white beard; horns short.

The Koodoo (*Strepsiceros kudu*).

Gulis Range, Gadabursi Mountains, Hargaisa, and the mountains of the
Booŕgha country.

These magnificent animals, possessing the grandest horn trophies in Africa,
measure as much as 5 feet at the withers.   Colour gray, striped on sides
with thin bars of white.   Bulls have fine long mane, and beard of dark
brown; females hornless.   Hair of beard measures as much as 9 inches
in length in a good specimen; breadth of ear, 7 inches (round back of).
When alarmed these animals 'bark' like our Highland red deer.   The
immature are fawn-coloured.

Measurements of horns collected by me (length in inches):

Straight line.	On outside curve.	Circumference.	Tip to tip.
42	$54\frac{1}{2}$	$9\frac{1}{2}$	$32\frac{1}{2}$
40	54	$10\frac{1}{4}$	26
$37\frac{3}{4}$	$49\frac{1}{2}$	$10\frac{1}{2}$	$19\frac{1}{2}$
34	$47\frac{1}{2}$	$8\frac{3}{4}$	$23\frac{1}{2}$

Lesser Koodoo (*S. imberbis*).

Base of the Gulis Range; parts of Ogaden; Gaboon, in the Haweea country;
base of Bur Gabo Range, in the Marehan country.

One of the prettiest animals in Somaliland.

Length from tip of nose to end of tail			...	6 feet	8 inches.	
,, ,, ,, ,,		dressed	6	,,	$11\frac{1}{2}$	,,
Length of horns ...	...	...	...	...	24	,,
Tip to tip	...	...	...	...	$13\frac{1}{2}$	,,
Round base	...	...	...	...	$6\frac{3}{4}$	,,
Lengths of other horns collected by me			...	23, 21, 18	,,	

HARTEBEEST.   DIK-DIK.   KOODOO.   DIK-DIK.   LESSER KOODOO.

ORYX.   ORYX.   WALLER'S GAZELLE.   CLARKE'S GAZELLE.

SPEKE'S GAZELLE.   PELZELN'S GAZELLE.   KLIPSPRINGER.   LIONS.

WART HOG.   KOODOO.   WART HOG.

LIONS.

Colour of head and body dark gray; forehead fawn; nose dark brown; short mane; no beard, as in the big koodoo; breadth of ear, $5\frac{1}{4}$ inches; chin pure white, followed underneath by dark brown, followed by a pure white band, $2\frac{1}{4}$ inches broad, followed by gray. At the base of the front of the neck is a band of pure white, $3\frac{1}{2}$ inches broad. From the corners of the eye come two white bands, as though to meet in front of face, $1\frac{1}{4}$ inches long. On either side on cheeks is a pure white spot. Along the body is a white dorsal stripe, from which run twelve or thirteen white stripes down each side. Tail fawn above, white below, and has a black tip; legs a rich fawn.

Bush Buck (*Tragelaphus decula*).

Dense bush fringing the Webbi Shebeyli.

Length of horns, 14 inches. Colour dark gray with a tinge of red, spotted and striped faintly with white on sides; old males get darker. Females hornless. Horns of male have a peculiarly beautiful twist.

The Beisa (*Oryx beisa*).

Found in vast herds on all the large open plains in Somaliland. Also on the stony ground of the Boorgha country, and along the north bank of the Webbi Shebeyli. Very scarce in the Midjertain, Haweea and Marehan countries, South-East Somaliland.

Length of fine male from tip of nose to end of tail: before skinning ... ... 7 feet 8 inches.

Length of fine male from tip of nose to end of tail: after skinning ... ... 8 ,, 3 ,,

Length of fine female: before skinning ... 7 ,, 3 ,,

dressed skin ... 7 ,, 11 ,,

Lengths of horns shot by me: Females ... $\begin{cases} 33\frac{1}{4} \text{ ,,} \\ 32\frac{1}{2} \text{ ,,} \\ 32 \text{ ,,} \end{cases}$

Males ... $\begin{cases} 31\frac{1}{2} \text{ ,,} \\ 30 \text{ ,,} \\ 30 \text{ ,,} \end{cases}$

Circumference of best horns ... ... $5\frac{3}{4}$,,

Tip to tip ... ... $5\frac{3}{4}$,,

Colour: body French gray; black stripe along middle of back; black patch on front of face; black stripe under neck, which divides and goes up nearly to root of ears on either side; tip of tail bushy and black; black patch on knees and on sides of body; belly white; black stripe through eye, which stripe does *not* unite with the front black patch, as in the gemsbok (*Oryx gazella*). One of my heads possesses a patch of sandy yellow, just below the horns, in the middle of the black.

Speke's Gazelle (*Gazella spekei*).

Found in small herds in great plenty just north of the Gulis Range. Great collections of herds seen together a few miles south of Lehello and north of Odewein. A few to be found on the edge of the Bun Giggiga.

Length from tip of nose to end of tail: before skinning, 3 feet 11 inches; dressed skin, 4 feet $3\frac{1}{2}$ inches.

Lengths of horns	Males	10½ inches		Circumference	Males	3¾ inches.
		9¾ ,,				3½ ,,
		9¾ ,,				
	Female	8¾ ,,				2½ ,,

Colour of body dark fawn, with two bands or stripes of a darker hue at sides ; rump and belly white; tail short and almost black ; nose has peculiar loose flaps of skin upon it ; skin extremely shiny and soft to the touch.

Pelzeln's Gazelle (*Gazella pelzelni*).

Found upon the maritime plain from the sea to the base of the Gulis Range, in Guban, the hot desert.

Length from tip of nose to end of tail : before skinning, 3 feet 9 inches ; dressed skin, 4 feet 1½ inches.

Length of horns : Males, 10¼ inches, 10 inches; Female, 7¾ inches.

Colour : back and sides light fawn ; no dark bands on sides, as in Speke's gazelle, nor loose flaps of skin on nose ; tail black ; belly white.

Soemmering's Gazelle (*G. soemmeringi*).

Native name : *owl*.

Found in huge herds upon all the big open plains in Somaliland—*i.e.*, in the Saylah Bun, the Toyo Bun, the Jiggiga Bun, the Arori Bun, and the Feroli Bun ; upon every little open space in Ogaden, less common in the Boorgha country, and extremely rare in the Midjertain, Haweea and Marehan countries, South-East Somaliland.

Length of male from tip of nose to end of tail : before skinning	5 feet 5	inches.
Length of male : dressed skin	5 ,, 10	.,
Length of female : before skinning ...	5 ,, 2	,,
dressed skin	5 ,, 8	,,

Measurements of horns :

Length on curve : Male	17¾	,,
Female	14½	,,
Circumference : Male	6	,,
Female	3¼	,,
Tip to tip : Male	6	,,
Female	9¾	,,

Horns vary in a remarkable manner. I have specimens the tips of which turn outwards, inwards, and backwards.

Body colour a light fawn-yellow ; white buttocks and belly. The white just above the tail is cut in the shape of the leaf-sight of a rifle. One of the skins I have is most beautifully 'watered' like a piece of silk. This is one of the least shy, and therefore most easily bagged, of the antelopes of Somaliland.

Clarke's Gazelle (*Ammodorcas clarkei*).

Native name : *dibitag*.

This animal takes the place of Waller's gazelle in Eastern and South-Eastern Somaliland ; very common at Eik, Bally Maroli, and found throughout the Midjertain, Marehan, and Haweea countries, South-East Somaliland.

MAMMALS

This animal holds its long tail straight up in the air when alarmed or when trotting, the tip of the tail *only* being bent towards the neck. Length of tail, 13 inches. Length of horns shot by me: 10¾ inches, 10 inches, 10 inches, 9¾ inches, 9 inches, 8¼ inches, etc. Females hornless. Colour of body, back, and sides purple-gray ; belly white ; tail dark brown ; legs rich fawn ; front of face rich fawn, followed by a white band on either side of face and round eyes ; chin and under lower jaw white ; cheek and neck dull fawn.

The Gerenook, or Waller's Gazelle (*Lithocranius walleri*).

Takes the place of Clarke's gazelle in the *West* of Somaliland ; found everywhere in the west where there is thick bush. Localities for this, the most difficult antelope to shoot in Somaliland, are : Lehello, Hargaisa, Abriordi Garodi, Daghatto and Sule Rivers in the Boorgha country, Bun Feroli, and along the north bank of the Webbi Shebeyli.

Length from tip of nose to end of tail :

Before skinning	5 feet 2 inches.
Dressed skin	5 „ 6½ „

Measurements of horns :

Length on curve	13¾ „
Circumference	5 „
Tip to tip	7½* „

Other horns shot by me : length on curves, 12¼ inches, 12 inches, 11¾ inches, 11 inches, 10¾ inches, etc.

Colour : back dark red, sides lighter, belly white ; tail short ; neck extremely long. Females hornless.

The Water Buck (*Cobus ellipsiprymnus*).

Native name : *balango*.

Found all along the north bank of the Webbi Shebeyli.

Length of body, 42 inches ; height, 38½ inches ; colour dark brown ; size of red deer ; length of horns, 20 inches ; small in comparison to those from South Africa.

Grant's Gazelle (*Gazella granti*).

Ganana River.

Horns of male curve backwards and then outwards ; horns of female nearly straight, and thinner ; a little smaller than a fallow buck ; colour light fawn.

Horns : Male, 19⅝ inches ; female, 12⅝ inches (ROWLAND WARD).

The Klipspringer (*Oreotragus saltator*).

Found sparsely in the Gulis Range and in the rocky mountains of the Boorgha country, West Somaliland.

Length : dressed skin (male)	3 feet 6½ inches.
'green' skin (female)	3 „ 2 „

Colour olive ; peculiar hollow hoofs and hollow bristly hair ; horns nearly straight. Length of horns, 4¼, 3¾, and 3¼ inches. Females hornless.

* Very wide, usually about 4½ inches.

The Abyssinian Duiker (*Cephalophus abyssinicus*).

Collected by Mr. Gillet at Sheik Mahomed.

Colour grizzled grayish-brown.

Swayne's Dik-dik (*Madoqua swaynei*).

Somali name : *guyu*.

Found for the most part on rocky ground close to water. Localities : Well Wall, Wardare, Galadi (Midjertain country), Sinnadogho (Marehan country), and Joh (Haweea country).

Length of male, 19½ inches from tip of nose to end of tail. This is the smallest of the three Somali dik-diks. Colour : body same as Gunther's dik-dik, but has slightly red-fawn-coloured sides, but not so red nor so much of it as in Phillip's dik-dik. Length of horns, 2½ inches and 1½ inches.

Kirk's Dik-dik (*Madoqua kirki.*)

Found by Sir John Kirk at Brava coast, South-East Somaliland.

Gray ; not much rufous on sides. Measurements of horns, 2½ inches.

Phillip's Dik-dik (*Madoqua phillipsi*).

Somali name, *Gol ass.*

Found from the maritime plain in Guban right away to the Webbi Shebeyli ; common in the west, in the Boorgha country, to Sinnadogho, in the Marehan country, in the south-east.

Length of males, 21½ inches ; length of horns, 2½ inches, 2½ inches, and 2¼ inches. Females hornless. Neck and cheeks gray ; back gray-brown ; sides of body have broad bands of bright rufous ; legs fawn-coloured ; snout and front of face reddish-fawn ; belly white ; back of ears fawn ; under neck fawn. This animal is larger than *Madoqua swaynei*, but smaller than *Madoqua guentheri*. It is the commonest of the four dik-diks, and found nearly all over Somaliland.

Gunther's Dik-dik (*Madoqua guentheri*).

Somali name : *gussuli.*

Same localities as *Madoqua swaynei*—Well Wall, Wardare, Galadi, Sinnadogho, and Joh (Haweea country, south-east). At Sinnadogho I shot the three different species of dik-dik.

Length of male, 21½ inches to 23 inches ; length of horns, 3¼ inches, 3¼ inches, 3 inches, 2¾ inches. Females hornless. These tiny antelopes, which run about in triplets and weigh less than a hare, are the largest of the dik-dik, and can easily be distinguished from the two others by the extraordinary tapir-like snout or ' Roman ' nose, the use of which has never been satisfactorily explained. Colour of body gray ; belly white ; no red in body as in other two ; long hairs between horns ; back of ears and snout fawn ; legs fawn ; chin white.

The Baira Antelope (*Oreatragus megalotis*).

Ali-Mahan, Gadabursi country, Wagar Mountain in the Gulis Range, and on Negegr, forty miles south-south-east of Berbera (SWAYNE).

Major H. Swayne says of this antelope : ' Nearly as large as an ordinary plateau gazelle, but reddish. Small straight horns. Shy and difficult to shoot.'

Discovered 1894. Height at withers, 20 inches. Colour of neck and back purple-gray; head fawn; white ring round eyes; short bushy purple-gray tail. Measurement of horn, 4½ inches.

Swayne's Hartebeest (*Bubalis swaynei*).

Native name : *seek*.

Found in vast herds on all the big open *buns* (plains) of Somaliland north of Ogaden, such as Bun Jiggiga (where there are thousands), Bun Toyo, Bun Saylah, and Bun Arori.

Length of a fine male before skinning ... 8 feet 1½ inches.
Length of a fine female before skinning ... 7 feet.

Horn measurements :

Length on front curve	{ My best male ...	... 17½ inches.
	{ ,, ,, female	... 13¼ ,,
Circumference ...	{ My best male ...	... 9 ,,
	{ ,, ,, female	... 7 ,,
Tip to tip	{ My best male ...	... 19½ ,,
	{ ,, ,, female	... 19 ,.

Male head dark red-brown, getting lighter down the body until reaching the rump, which is a very light fawn; broad black or very dark brown mark down front of face and above the knees; tail has tip of long black hairs. Female much lighter in colour; horns thinner; no dark marking down face. These animals when moving away from one look very much like red deer. They stand upon the open plains for hours as though asleep, without moving, and in a very odd attitude, resembling large donkeys.

Hunter's Hartebeest (*B. hunteri*).

North bank of Tana River, South Somaliland.

Colour of whole body rufous, except a white line on forehead, extending from eye to eye. Length of horns, 25 inches.

The Giraffe (*Giraffa camelopardalis*).

Aulihan country, south of the Webbi Shebeyli, and generally between that river and the Ganana.

Colour light yellow; less spotted than the South African variety. Height, 18 feet.

The Camel (*Camelus dromedarius*).

Found all over Somaliland.

A dirty yellow coat of short hairs. Height, 6½ to 7 feet. One hump. Young have curly woolly coats. These animals will go for over a month without water, if they have no work and plenty of green grass. Amount of water in stomach of one killed which had drunk a week before and had light work, two bucketfuls; amount of water in stomach of one killed after a week's hard work, with no *green* grass and no water, 2 pints. Camels are bred extensively by the Somalis for eating purposes. The animals are very fat, and have enormous humps; they do not work. The meat is greatly esteemed by the Somalis, and I quite agree with them that it is the best meat in the country.

The Wart Hog (*Phacochœrus œthiopicus*).

Found in the Boorgha country, at Bun Feroli, and at Lehello and Upper
Sheik, just over the tops of the Gulis Range, also at the foot of the range.
Height at shoulders, 30 inches. Colour dirty slate gray; two large
warts under eyes, and two lower down on sides of snout; long dirty
yellow bristles down back of head, neck, and back; bristles at end of
long thin tail. It carries its tail erected on high when alarmed, and is
a most comical object as it scampers off. Old boars carry enormous
tusks; sows also carry fine tusks. Record length of tusks, 27 and 26
inches (R. WARD).

The Hippopotamus (*Hippopotamus amphibius*).

Found in the Webbi Shebeyli, 400 miles south of the coast. Tracks seen
all along the banks.

Length 12 to 14 feet. Colour: sides reddish or yellow-brown; back blacker.
Average length of male tusks, 30 inches.

The Black Rhinoceros (*Rhinoceros bicornis*).

I found this animal very numerous in the Boorgha country at Biermuddo,
Gonsali, and Havooli, and along the north bank of the Webbi Shebeyli,
from Boholo Deno to Mount Culdush, and east bank of the Webbi
Daghatto. A few left in the Farfanyer district, and to the east of
Ogaden. A few near Galadi, in the Midjertain country, South-East
Somaliland; also in the Marehan country, south-east. Very numerous
between the Webbi Shebeyli and the Webbi Ganana.

Selous has clearly demonstrated that there are only two kinds of African
rhinoceros, *i.e.*, the 'black' rhinoceros (*Rhinoceros bicornis*) and the
'white' rhinoceros (*R. simus*). A friend of mine asked the attendant
at a well-known museum why the huge gray-black object he was contemplating was called white, and received the answer: 'Oh, because it has
a square mouth!' The black rhinoceros, as a matter of fact, is almost
the same colour as the white rhinoceros, but the difference lies in the
head and mouth. The head of the black 'rhino' is small in proportion
to its body; the head of the white 'rhino' is large in proportion to its
body. The white 'rhino' has a huge 'square' mouth, and the black 'rhino'
has the upper lip prehensile. Secondly, the black variety feeds on roots,
leaves, and branches of thorn-bush, whilst the white feeds exclusively
on grass.

Wherever I walked in the bush close to the Webbi Shebeyli, I noticed the
dung tossed all over the place by the horn of the black rhinoceros, and
a half egg-shaped hole scooped out of the ground about a foot deep.
These holes I at first attributed to the wish of the animal to make a bed
to lie in, but afterwards changed my opinion, as I have seen a rhinoceros
lying down, and on going up to examine the place after he had left it,
I found no such hole. The animal digs up all this earth with its horn
to cover the dung and scatter it, so as to destroy all trace of itself, on the
same principle as a dog does. As I have before remarked, I consider the
hunting of this animal, which is very easy of approach, is attended with
no little risk, especially in the Boorgha country, where there is nothing
in the shape of a tree-trunk to get behind, the miserable little thin thorn-
bushes affording no check to the rush of an infuriated and wounded rhino-

ceros. His sight being bad, he will often twist round and round, and then dash off in any direction, and often right into you. This, of course, is not a determined charge, but, nevertheless, when there are several men it is often very difficult for all to clear out of the monster's way, as he comes snorting and thundering by amid a cloud of dust. That this animal can be so infuriated as to make a determined charge I have before shown. I should advise hunters never to be conspicuous when firing at this animal, but to kneel or sit down if possible under shelter of some thorn-bush, however thin, or at least to have some thorn bush close at hand to which to repair after firing. Above all, never *show* yourself to a wounded rhinoceros—or any other animal, for the matter of that.

The skin of the rhinoceros comes off very easily, and looks on the inside, together with the denuded body, exactly like the peel and freshly-peeled

DEAD RHINOCEROS.

body of an orange. The skin dries to about half the thickness it possessed when first taken off the body, and becomes so hard that the edges will cut your hand if you do not lift a 'plate' of hide with care. The natives prize this skin, as it makes them excellent shields and whips, but they do not care for the flesh. When stripped of the *epidermis* and highly polished, the hide resembles clouded amber, and is semi-transparent. Dimensions of four killed by me in the Boorgha country :

Length from Tip of Nose to End of Tail.	Girth.	Length round Curve of Anterior Horn.	Length round Curve of Posterior Horn .
12 feet.	9 feet 10 inches	16½ inches.	7½ inches.
11 ,, 6 inches.	9 ,, 6 ,,	16½ ,,	7 ,,
11 ,, 6 ,,	9 ,, 6 ,,	11½ ,,	7 ,,
10 ,, 2 ,,	7 ,,	11¼ ,,	5½ ,,

The Horse (*Equus vulgaris*).

Bred by nearly every tribe in Somaliland.

Ugly-looking brute as a rule, but fine mover over rough ground. Stands about 13½ to 14 hands high; never shod. Used by the Somalis for fighting.

I saw a few handsome fat ponies being watered at Odewein.

Grévy's Zebra (*Equus grevyi*).

Found in the Boorgha country, South-West Somaliland, and from Bun Feroli (Zebra Plain) to the Webbi Shebeyli, where it is common. At Bun Feroli I frequently saw a herd, or collection of herds, numbering upwards of 80 to 100 animals.

Length of males from tip of nose to end of tail (head stretched out straight), 8 feet 8 inches, 10 feet 7 inches, 10 feet 6 inches; average girth, 4 feet 9 inches; breadth of ears, 7 inches. A magnificent-looking animal, very massively built, and far superior in size and beauty of marking to the comparatively miserable looking Burchell's zebra seen in shows. Ears enormously broad, tipped with white, and having a band of dark brown below and behind, 4¼ inches broad; broad bands of dark brown on neck, from ¾ inch to 3¼ inches broad; front of face most beautifully marked in white and brown stripes; bands broader on body, narrow on legs; dark brown band down back and tail, the latter striped and spotted with brown. Stripes vary enormously in different skins.

Somali Wild Ass (*Equus nubianus somalicus*).

Found in Guban, the great maritime plain between the sea and the Gulis range of mountains. I encountered one herd between Hargaisa and Berbera, two out of which I bagged with difficulty. Said to be found south of Upper Sheik, but I never encountered their tracks there.

Length before skinning from tip of nose to end of tail, 7 feet 2 inches; greatest girth, 3 feet 9 inches. Colour a beautiful French gray; no black stripe down the back and across the shoulders; belly white; white round eyes, and white nose; ears long and narrow; dark brown mane; legs white, striped narrowly with irregular bands of dark brown. A massive and handsome animal, very difficult to approach.

The Abyssinian Hyrax (*Procavia abyssinica*).

To be looked for on the Abyssinian and Shoan boundaries.

'Fur coarse and fairly long; colour mottled gray-brown, varying towards either olive or ferruginous; some specimens marked by rufous over the greater part of the back; the hairs dark brown at their bases and black at their tips, with a broad subterminal band of dirty yellow; dorsal spot very small, oval, more inconspicuous than in any other species, and sometimes scarcely to be found.'

The Shoan Hyrax (*Procavia shoana*).

Shoan boundaries, among rocks.

Fur very long, soft and fine. 'Size very large; form stout and heavy; general colour grizzled olivaceous gray. The greater breadth of the yellow ring, and the larger number of the straight hairs as compared with the woolly under fur, quite take away the appearance of fine speckling, and produce a coarse mottled appearance. Belly dirty yellow or brownish; dorsal spot very large and diffuse, wholly black, prominent. Almost the largest of the genus.'

Bruce's Hyrax (*Procavia brucei somalica*).

Seen sitting upon rocks and large boulders in Guban. I collected some at Daraweina, on the caravan road to Hargaisa.

A dirty yellow-gray; fur like a rabbit; no tail; size small; a long, narrow spot on back.

The Pale Hyrax (*Procavia pallida*).

Guban, North Somaliland.

'Size small; form stout and squat; fur very short, close and crisp; colour pale sandy-gray, the hairs chocolate brown basally, with a broad cream-coloured subterminal ring and a black tip; rump rather more rufescent; dorsal spot small, oval, pale creamy-yellow; the peripheral hairs with a broader, and the central ones with a narrower, brown basal part, and none of them with darker tips.'

The Elephant (*Elephas africanus*).

I saw plenty of elephant tracks about Boholo Deno, and all along the Webbi Shebeyli bank to Mount Culdush; but the animals themselves had all migrated across the Daghatto River, to the west of the Boorgha country. I do not believe there is a single elephant to-day in Ogaden. They have all been killed or driven far to the west, to the Shoan boundaries. I saw tracks of elephants in the Haweea country, South-East Somaliland, at Joh and at Sinnadogho, in the Marehan country, but never set eyes on the animals themselves. I heard of elephants in 'the reserve,' in the Gadabursi country, but did not credit it.

Measurements of male shot in Somaliland:

Height at shoulder	...	...	...	9 feet 10½ inches.
Girth	...	...	...	16 ,, 2 ,,
Girth of foot	...	...	...	4 ,, 5 ,,
Total length	...	...	...	23 ,, 4 ,,
Height of female shot in Somaliland	...			8 ,,

The tusks of Somali elephants are comparatively small: 4 feet 11 inches, 4 feet 9½ inches, and 4 feet 5 inches, Rowland Ward records as the best, weighing 26 pounds, 33½ pounds, and — pounds respectively.

RODENTS.

The Abyssinian Spiny Squirrel (*Xerus rutilus*).

To be looked for along the Shoan boundaries among rocky ground.
Colour yellowish-red. Long bushy tail.

Spiny Squirrel (*Xerus dabagala*).

Collected at Lehello.
Colour reddish-fawn.

Ochre-footed Scrub Squirrel (*Sciurus ganana*).

Webbi Ganana.

'Above, uniform tawny ochre, faintly grizzled with black. Below, tawny white. Upper tail coloured like back, lower tail with broad mesial stripe of clear rusty ochre.'—RHOADS.

The Bright Red Gerbil (*Gerbillus ruberrimus*).

Caught at Bally Maroli (5,000 feet), a little west of Eik.

Rich fawn-coloured back; belly white. Length 2¼ inches. Very long tail.

The Dust-coloured Gerbil (*Gerbillus pulvinatus*).

'Soles and toes of fore and hind feet cushioned throughout with hairs, like those of the upper surfaces of the feet. Colour above, from nose to tail, fawn, sparingly lined with black-tipped hairs ; much blacker across rump and thighs ; upper tail fawn, becoming blackish-brown toward pencillate tip, the underside white almost to tip ; all lower parts and feet white ; head and body 99, tail 135, hind-foot 26·5 inches.'—RHOADS.

The Unwarlike Gerbil (*Gerbillus imbellis*), *sp. n.*

Discovered by the author at Goodar (4,500 feet).

Mr. W. E. de Winton says of this animal (*Annals and Magazine of Natural History*, ser. 7, vol. i., March, 1898) : ' Size medium ; colour rich dark fawn, most of the hairs on the back tipped with black, sides purer ; bases of the hairs on the back and the top of the head slate-coloured ; all the underparts pure white ; on the eyebrows, cheeks, and front of fore-legs, the white hairs are tipped with fawn ; the white spots at the base of the ears and above the eyes distinct ; tail darker above than below ; rather sparingly haired ; feet not very thickly covered with white hairs ; nails darkish horn-colour ; soles, toes, and pads very pale, closely covered with very conspicuous scale-like granulations ; the toes have a few stiff white hairs on the lower side ; pads and soles quite naked. Measurements (taken from dried skin) : head and body (c.) 110 millimetres ; tail ? (broken) ; hind-foot (c.) 26·5 ; ear (c.) 14 ; skull, greatest length 32·5, greatest breadth 16·5 ; nasals 13·2 × 2·9 ; etc. The extraordinary weakness of the lower jaw suggests the specific name that is given, gerbils being noted for fighting among themselves. It will be interesting to know upon what this animal lives, for its food can hardly be of the same nature as that of the family generally.'

Peel's Gerbil (*Gerbillus peeli*), *sp. n.*

Discovered by the author at Eik (4,500 feet), July 4.

Mr. de Winton says of this animal (*Annals and Magazine of Natural History*, ser. 7, vol. i., March, 1898) : ' Size small ; colour above, rich fawn, most of the hairs tipped with blackish ; the bases of the hairs slate-coloured ; all the underparts, to the bases of the hairs, pure white ; feet and hands well clothed with white hairs ; nails horn-coloured ; fingers and toes sparingly covered with hairs on the lower sides ; soles and pads quite naked ; tail bicoloured, blackish brown above, deepening in intensity towards the tip, buffish-white beneath. Measurements (taken from the dried skin) : head and body (c.) 70 millimetres ; tail (c.) 50 ; hind-foot (c.) 24 ; skull, greatest length 26 ; greatest breadth 14·5 ; etc. The skull is peculiarly square and short, and, unlike any other gerbil I know, the zygomatic processes start out very abruptly in front, recalling the skull of Malacothrix ; the nasals, however, are short ; the bullæ are rather large, and very thin in texture. The palate is peculiar, the palatal (in distinction to the incisive) foramina being unusually large, etc. I have great pleasure in associating the name of the collector with this very interesting new form.'

Phillips' Gerbil (*Gerbillus [Tatera] phillipsi*).

Discovered by Mr. E. Lort Phillips, March 8, 1897, at Hanka Dadi.

Mr. E. de Winton says of this gerbil : ' Colour of the upper parts fawn ; most of the hairs on the top of the head and on the back are tipped with dusky ; scarcely any sign of eye or ear patches ; the fur gray at the base except on the eyebrows and cheeks ; all the underparts to the base of the fur, with the feet and hands, pure white ; the tail is bicoloured, much like the back, above, white beneath ; the feet and hands are not very thickly covered with hair, and the tail has only short hair upon it. The pads of the fore-feet (in the dry skin) are darker than the soles generally, and the soles and pads of the hind-feet are dusky-brown or almost soot-coloured.' Measurements (in flesh) : head and body 120 millimetres ; tail 163 ; hind-foot 32 ; ear 20.

(*Gerbillus [Tatera] murinus.*)

The African Crested Rat (*Lophiomys imhausi*).

Shoan boundaries.

Long hairs some 3½ inches in length, white at ends and base, and black in the middle, run down the back and tail. Colour dark brown ; white spot on forehead and a white line under the eyes ; tip of tail white.

Smith's Crested Rat (*Lophiomys smithi*).

Sheik Husein.

Discovered by Dr. Donaldson Smith. Length 14 inches.

' Covered with long silvery white fur.'—SMITH.

Long crest down back and tail as in the African crested rat.

The Black Rat (*Mus rattus*).

Ogaden and the Boorgha country.

Back yellowish brown ; belly white. Length 15 inches.

The House Mouse (*Mus musculus*).

Coast towns, Berbera, Zeila and Bulhar.

Colour brown. Ears large ; tail long.

(*Mus gentilis.*)

Guban.

This is the desert form of *M. musculus*. Paler and yellower than the house mouse, with a paler, almost white, belly (BRANTS).

(*Mus macrolopis*).

Guban.

Head and body, 130 ; tail, 126 ; hind foot, 27. Colour gray.

Mrs. Phillips' Spiny Mouse (*Acomys louisœ*).

Hawaina Plain.

'General colour grayish fawn; fur scarcely spinous, quite different from that of its allies; under surface and limbs pure white. Head and body 65; tail 79; hind-foot 16·1; ear 13·5.'—Thomas.

The Ash-coloured Spiny Mouse (*Acomys cinerascens*).

'Above blue ash-gray, also the outer sides of the feet; nose, chin, whole under side and inner side of feet pure white; colours of upper and under parts sharply defined.'—Reide.

Head and body (c.) 85; tail 70.

Field Rat (*Arvicanthis variegatus*).

West Somaliland.

'Coarsely grizzled black, brown, and yellow, faint black stripes down centre of back; belly rather lighter and more thinly haired; tail dark above, paler beneath.'

Head and body (c.) 150; tail 140.

'Very variable in proportion of tail and size.'

Tree Mouse (*Deudromys mesomelas*).

'This little beast lives in reeds.'

'Reddish chestnut-brown on the upper part of the body, with a black stripe along the centre of the back; lower parts white; upper incisors grooved.'

Head and body (c.) 90; tail (c.) 70.

The Naked Sand Rat (*Heterocephalus glaber*).

Found nearly all over Somaliland where there is soft soil. One caught at Sassabanah by Dr. Donaldson Smith.

'Their runs are a foot underground, and at frequent intervals they make holes to the exterior, through which you may see the earth being kicked up in little jets, that cause one to look on in astonishment if one does not know the origin of these little volcanoes.'—Smith.

Size of common mouse; almost naked skin; very small eye, and no external ears. Colour dirty yellow.

Phillips' Naked Sand Rat (*Heterocephalus phillipsi*).

Discovered by Mr. E. Lort Phillips.

A size smaller than the above.

The Pectinator (*Pectinator spekei*).

Collected at Lehello.

This animal was first discovered in Somaliland by Captain Speke. I found it living in large families among the rocks in the desert of Guban and just south of the Gulis Range, in the same manner as the hyraces. Some were to be seen basking upon large boulders, and when disturbed they ran into holes underneath the rocks.

Colour dark-gray; fur thick and soft; the tail, which is very short, is continually twitched up and down; skin so tender that I pulled the tail off when skinning it. Length from tip of nose to end of tail 1 foot.

The Common Porcupine (*Hystrix cristata*).
Found in Guban, Ogaden, and the Boorgha country.
Length 30 inches. Colour dark-brown; white band round neck; most of the quills are ringed with black and white.

The Somali Hare (*Lepus somalensis*).
Collected at Lehello.
Fawn colour; very long ears; belly white; the upper incisors have the grooves entirely filled with cement level with the surface.

The Berbera Hare (*Lepus berberanus*).
Found in Guban.
Colour fawn; belly white; long ears.

BIRDS.

Thanks to the untiring energy of that great sportsman-naturalist, Mr. E. Lort Phillips, the birds of Somaliland are pretty well known. In the following list the birds which I have not personally examined in the flesh or skin are partly described from Layard's 'Birds of South Africa,' 'The Ibis,' 'The Proceedings of the Zoological Society, London,' 'The Royal Natural History' (Lydekker), and Blandford's 'Zoology of Abyssinia.'

PASSERES (PERCHING BIRDS).

The Thick-billed Raven (*Corvus crassirostris*).
Sheik Husein.
Size large; iris very dark-brown; bill and legs black.

The Short-tailed Raven (*Rhinocorax affinis*).
Iris dark-brown; bill and legs black; tail short; long secondary quills; croak much deeper than that of most crows.

Miss Edith Cole's Crow (*Corone edithæ*).
Deragodeley, Leferuke, Ogaden.
Size small; colour brown; iris brown.

Wattled Starling (*Dilophus carnuculatus*.)
Hargaisa.
Colour ash; shoulders and upper part of wings white, rest of wing and tail green-black; iris light-brown. Female has not a naked head; length 8 inches.

Blythe's Grakle (*Amydrus blythii*).
Sheik Mohamed.
Whole head and neck ash-gray; male 7 inches; female 6·37 inches; iris bright red; above and below slight green gloss; bill comparatively short.

Grakle (*Amydrus morio*).

Sheik Mohamed.

Iris bright red ; general colour dark steel-blue ; tail brownish ; wings deep rufous, the large feathers more or less tipped with brown-black. Length 13 inches.

White-headed Starling (*Heteropsar albicapillus*).

Bally Maroli.

Length of skin 10¼ inches ; wings, back, and tail a metallic green-blue ; secondary coverts white ; back of head white ; chin, chest, and breast brown, pencilled with white streaks ; under tail-coverts white ; beak and legs black ; iris white.

Red-billed Ox-pecker (*Buphaga erythrorhyncha*).

Throughout Ogaden and the Boorgha country and along the banks of the Webbi Shebeyli.

Length of skin 7½ inches; bright red beak ; back, wings and tail brown ; under parts buff; iris orange.

Green Glossy Starling (*Lamprocolius chalybeus*).

Dabulli.

Iris golden yellow ; colour metallic blue-green ; a dark spot near the ear and at the end of the feathers of the upper wing coverts and secondaries. In the young the upper parts alone are metallic, the lower parts being a dark gray-brown.

Glossy Starling (*Lamprotornis porphyropterus*).

Sheik Husein.

Tail long ; under tail-coverts and flanks purple-red ; bill and feet black ; iris pale yellow. Length 14 inches.

Superb Glossy Starling (*Lamprotornis superbus*).

Guban, between Berbera and Hargaisa, and throughout Ogaden.

Length of skin 6½ inches ; head, back, wings, and tail metallic blue, followed by a band of white ; lower part of breast dark-red ; iris cream.

Yellow-bellied Glossy Starling (*Cosmopsarus regius*).

Lehello.

Length of skin 10¾ inches. One of the handsomest and tamest birds in Somaliland. Head metallic green ; back metallic blue ; tail blue-black ; upper part of breast metallic red ; lower part and under tail-coverts brilliant orange ; iris white.

Shelley's Glossy Starling (*Spres shelleyi*).

Lehello.

Length of skin 5¾ inches ; back of head and tail, back and wings, glossy blue-black ; chin and breast dark-red ; bill and feet black ; iris orange.

Drongo (*Buchanga assimilis*).

Lehello.

Length of skin 9 inches ; colour blue-black ; beak and legs black ; black bristles round beak.

Black-headed Oriole (*Oriolus larvatus*).
Odewein, Wells of Farfanyer, Boorgha country.
Head and breast dark-black ; neck, back, and rump bright yellow ; wing-coverts black ; feet gray ; iris red. Length 9 inches.

Weaver (*Galeopsar salvadorii*).
Ehrer River, near Shebeyli.

White-headed Weaver (*D. leucocephala*).
Ogaden, Boorgha country.
Length 8¾ inches ; head and breast white ; wings and tail brown ; secondary wing-coverts white ; rump and under tail-coverts brilliant vermilion.

Yellow Weaver Bird (*Hyphantornis spekii*).
Bally Maroli.
Length of skin 5½ inches ; back of head and breast a brilliant yellow ; chin black ; back and wings brown and yellow ; iris white. This bird builds a curious retort-shaped nest. The eggs are blue.

Wire-tailed Weaver (*Linura fischeri*).
Eik.
Length 10¼ inches, of which 7 inches are taken up by the tail ; rufous crest on head ; iris yellow ; throat, back, and wings black ; breast yellow-white ; long tail of four yellow-white thin feathers ; bill red.

Red-beaked Weaver (*G. ianshinogaster*).
Lehello.
Thick red beak ; rufous throat, head, and back ; blue breast, forehead, and rump ; iris red.

Sociable Weaver (*Philetærus cabanisi*).
Dabulli.
Bill silvery-white ; feet brownish flesh-colour ; iris orange ; flanks with a blackish patch, the feathers of which are margined with whitish ; chin black ; plumage above drab-brown. Length 5 inches.

Weaver (*Quelea æthiopica*).
Shebeyli River.
Male : bill red ; feet dark flesh ; iris light-brown. Female : bill and legs much paler.

Cut-throat Weaver (*Amadina fasciata*).
Goura.
Bill gray ; feet flesh ; iris red-brown ; the throat is marked by a crimson band extending to the ear-coverts.

Weaver (*Ædemosyne cantaris*).
Sule River.
Bill dark slate ; feet light slate ; iris dark-brown.

Blood Weaver Finch (*Estrelda rhodopyga*).
Webbi Shebeyli.
Iris light-brown ; feet dark-gray. These finches take their name from the prevalence of scarlet in their coloration.

20—2

Waxbill (*Zonogastris melba affinis*).

Ogaden.

Under tail-coverts barred; throat and forehead deep-red; white spot on breast clearly perceptible through the overlying yellow.

Waxbill (*Estrelda nigumentum*).

Bussarla.

Iris red-brown; bill gray.

Waxbill (*Estrelda phœnicotis*).

Sheik Husein.

Male: Iris red; bill dark pink, tip black; feet light brown. Female: Iris light brown.

(*Heteropyphantes emini.*)

Sheik Mohamed.

Feet light brown; bill black; iris white.

Long-tailed Paradise Whydah Bird (*Vidua paradisea*).

Boorgha country.

Length 12 inches, 8½ inches of which is taken up by the tail; two feathers of the tail very long and thin; two other feathers of the tail short and rounded. Tail, head, back, and wings black; back of neck buff-yellow; breast rufous; under tail-coverts buff-yellow; females light brown and have not long tails.

Common Widow Bird (*Vidua principalis*).

Sheik Husein.

Colour deep black; collar, wings, and scapulars white; lower parts of back and rump white; large patch of white on wings; side of head and underparts white; bill red; iris dark brown. Length 10 inches.

Abyssinian Weaver (*Hyphantornis galbula*).

Boholo Garshan.

Iris orange brown; bill black; legs flesh coloured.

Lichtenstein's Weaver (*Hyphantornis vitellina*).

Darror Mountains.

Size small. Sides of head and chin black; only the upper part of the throat black; iris orange.

Weaver (*Cinnanopteryx rubiginosa*).

Above chestnut; tail-coverts paler; scapulars chestnut with black centres; lesser wing-coverts ash-brown; cheeks and throat black; bill black; feet red. Length 7 inches.

Red-rumped Weaver (*Dinemellia dinemelli*).

Hargaisa.

Head and under parts white; back, wings, and tail brown, the wings having a white bar; rump and tail-coverts bright red.

Red Bishop Bird (*Pyromelana oryx*).

Found nesting at Bally Maroli.
Back of head, back, and upper breast brilliant vermilion; wings and tail brown; front of face and lower breast deep black.

Red-breasted Finch (*Pyromelana franciscana*).

Webbi Shebeyli.
Above bright red; crown, sides of face, and lores black; cheeks, throat, and breast bright red; remainder of under surface black, except flanks, vent, and under tail-coverts, which are red; lesser wing-coverts brown; bill black; feet red. Length 4·5 inches.

Black and Yellow Bishop Bird (*Pyromelana xanthomelæna*).

Budda.
Colour rich velvet black; rump and shoulders rich yellow; feet light brown; iris dark brown. Length .5¾ inches.

Yellow-throated Sparrow (*Petronia pyrgita*).

Webbi Shebeyli.
Iris dark brown; colour uniform brown. Size large; length 6 inches.

Sparrow (*Passer castanopterus*).

Berbera.
Above ash-brown with an olive tinge; under surface bright yellow. Length 5·2 inches.

Gray-headed Sparrow (*Passer diffusus*).

Sheik.
Head and neck gray; wing-coverts, rump, and back dark brown; chin, throat, and flanks pale brown; belly dirty white; bill black. Length 5 inches.

Yellow-bellied Canary (*Serinus maculicollis*).

Lehello.
Breast yellow; back gray; forehead yellow; thick beak; throat white, brown band round throat; lower breast white.

Donaldson Smith's Seed Finch (*Serinus donaldsoni*).

Smith River.
Primaries brown; back yellow and brown; breast light yellow; iris dark brown; bill flesh-colour and very thick; flanks streaked with dusky blackish; no yellow frontal patch, but eyebrow yellow. Size large.

White-browed Finch (*Poliospiza pallidior*).

Sheik.
Very gray on breast and sides of body; abdomen white; bill dark.

Bunting (*Emberiza poliopleura*).

Sheik Husein; Haud.
Iris dark brown.

Finch (*Tephrocorys ruficeps*).
Sheik Mohamed.
Legs and iris brown.

Mrs. Phillips' Finch (*Rhynchostruthus louisæ*).
Ear coverts and cheeks, sides of neck, and breast ashy-gray; no white cheek spot; wings green and yellow; primaries black; tail black and yellow; bill thick, short, and lead-coloured.

Rock Bunting (*Fringillaria septemstriata*).
Waggar Mountain.
Iris black.

Rock Bunting (*Fringillaria tahapisi*).
Waggar Mountain.
Iris brown; head and throat black, head striped with white; back light brown; belly lighter.

Lark (*Spizorcorys personata*).
Sassabanah.
Breast and abdomen vinous; ear-coverts and sides of neck gray; lores black.

Bush Lark (*Mirafra intercedens*).
Dagaboor; Ogaden.

Dr. Sharpe's Bush Lark (*Mirafra sharpii*).
Silo Bun.
Head rufous; feathers have black spot at tip; nape and sides of neck dark rufous, feathers edged with pale buff; back dark rufous; rump similar to back; primaries light chestnut; throat and sides of neck white; breast buff-streaked and spotted with brown-black, lower parts pale buff; length 6·10 inches.

Elliot's Lark (*Galerita ellioti*).
Dagaboor.
Top of head pale rufous with crest; primaries dark brown; secondaries black-brown; upper tail coverts buff with black central streaks; front white, breast pale buff spotted with black; under parts pale white; length 6·40 inches.

Lark (*Pyrrhulauda melanarchen*).
Berbera.
Male: wing 3·05 inches; tail 1·95 inches; tarsus 0·7 inch. Female: wing 3·1 inches; tail 1·95 inches; tarsus 0·75 inch.

Gillet's Lark (*Mirafra gilleti*).
Eik.
Light ashy-brown rump and upper tail-coverts; long crest on head.

Somali Short-toed Lark (*Alaudula somalica*).
Berbera Plain.
Back light brown; small crest on head; breast lighter; dark band round throat of male.

Desert Lark (*Alæmon alaudipes*).
Berbera Plain.
White wing patches.

Desert Lark (*Pseudalæmon fremanthii*).
Gedais.
Iris light yellow; bill long; colour sandy; back streaked with dark brown.

Lark (*Ammonanes arkeleyi*).
Berbera.
Front and top of head rufous brown; rump golden buff; primaries dark brown; throat white; under parts buff. Length 5 inches.

Cape Wagtail (*Motacilla melanope*).
Guban.
Head gray; throat white; tail and wings brown and white; breast dull white; iris black.

Pied Wagtail (*Motacilla vidua*).
Shebeyli River.
Colour above jet black; patch of white on shoulders; under parts white; iris brown. Length 8 inches.

Yellow Wagtail (*Motacilla flava*).
Sheik Husein.
Iris and feet dark brown; head and upper parts of body olive green; few black spots on throat; under parts light yellow. Length 6½ inches.

Yellow Wagtail (*Motacilla campestris*).
Berbera.
Back olive green; quills and wing-coverts brown; under parts yellow. Length 6 inches.

Wagtail (*Motacilla borealis*).
Berbera.
Male has a black crown and no eye-streak.

Wagtail (*Motacilla cinereicapilla*).
Berbera.
Gray crown; very little eye-streak.

Yellow-breasted Pipit (*T. tenellus*).
Eik.
Head, back, tail, and wings brown and yellow; breast and under wings bright canary yellow; iris dark brown.

Pipit (*Anthus campestris*).
Sheik.
Distinguished from others by two nearly white outer tail-feathers.

Pipit (*Anthus sordidus*).
Sheik Pass.
Very distinctly mottled on the back; iris brown.

Red-throated Pipit (*Anthus cervinus*).
Sogsoda.
Iris hazel ; male rufous brown on upper parts ; broad eye-stripe rufous buff ; chin, throat, sides of neck, and breast chestnut.

The Tree Pipit (*Anthus trivialis*).
Sheik Husein.
Legs and under mandible very light gray : iris dark brown ; eye-stripe buff; upper parts brown, with darker streaks ; wing-coverts and secondaries dark brown ; chin white ; breast buff.

Sun-bird (*Anthrothreptes orientalis*).
Rugger Pass.
Iris black.

Sun-bird (*Cinnyris osiris*).
Maradyeh.

Sun-bird (*Cinnyris habessinicus*).
Sheik Pass.
Iris light hazel.

White-bellied Sun-bird (*Cinnyris albiventris*).
Berbera Plain.
Iris dark brown ; lower breast, sides of abdomen, under tail-coverts, and thighs buff; pectoral tufts orange and pale yellow ; tail metallic-black ; rest of plumage metallic black.

Hunter's Red-chested Sun-bird (*Cinnyris hunteri*).
Of this little gem I collected a male on the Marehan waterless plain and a female at Eik.
Male : back and wings dark olive green ; lesser wing-coverts and rump metallic green ; upper part of breast bright vermilion, surrounded by a thin fringe of metallic blue. The base of these red feathers of the breast has a thin band of copper, showing in some lights green, in others yellow ; long curved black beak; lower part of the breast and throat rich black ; legs black ; iris brown. Length 4¾ inches.
Female : dull brown, breast tinged with green.

Little Long-tailed Sun-bird (*Nectarinia metallica*).
Maritime Plain.
Head and back metallic green ; rump and tail metallic blue ; breast brilliant orange and lemon yellow.

Lesser Gray Shrike (*Lanius minor*).
Guban.
Back gray; wing-coverts black ; quills black ; broad black band across forehead; under parts white; bill and feet black ; iris hazel. Length 8 inches.

Black and Gray Shrike (*Lanius antinorii*).
Lehello.
Length of skin 7½ inches ; head, wings, and tail deep black ; back light slate gray ; breast pure white.

The Isabelline Shrike (*Lanius isabellinus*).

Bun Dagaboor.

Iris brown; female has the head much less rufous, only a trace of a white band on the primaries, and the under parts pale brownish with a pink tinge. Male wing 3·7 inches; tail 3·55 inches. Female wing 3·8 inches; tail 3·7 inches.

Shrike (*Lanius humeralis*).

Tuago.

Iris dark brown; pupil large. Male wing 3·7 inches; tail 4·6 inches. Female wing 3·7 inches; tail 4·85 inches.

Rufous-tailed Shrike (*Lanius phœnicuroides*).

Gulis, Berbera.

Iris brown; legs red; bill black; a narrow white eyebrow; upper parts pale rufous gray; under parts rufous white. Length: male 7½ inches; female 7 inches.

Honey-eater, or White Eye (*Zosterops flavilateralis*).

Sule River.

Iris light brown; feet dark gray.

Honey-eater, or White Eye (*Zosterops poliogaster*).

Bohologarshan.

Tit (*Parus thruppi*).

Sogsoda Plain.

Iris black.

Tit (*Ægithalus musculus*).

Haud.

Iris brown; bill pointed; wings short and rounded.

Small Brown-headed Bush Shrike (*Telephonus jamesii*).

Eik.

Length of skin 6¾ inches. Head light brown, with black line from beak to body down centre; back brown; tail darker; lesser wing-coverts rufous; breast white; legs gray; iris brown.

Blandford's Bush Shrike (*Telephonus blandfordi*).

Sheik Husein.

Iris purple; legs blue-gray.

Yellow-breasted Shrike (*Laniarius poliocephalus*).

Webbi Shebeyli.

Back light olive green; wing-coverts tipped with yellow; head, sides, and face gray; under parts bright yellow. Length 9½ inches.

Shrike (*Laniarius cruentus*).

Berbera Plain; Haud.

Iris brown; legs light gray.

Bush Shrike (*Dryoscopus œthiopicus*).

Waggar Mountain.

Iris hazel.

Bush Shrike (*Dryoscopus funebris*).
Waggar Mountain.
Iris dark brown.

Bush Shrike (*Dryoscopus gambensis*).
Walenso.
Bill under mandible gray; upper mandible black; iris red; legs gray.

Bush Shrike (*Dryoscopus rufinnchalis*).
Dabulli.
Forehead and fore-part of crown black; iris dark brown; legs gray.

Rueppell's Wood Shrike (*Eurocephalus rueppelli*).
Gedais.
Iris brown.

Bush Shrike (*Nilaus minor*).
Leferuke.
Iris hazel.

Helmet Shrike (*Prionops cristatus*).
Haud.
Iris yellow; legs red; frontal feathers overhanging the nostrils.

Flycatcher (*Bradyornis pumilus*).
Hargaisa.
Grayer than *B. pallidus*.

Rueppell's Flycatcher (*Bradyornis rueppelli*).
Hullier.
Head and rump white; back dark brown.

Rufous Warbler (*Ædon familiaris*).
Gedais.
Iris brown; upper parts light rufous; central pair of tail feathers brown.

Willow Wren (*Phylloscopus trochilus*).
Sheik Mohamed.
General colour above olive brown; tail ash brown; chest distinctly washed with yellow; iris dark brown; legs brown. Length 4·8 inches.

Chiff-chaff (*Phylloscopus rufus*).
Waggar Mountain.
Iris black; upper parts olive green; rump yellower; above eye yellow streak; wing-coverts and tail brown; under parts white; bill brown.

Common White Throat (*Sylvia cinerea*).
Sheik.
Chin and throat white; belly dirty white; wing-coverts edged with pale brown; iris black.

Blandford's Warbler (*Sylvia blandfordi*).
Berbera Plain.
Wing 2·5 inches; tail 2·35 inches. Legs dark; iris black.

Desert Warbler (*sylvia nana*).
Berbera Plain.
Iris light yellow.

Warbler (*Hypolais languida*).
Silo Plain; Berbera Plain.
Length 3 inches. Iris black; first primary very pointed.

Warbler (*Hypolais pallida*).
Berbera; Guban.
Iris hazel.

Bush Warbler (*Eremomela flavicrissalis*).
Dagaboor; Sheik.
Iris black.

The Short-tailed Bush Warbler (*Camaroptera brevicaudata*).
Gulis.
Iris light hazel; pupil small; orbit pinkish-brown; legs flesh colour; bill black; female iris pale gray; colour of plumage duller and more uniform; throat whiter.

Warbler (*Camonastes simplex*).
Gulis.
Iris hazel.

Isabelline Warbler (*Sylviella isabellina*).
Le Good.
Head, entire upper parts, and tail dark slaty gray with a green tinge; rump buff; under parts buff-white; bill black. Length 3·40 inches.

Mrs. Phillips' Blackbird (*Merula ludoviciæ*).
Waggar Mountain.
Head, neck, and tail black; other parts slaty black; legs and beak yellow; iris brown.

Rock Thrush (*Monticola saxatilis*).
Sheik.
Iris brown; adult male head and neck ash blue; scapulars blackish washed with blue; centre of back white; tail and upper tail-coverts light red; throat ash-blue; rest of under parts rufous orange.

Blue Rock Thrush (*Monticola cyanus*).
Sheik.
Adult male: above dull blue; silvery gloss on head and breast; under parts dull blue; iris black. Female: above gray-brown tinted with blue; lower parts buff.

Rock Thrush (*Monticola rufocinereus*).
Sheik.
Iris brown.

(*Irania gutturalis.*)
Gulis.
Iris brown; upper parts slate gray; lores and ear-coverts black; eye-stripe white; chin and upper throat white; under parts chestnut; bill black.

Somali Wheatear (*Saxicola somalica*).
Doda.
Rump uniform ash ; no rufous on wings ; iris brown.

Wheatear (*Saxicola œnanthus*).
Sheik Husein.
Iris dark brown ; male : crown and upper parts gray-blue ; lores and ear-coverts black ; upper tail-coverts white ; tail black and white ; under parts buff-white.

The Isabelline Wheatear (*Saxicola isabellina*).
Silo Plain.
Iris brown ; size large ; colour red-brown ; rufous brown on rump.

Phillips' Wheatear (*Saxicola phillipsi*).
Bohologarshan.
Iris dark brown.

Wheatear (*Saxicola morio*).
Waggar.
Iris plain black.

Desert Wheatear (*Saxicola deserti*).
Berbera.
Iris black ; head gray ; back and lower wing-coverts buff ; primaries black ; secondaries brown ; tail black ; under parts white.

Black-tailed Chat (*Saxicola melanura*).
Lehello.
Length of skin, 4¾ inches. Light brown, tail darker ; breast whitish ; iris black.

Redstart (*Ruticilla semirufa*).
Sheik.
Iris black ; very little white on forehead ; black on throat extends over chest ; rump and under parts deep chestnut.

Little Red-headed Warbler (*Dryodromas smithii*).
Lehello.
Length 4¼ inches. Head rufous ; back and wings light brown ; tail black ; breast white ; iris light brown ; legs pink.

Red-tailed Redstart or Fantail (*E. leucoptera*).
Lehello.
Length 5½ inches. Back and tail dark red ; iris black ; wings black and white ; breast white.

Black-tailed Chat (*M. melanura*).
Lehello.
Length of skin, 4¾ inches. Colour light brown, tail darker ; breast whitish ; iris black.

(*Burnesia somalica.*)
Dagaboor ; Berbera Plain.
Head and upper parts, wing-coverts, primaries and secondaries ashy brown ; under wing-coverts white ; tail ashy brown above, blue-gray beneath ; sides of face and under parts white ; bill black ; iris light hazel. Length 5·90 inches.

Bulbul (*Pycnonotus arsinoë*).

Length of skin, 7 inches. Head and beak black; back of tail and wings brown; breast: upper light brown, lower white. Feeds on buds and fruits.

Dodson's Bulbul (*Pycnonotus dodsoni*).

Sule River.

Under surface very white; black on head and throat well defined; back mottled black-brown; fore-neck white; iris black.

The Little Bulbul (*Phyllostrophus pauper*).

Shebeyli.

Tail brown; no olive shade in plumage; iris red.

Reed Warbler (*Acrocephalus phragmites*).

Las Durbar.

Reed Warbler (*Acrocephalus streperus*).

Las Durbar.

Upper parts rufous brown; chin and throat dull white; breast and flanks pale buff.

Thrush (*Pratincola albifasciata*).

Sheik Mohamed.

Iris dark brown.

Smith's Babbling Thrush (*Crateropus smithii*).

Sheik Husein.

Iris gray-brown; legs brown; lores white; throat and breast gray with white margins; upper parts very dark.

Babbling Thrush (*Argya rubiginosa*).

Shebeyli.

Tail brown; no olive shade in plumage.

Alymer's Babbling Thrush (*Argya alymeri*).

Hullier.

Bill white; iris cream; bare skin about eye blue-white; legs light brown.

Flycatcher (*Pachyprora bella*).

Le Good.

Iris yellow; head and back dark blue-gray; two white spots on forehead; secondaries black, margined with white; primaries dark brown; black stripe from bill to nape; throat white; broad blue-black band across breast; tail blue-black; bill, tarsi, and feet black. Length 4·50 inches.

Flycatcher (*Pachyprora orientalis*).

Sheik.

Iris yellow.

Flycatcher (*Parisome boehmi*).

Hargaisa.

Iris light yellow.

Spott•d Flycatcher (*Muscicapra grisola*).
Sheik Husein.
Iris dark brown ; colour brown ; tail and primaries dark brown ; ring of
dirty yellow round eye ; cheeks and under parts dirty white. Length
5·4 inches.

Flycatcher (*Terpsiphone cristata*).
Length 4 inches. Upper parts umber, marked with white and yellow ; breast
and belly pale yellow ; iris dark purple.

Flycatcher (*Pachyprora puella*).
Okoto.
Iris yellow.

Warbler (*Sylviella micrura*).
Fehja.
Iris red ; legs light brown ; rump feathers nearly hide the tail.

Dodson's Warbler (*Cisticola dodsoni*).
Haud.

Warbler (*Cisticola marginalis*).
Sheik Mohamed.

Warbler (*Cisticola cisticola*).
Silo Plain.
Distinct shade of rufous on the tail before the subterminal bar.

Somali Warbler (*Cisticola somalica*).
Milmil.
Rump uniform ash.

(*Erythopyia leucoptera.*)
Shebeyli.
Length 6·5 inches. Iris dark brown ; above dark cinnamon ; under parts
white ; upper part head and neck gray ; wings dull black ; wing-coverts
and secondary quills margined with white ; tail feathers light rufous.

Donaldson Smith's Chat-thrush (*Cossypha donaldsoni*).
Sheik Husein.
Iris dark brown.

Chat-thrush (*Cichladusa gullata*).
Moodenar.
Iris red-brown.

Ground Thrush (*Geocichla simensis*).
Sheik Mohamed.
Iris dark brown ; bill long, thick, and slightly hooked.

Abyssinian Thrush (*Turdus abyssiniens*).
Sheik Mohamed.
Iris dark brown.

Swallow (*Hirundo æthiopica*).

Hargaisa.

Length 7 inches. Upper parts dark blue ; above beak yellow-brown ; black collar ; chin and breast white ; iris dark brown.

Common Swallow (*Hirundo rustica*).

Eik.

Metallic-blue back ; breast white ; tail forked.

Rock Martin (*Cotile obsoleta*).

Waggar.

Iris black.

PICARIÆ (WOODPECKERS, CUCKOOS, HORNBILLS).

Larger Woodpecker (*Thripias schoënsis*).

Lehello ; Boorgha country.

Iris dark red. Back brown, spotted with white ; back of head brilliant scarlet ; under parts gray and brown ; legs and beak black ; tail and wings have bright yellow quills.

Small Woodpecker (*Dendropsicus hemprichi*).

Lehello ; Hargaisa.

Length of skin, 4¾ inches ; back brown spotted with white ; back of head bright red ; under parts gray and brown ; legs and beak black ; tail and wings have bright yellow quills.

Woodpecker (*Campothera nubica*).

Shebeyli ; Sogsoda.

Iris red ; above olive green ; tail barred with six bands of yellow ; head gray·black, tipped with red ; crest bright red ; fòre-cheeks red; rest of sides, face, and neck dirty white ; under parts yellow spotted with black. Length 8 inches.

Lesser Honey Guide (*Indicator minor*).

Waggar Mountain.

Iris brown ; upper parts yellow-brown ; feathers of wing bright yellow ; chin, sides of face, breast, and belly ash. Length 5¼ inches.

Yellow-spangled Barbet (*Trachyphonus shelleyi*).

El Dara.

Size of a redwing ; wings dark brown ; back and tail spotted with light brown and white ; head red, yellow, and brown ; iris brown ; rump yellow, followed by red towards the tail.

Barbet (*Trachyphonus margaritatus*).

Sheik.

Bill pale reddish-brown ; legs greenish horn-coloured ; iris brown.

Barbet (*Barbatula affinis*).
Northern Haud.

Bland's Barbet (*Tricholæma blandi*).
Gulis.
Bill lead-coloured ; back of head and throat brown tipped with white ;
back, wings, and tail brown and yellow ; breast white ; brown streak from
eye to shoulder ; no red spot on breast ; iris brown.

Barbet (*Tricholæma stigmatothorax*).
Le Good.
Iris black ; legs dark slate ; long black bristles below the beak and in front
of the eye.

Large Crested Cuckoo (*Coccystes caffer*).
Dogga Mountain.
Upper parts greenish-black ; long crest on head ; secondaries and tail
greenish-black ; broad white tip to tail ; under parts dirty white ; bill
black ; feet brown ; iris olive.   Length 15 inches.

Cuckoo (*Centropus superciliosus*).
Tooloo.
Length 14 inches ; wing 6 inches ; tail 8 inches.   Iris red ; legs gray ; bill
black.

Cuckoo (*Cuculus gularis*).
Gulis.
Upper parts blue-gray ; wing-coverts dark gray-brown ; under parts dirty
white ; bill and feet yellow.   Length 12 inches.

European Cuckoo (*Cuculus canorus*).
Sheik Mohamed.
Length 13 inches.   Upper parts ash gray ; sides of face, throat and neck
blue-gray ; back glossy green ; wing-coverts dark gray ; under parts
white ; iris brown.

White-bellied Plantain-eater (*Schizœrhis leucogaster*).
Gulis ; Milmil ; Sheik.
Crest on head ; iris dark brown.

Donaldson Smith's Plantain-eater (*Turacus donaldsoni*).
Sheik Mohamed ; Darro Mountain.
Iris brown ; bill and eye wattle red ; crest on head green and red-brown ;
white patch between eye and beak, and white streak down side of head ;
upper parts of breast and back green ; belly slate ; lower part of back
and tail blue ; primaries dark red.

Coly (*Colius leucotis*).
Sheik Husein.
Orbits gray ; legs red ; iris blue-gray ; ear-coverts white.

Coly (*Colius macrura*).
Bohologarshan.
Feet, face and base of bill red ; iris red.

Little Swift (*Tachornis parva*).
Shebeyli.

Nubian Nightjar (*Caprimulgus nubicus*).
Haud.
Iris black; pupil white.

Donaldson Smith's Nightjar (*Caprimulgus donaldsoni*).
Hargaisa.
Very long rictal bristles; red collar round back; neck mottled.

Nightjar (*Caprimulgus inornatus*).
Zeilah; Waggar Mountain.
Iris black. Wing 6 inches; tail 4·7 inches.

Carmine-throated Bee-eater (*Merops nubicus*).
Webbi Shebeyli; Gulis.
Length 13½ inches. Tail red; under parts pink; iris dark red.

Revoil's Bee-eater (*Merops revoili*).
Lehello.
Length 5½ inches. Head, back, wings and tail metallic green; rump bright
blue; chin white; breast rufous.

Common Bee-eater (*Merops apiaster*).
Luku.
Distinguished from other bee-eaters by its yellow forehead and throat and
yellow scapulars; iris red-brown. Length 11 inches.

White-throated Bee-eater (*Merops albicollis*).
Berbera.
Iris red; above pale green; upper tail-coverts and tail pale blue; forehead
and a broad line over eye white, with a black band across lower throat,
then a line of pale blue; crown of head black; throat white; under
wing-coverts pale buff; bill black. Length 11 inches.

Bee-eater (*Melithophagus cyonostictus*).
Shebeyli River; Gulis.
Iris red.

Somali Hoopoe (*Upupa somaliensis*).
Hargaisa; Well Wall; Odewein.
Length 11 inches. Long yellow crest on head tipped with black; head
yellow; back gray-brown; rump white; tail black and white; wings
barred with black and white; iris yellow.

Yellow-billed Wood Hoopoe (*Rhinopomastes minor*).
Milmil; Lehello.
Length 7½ inches. Curved yellow beak; breast black; back, wings, and
tail dark blue; white bar on wings; iris brown.

Wood Hoopoe (*Irrisor erythorynchus*).
Shebeyli.
Upper parts metallic green; white bars on wings; white spots on tail; bill
curved; bill and feet red; iris brown; legs dull pink. Length 15 inches.

21

Abyssinian Hornbill (*Buchorax abyssinicus*).

Sheik Mohamed.

Legs black ; iris dark brown ; bill black and 9 inches long; helmet on bill ;
plumage black; large quills white. Length 3 feet 2 inches.

Hornbill (*Lophoceros flavirostris*).

Gulis; Smith River.

Throat black; bill yellow ; iris yellow.

Hornbill (*Lophoceros medianus*).

Gulis.

Iris brown; orbits white, shaded with pink-gray; bill red; base of bill
white.

Yellow-billed Hornbill (*Lophoceros melanoleucus*).

Ogaden.

Length 21 inches; length of tail 9 inches. Bill brilliant red or yellow ;
head gray; back and lesser wing-coverts spotted brown and white; breast
and tail brown and white.

Hornbill (*Lophoceros hemprichi*).

Darro Mountains.

Bill red-brown, under mandible brighter ; iris yellow-brown.

Red-billed Hornbill (*Lophoceros erythrorhynchus*).

Smith River.

Iris yellow; bill red, and not much arched; head and throat dirty white;
crest on head; upper parts gray; under parts white. Length 20 inches.

The Sibi Hornbill (*Lophoceros sibbensis*).

Sibi.

Feet black ; soles yellow-white ; bare skin of neck light blue ; red next bill;
iris brown.

African White-breasted Kingfisher (*Halcyon semicœrulea*).

Webbi Shebeyli; Gunder Libah.

Beak red; head gray; breast and under wing-coverts chestnut; back black;
rump blue; tail blue; breast gray. Length 8 inches.

Striped Kingfisher (*Halcyon chelicutensis*).

Milmil.

Head brown ; upper back, scapulars and wing coverts brown ; lower back,
rump and upper tail-coverts blue; tail dark green above, gray-brown
beneath ; under parts white; upper breast crossed with brown ; bill and
feet red. Length 6½ inches.

Pied Kingfisher (*Ceryle rudis*).

Shebeyli River; Bainhou.

Head black striped with white ; body black and white ; under parts white
with two black bands across breast; bill and feet black; iris brown.

Kingfisher (*Ispidina picta*).

Mount Kuldush.

Bill and legs orange ; iris brown.

Phillips' Roller (*Coracias lorti*).

Leferuke ; Sheik ; Hargaisa.

Legs yellow.

White-naped Roller (*Coracias nævia*).

Gedais.

Upper parts red-brown with olive gloss; under parts dull brown streaked with white ; wings dull green ; tail dark blue ; cheeks red with white streaks ; bill black.   Length 13 inches.

Common Roller (*Coracias garrula*).

Hargaisa ; Ogaden.

Length of skin, 12 inches.   A strikingly handsome bird ; back of head and under parts green ; cheeks and chin lilac ; back brown; rump, lesser wing-coverts and secondaries Oxford blue ; median wing-coverts and tail Cambridge blue ; the two outer feathers of the tail elongated.

PSITTACI (Parrots).

Red-bellied Parrot (*P. rufiventris*).

Hargaisa ; Ogaden and the Boorgha country.

Length of skin, 8¼ inches.   Head, back and wings green-gray; upper part of breast rufous gray ; lower part brilliant orange ; under tail-coverts and rump brilliant green.

STRIGES (Owls).

Little Owl (*Carine spilogaster*).

Eik.

Length of skin, 6¾ inches.   Back and wings a tawny brown with large spots of white ; back of head and neck dull yellow ; chin white ; breast white slashed with tawny brown ; claws well feathered with yellowish-white ; beak yellow ; iris yellow.

Verreaux's Eagle Owl (*Bubo lacteus*).

Galadi ; Sheik Mohamed.

This magnificent owl has a general colour of brownish-gray ; a white mark from shoulder half-way down back ; on wing-coverts several white blotches ; cere blue-gray ; bill ash ; eyelid pink ; iris dark brown.   Length 26 inches.

Pigmy Owl (*Glaucidium perlatum*).

Darror Mountain.

Bill green-yellow ; iris straw.

Cape Scops Owl (*Scops capensis*).

Daboÿe.

Size small; colour dark mottled gray with black cross-lines; ear-tufts distinct; under parts paler, more white on abdomen than on breast; iris yellow; feet gray. Length 7·5 inches.

ACCIPITRES (Birds of Prey).

African Falconet (*Poliohierax semitorquatus*).

Sogsoda.

Upper parts blue-gray; behind neck and upper tail-coverts white; legs orange; bill yellow; iris brown. Length 7½ inches.

Kestrel (*Cerchneis fieldi*).

Upper parts light rufous; head and nape streaked with narrow black lines; primaries black edged with light buff; tail ash gray; bill pale blue. Length 12·50 inches.

Eastern Red-footed Kestrel (*Cerchneis tinnunculus*).

Length 9½ inches. Above lead-coloured; wing-coverts and primaries gray; under parts gray; thigh, vent, and under tail-coverts chestnut; iris light yellow.

The Short-legged Kestrel (*Butorides brevipes*).

Berbera.

The Lesser Falcon (*Falco minor*).

Sinnadogho, Marehan country.

Size of a hen harrier; eye brown; base of beak and round eye brown; legs bright lemon yellow; head and back of wings dark brown; back slate gray; breast buff, barred with dark brown; huge talons and black claws.

Naked-cheeked Hawk (*Polyboroides typicus*).

Sheik Mohamed.

Throat and neck dark gray; rest of under parts marked with broad black and white bands; head crested; tail black with narrow white tip, and above a broad white band. Length: Male, 2 feet; female, 2 feet 3½ inches.

Pallid Harrier (*Circus macrurus*).

Gedais.

Pale blue-gray; lores and sides of face white; under parts gray-white; bill black; feet yellow; iris yellow. Length 17½ inches. Female brown; iris dark brown.

Chanting Goshawk (*Melierax poliopterus*).

Sheik.

Upper parts and breast gray; belly white and brown; rump white; tail tipped and barred with white; cere and legs red; iris brown. Length 24 inches.

Black Goshawk (*Melierax niger*).
Waggar Mountain.
Male colour black ; tail has three white spots above and four below.
Length 11¼ inches ; female 13 inches.

Red-faced Goshawk (*Melierax gabar*).
Bohologarshan.
Upper parts and head gray ; throat and breast blue-gray ; belly white
barred with gray ; upper and under tail-coverts white ; iris orange.
Length 14 inches.

Goshawk (*Astur sphenurus*).
Ehrer River.
Iris red ; legs yellow.

Yellow-billed Kite (*Milvus ægyptius*).
Sheik.
Upper parts brown ; top and head, neck, cheeks, and throat light brown ;
wings long and pointed ; tail deeply forked ; iris brown ; bill and legs
yellow. Length 21 inches.

Black-winged Kite (*Elanus cœruleus*).
Budda.
Upper parts blue-gray ; under parts white ; shoulders black ; feet bright
yellow ; iris red. Length 12 inches.

African Sea Eagle (*Haliœtus vocifer*).
Berbera.
Head, breast, top of back, and tail pure white ; wings and back very dark
brown ; belly and thighs deep red-brown ; cere and legs yellow ; iris
brown. Length 2 feet 8 inches.

The Bateleur Eagle (*Helotarsus ecaudatus*).
All over the Marehan and Haweea countries.
This very handsome bird has a large crest upon its head ; back and tail
chestnut ; head, neck, and breast deep black ; wing-coverts bronze ;
secondaries gray ; cere and parts in front of eye which are naked a
brilliant red ; legs brilliant red ; iris rich brown.
This bird is much sought after by Somalis for female complaints. The flesh
is dried hard in the sun and given as a medicine.

(*Entolnœtus spilogaster*.)
Feet green-yellow ; iris yellow ; bill light gray.

Tawny Eagle (*Aquila rapax*).
Waggar.
Colour red-brown ; tail and wings dark brown ; legs feathered to the toes.
Length, 2 feet 8 inches.

Augur Buzzard (*Buteo augur*).
Sheik Mohamed.
Colour black ; base of quills ashy gray with black bars ; tail reddish and
marked at tip with black ; iris brown. Length 20 inches.

Abyssinian Vulture (*Lophogyps occipitalis*).

Mandera.

Colour dark brown; distinguished by the head being covered with down, which forms a ridge on the occiput, and by the absence of the neck lappets; size small.

Egyptian Vulture (*Neophron percuopterus*).

Berbera, and along sea-coast.

Colour white; no feathers on head and neck, which are yellow; primaries black; legs flesh-coloured. The young are dark brown.

Secretary Vulture (*Serpentarius secretarius*).

Silo Bun.

Colour light gray; quills and primary coverts black; upper tail-coverts white; under parts gray-white; thighs and abdomen black; under tail-coverts white; legs yellow; iris gray; height 4 feet; crest of plumes at back of head; legs very long and thin; two middle feathers of the tail very long, sometimes nearly 3 feet.

STEGANOPODES (Pelicans).

Common Pelican (*Pelicanis onocrotalus*).

Sea-shore, Berbera.

Crest in breeding season; upper mandible red at the base, yellow at tip; lower mandible pale red; pouch flesh-coloured; primaries black. Length 5 feet.

HERODIONES (Herons, Storks, Ibises).

Common Heron (*Ardea cinerea*).

Wells of Farfanyer; Webbi Shebeyli.

Colour slate gray; under parts gray. Length 3 feet.

The Little Egret (*Ardea garzetta*).

Marehan country; Webbi Shebeyli.

Body white; legs and beak black; crest of two feathers.

Egret (*Lepterodias gularis*).

Berbera.

Iris light yellow; colour dusky slate; throat white; plumes on scapulars and breast small; crest in breeding season.

The Common Bittern (*Botaurus stellaris*).

Webbi Shebeyli.

Colour buff barred with black; ruff round neck. Length 30 inches.

Buff-backed Egret (*Bubuleus ibis*).

Webbi Shebeyli.

General colour white; crest in breeding season; top of head, crest, and feathers on breast buff; bill and legs yellow; iris white.

The Hammer-head (*Scopus umbrella*).

Sheik Husein.

Length 25 inches. Head very large; beak longer than head; neck short and thick; broad and bushy crest on head; colour umber-brown; brighter on the under surface; beak black; legs and feet brown or black; iris dark brown.

White Stork (*Ciconia alba*).

Colour white; quills black. Length 42 inches.

African Marabou Stork (*Leptoptilus criminiferus*).

Bun Feroli; common in the Boorgha country; Well Wall.

Length from tip of beak to tip of toe, 4 feet 7½ inches; length of beak, 12 inches. One enormous male killed by me at Well Wall measured 6 feet 1½ inches from tip of beak to tip of toe, and exactly 9 feet from tip to tip of wings. Large naked head, neck, and pouch, latter brilliantly coloured red and blue, which is lost when skinned; wings and back dark blue-black; breast black and white; fluffy white feathers between the legs, the ' marabou ' feathers of commerce.

The Sacred Ibis (*Ibis æthiopica*).

Bainhou.

Bill very long; short twelve-feathered tail. Colour pure white; tips of wings dark green. Length 29 inches. Iris brown; naked head and neck black; plumes on the back and tips of the quills greenish-black; rest of plumage white tinged with buff.

Hadadah Ibis (*Hagedashia hagedash*).

Bainhou.

So called from its cry, ' Ha—ha—hadadah.' Above glossy brown-green; under parts, head, and neck gray-brown; bill red and black; legs red-brown; iris white. Length 2 feet 5 inches.

ANSERES (The Ducks).

Egyptian Goose (*Chenalopex ægyptiaca*).

Found breeding on all suitable lakes and rivers in Somaliland; on the Jiggiga Plain, Webbi Shebeyli, Sinnadogho in the Marehan country, Allahballah.

Length 28 inches. Back brown; rump black; back of neck reddish-brown; breast gray; under tail-coverts buff; wing-coverts white barred with a black line; secondaries metallic green; iris orange.

Tree Duck (?).

Abdin Libah.

Size of a widgeon; wings and breast colour of female teal; legs black; iris brown; top of head brown under buff.

Common Teal (*Querquedula crecca*).

Mud flats close to the harbour at Berbera.

Head brown and metallic blue; body gray barred with brown; breast gray-buff spotted with brown.

Duck (*Anas undata*).

Sheik Mohamed.

Iris light brown ; bill yellow and black.

Duck (*?*).

Allahballah.

Iris brown; back rufous ; sides like a ' gray hen ' ; breast black; head and neck black and white.

COLUMBÆ (Pigeons).

The Abyssinian Walia or Fruit Pigeon (*Vinago walia*).

Foot of the Girato Pass ; Gulis Mountains.

Length of skin, 10¾ inches. Head and upper parts of breast slaty green; back brilliant green ; tip of tail slate ; lesser wing-coverts lilac; tips of wings brown ; lower portion of breast brilliant yellow ; iris pink; feet yellow.

African Ground Dove (*Chalcopelia afra*).

Sheik Husein ; Mount Kuldush.

Colour above ash brown ; top of head lead-colour; white stripe across lower part of back ; iris brown; two or three large spots of bright purple and green on centre of wings; under tail black. Length 7½ inches.

Spotted Pigeon (*Columba guineæ*).

Wardare.

Dark red back and wings, latter spotted with white ; iris yellow ; rump, tail, and breast French gray; pointed feathers on chest.

Pale Ring Dove (*Turtur damarensis*).

Eik.

Colour gray ; black band on back of neck ; eye brown; belly white.

Turtle Dove (*Turtur senegalensis*).

Wardare.

Length of skin, 9½ inches. Head and neck reddish-brown ; lesser wing-coverts bright slate blue ; lower back red-brown ; breast reddish, turning to white at tail ; upper tail gray ; under parts black and white.

Turtle Dove (*Turtur lugens*).

Sheik Husein.

Iris bright yellow ; feet pink ; bill dusky red.

Turtle Dove (*Turtur roseogriseus*).

Hullier.

Feet brown; bill black ; iris chestnut ; head and neck pink ; chin, throat, under tail-coverts, and vent white ; no black streak on lores ; on hind-neck a broad black collar ; rump and upper tail-coverts pale gray-brown ; primaries brown-black. Length 12·5 inches.

Pigeon (*Columba albitorques*).

Legs red ; iris dark brown.

Little Long-tailed Dove (*Œna capensis*).
Eik.

Length 9 inches. A remarkably pretty bird ; back of head and wing-coverts light slate gray ; back gray-brown ; chin and throat deep black ; breast white ; tail very long and slate-coloured ; beak and legs red ; under wing and secondaries dull brick red ; iris brown.

Lichtenstein's Sand Grouse (*Pterocles lichtensteini*).
Habr Heshi.

Light brown with black tips to wings ; colour of back and neck like hen pheasant ; breast white ; sides of body black ; iris brown ; bill and feet orange ; flight like partridge.

Sand Grouse (*Pterocles decoratus*).
Okoto.

Feet gray ; bill horn colour ; colour sandy ; female barred above and spotted below with black ; throat dirty white.

Sand Grouse (*Pterocles exustus*).
Berbera ; Milmil.

GALLINÆ (GAME BIRDS).

Bare-throated Francolin (*Pternistes infuscatus*).
Foot of Gerato Pass ; Gulis Mountains.

Length of skin, 15 inches. Wattles yellow ; brown back streaked with white ; legs black ; breast speckled with brown and red brown ; lores red.

Kirk's Francolin (*Francolinus kirki*).
Sogsoda.
Iris brown.

Lort Phillips' Francolin (*Francolinus lorti*).
Waggar Mountains (9,000 feet).

White patch on sides of neck, spotted with black ; deep chestnut patches on feathers of fore-neck ; spots on breast deep chestnut ; throat white ; back of head and round eye chestnut. Length 12·5 inches.

Francolin (*Francolinus castamericollis*).
Sheik Mohamed.
Iris brown.

Harlequin Quail (*Coturnix delegorquei*).
Very plentiful at Eik.

An extremely handsome bird. Length of skin, 6 inches. Rich chestnut and black breast ; mottled brown back streaked with yellowish-white ; throat white, having a black marking on it ; legs dull yellow ; iris brown.

Vulture-like Guinea-fowl (*Acryllium vulturinum*).
Common in the Boorgha country, West Somaliland and in Central Ogaden.

A strikingly handsome bird. Head and neck naked like a vulture, and cobalt blue ; back of neck has soft brown velvety feathers ; breast feathers pointed and coloured blue and black with a white streak ; back and tail black covered with white spots ; wings black and purple.

The Abyssinian Guinea-fowl (*Numida ptilorhyncha*).

Boorgha country.

Distinguished by a bunch of horny bristles at the base of the upper mandible.

FULICARIÆ (THE RAILS).

The Red-knobbed Coot (*Fulica cristata*).

Sheik Mohamed.

Head and neck black ; rest of plumage dull slate ; legs and bill gray ; above the white shield on the head are two knobs of chestnut ; pink bands just under feathers of thigh.   Length 16 inches.

ALECTORIDES (BUSTARDS, CRANES, ETC.).

Small Bustard (*Lophotis gindiana*).

Leferuke ; Guban.

Iris yellow.

Arabian Bustard (*E. arabs*).

Ogaden.

A very handsome bird.   Length 29¼ inches.   Back brown ; long brown crest on head ; beak dark green ; neck speckled gray and white ; breast white ; wings brown spotted with white ; legs greenish-yellow.

Large Bustard (*N. heuglini*).

Lehello.

Iris brown ; crest dark brown ; throat and neck light slate blue, verging into rufous brown on chest ; breast and belly white ; back and wing-coverts mottled olive and black.

Small Bustard (*Heterotetrax humilis*).

Upper Sheik and on the Berbera-Hargaisa road.

Breast white ; back and half of wings light brown, speckled like a gray hen ; rest dark brown ; legs and iris yellow.

Large Bustard (*Lissotis hartlaubi*).

Silo Plain.

Lesser back, rump, upper and under tail-coverts, and tail black.   Length 27 inches.

Bustard (*Trachelotis canicollis*).

Near Toyo Plain.

Length 22 inches.   Iris pale yellow ; under parts white ; long under tail-coverts buff barred with black ; bill dull white.

LIMICOLÆ (PLOVERS, SNIPE, ETC.).

The Small Courser (*C. somalensis*).

Dagaboor ; Sogsoda.

Colour light buff ; abdomen dirty white ; feathers of top of head have terminal black spots ; back and wings barred with black-brown ; throat dirty white ; tail buff barred with brown-black ; iris black.

Thick Knee (*Œdicnemus affinis*).
Sibi.
Iris yellow ; base of bill and feet yellow.

Common Thick Knee (*Œdicnemus scolopax*).
Sogsoda.
Iris yellow and large; plumage mottled and striated with shades of buff and brown.   Length 16 inches.

Courser (*Rhinoptilus cinctus*).
Dagaboor; Gedais.
Eyelids yellow; legs cream ; iris dark brown.

Somali Courser (*Rhinoptilus hartingi*).
Eik.
Length 8½ inches.   Head, wings, and back speckled with light red-brown ; upper breast barred with two or three dark brown lines; lower breast yellow-white ; black tips to wings.

Crab Plover (*Dromas ardeola*).
Sea shore, Berbera.
Colour white, with a black patch between the wings ; wings black; head mottled with black ; bill black and very strong ; legs black and very long ; feet half palmated.   Length 1 foot 3 inches.

Red-legged Plover (*Chettusia coronata*).
Lehello.
Length of skin, 12 inches ; brilliant red legs ; red and black beak ; back of head black and white ; back and wings yellow-gray ; tail white and black ; breast gray; belly white.

Spur-winged Plover (*Hoplopterus spinosus*).
Wells of Farfanyer ; Ogaden.
Colour black and white ; strong spur on each wing; iris red.

Golden Plover (*Charadrinus dominicus*).
Berbera.
Back and wings blackish, and spotted all over with yellow ; axillaries white ; no hind-toe ; breast white in winter, black in breeding season ; forehead white ; tail barred with brown.

Kentish Plover (*Ægialitis cantiana*)
Berbera.
Upper parts light brown-gray ; bill and claws black; iris brown.   Length 6 inches.

Common Ringed Plover (*Ægialitis hiaticula*).
Berbera.
Forehead and stripe behind each eye white ; fore-crown, lores, and under eye black ; chin, throat, and neck white followed by a black collar ; back brown ; lower breast white; bill black and yellow ; legs orange.   Length 7·75 inches.

Stilt Plover (*Himantopsus candidus*).

Allahballah.

Length 18 inches; beak 2½ inches; legs 9¾ inches. Long grayish-white neck; back and wings metallic black; breast white; legs pink; iris red; bill black.

(*Stephanibyx coronata.*)
Boodwain.
Legs and bill red; iris yellow.

Plover (*Oxyechus tricollaris*).

Leferuke; Gulis; sea-shore, Berbera.
Legs dull yellow; eyelids red.

Green Sandpiper (*Helodromas ochropus*).

Gulis; Sinnadogho.
Length of skin, 10½ inches. Iris hazel; long bill and legs black; breast and upper tail-coverts white; throat white speckled with gray; back and wings dull green.

Sanderling (*Calidris arenaria*).

Berbera.
Iris brown; upper parts pale gray with darker bars; under parts white. Length 7 inches.

Common Sandpiper (*Actitus hypolemeus*).

Sinnadogho.
Length 7 inches. Back gray; breast white; iris brown.

Curlew (*Numenius arquata*).

Along the sea-shore in hundreds at Berbera.
Long curved beak; colour gray, brown, and white.

Common Snipe (*Scolopax cœlestis*).

Wells of Farfanyer.
Upper parts brown and buff; under parts white; fourteen feathers in tail.

Snipe (*Scolopax* or *Terekia cinerea*).

Sea-shore, Berbera.
Length 10¼ inches. Tail of fourteen feathers.

Little Stint (*Tringa minuta*).

Sea-shore, Berbera.
Winter plumage: Above brown-gray; throat, neck, breast, and abdomen white; tail feathers ash gray edged with white. Summer plumage: Upper parts yellow-red. Length 5 inches.

The Dunlin (*Pelidna alpina*).

Sea-shore, Berbera,
Upper parts gray; upper breast and throat dull white with dark stripes; lower breast black; belly white. Length 8 inches.

Gull (*Larus hemprichi*).

Berbera.

Iris brown ; colour brown with a white collar.

PYGOPODES (GREBES).

Cape Grebe (*Tachybaptes capensis*).

Sheik Mohamed.

Iris brown.

RATITÆ (OSTRICHES).

The Somali Ostrich (*Struthio molybdophanes*).

Saylah Bun (waterless Haud) ; Dumberelli (Ogaden) ; Bun Feroli and Gobtelleli, Boorgha country.

Male : Head and neck covered with down ; naked legs, which are slate-coloured, with a bright red patch on the front of the legs above the feet ; feathers on body black, with white plumes on wings and tail ; two toes on each foot. Female : Feathers of body brown ; eggs a dirty white, indented with small circles. Height of male, about 3½ feet to top of back.

REPTILES.

The Crocodile (*C. niloticus*).

Swarming in the Webbi Shebeyli and Webbi Ganana.

Colour uniform dark olive ; skull comparatively smooth. A large one measured 13 feet long. In order to kill a crocodile and recover him, he must be shot in the brain, which is immediately behind the ear. The plates on the body are easily pierced by a bullet, but when hit obliquely the bullet will often ricochet.

TORTOISES.

LAND TORTOISE.

Leopard Tortoise (*Testudo pardalis*).

Hargaisa, Sibi, and the Boorgha country.

I picked up this extremely handsome tortoise in all sizes. The carapace of an adult was 32 inches long and 28 inches broad, both measurements being taken along the curve ; a young one measured 9½ inches long and 8½ inches broad, and a very young one, which was most beautifully marked, measured 4½ inches long and 4 inches broad. The young ones I found for the most part in stony ground, the large ones in the luxuriant grass. It was amusing to see a whole army of these monsters migrating from one patch of grass across a desert to another patch of fresh grass. The ground colour is yellow, with sexagonal rings of black, the sides being spotted with black ; under surface plain yellow.

WATER TORTOISE.

The Side-necked Tortoise (*Pelomedusa galeata*).

Common at the bottom of wells in the Boorgha country; in pools in the rock in Guban, and in rain lakes in Ogaden.

These side-neck tortoises are so called because they draw their head and neck sideways within the shell when alarmed. The carapace is much flatter than that of the land tortoises, and is of a dull yellow colour.

Measurements of two collected by me:

1. Length of carapace ... ... 6¼ inches.
   Breadth of ,, ... 6 ,,
2. Length of ,, ... 4¼ ,,
   Breadth of ,, ... 4 ,,

LIZARDS.

GECKOTIDÆ (THE GECKOS).

(*Platydactylus delalaudii.*)
(*Hemidactylus mabonia.*)
(*Hemidactylus verruculatus.*)

Turkish Gecko (*Hemidactylus turcicus.*)

Guban.

Claws compressed. Length 4 inches. Body covered with from fourteen to sixteen longitudinal rows of warts, of which some are white, others blackish; upper parts grayish-brown spotted with flesh colour.

(*Pristiurus flavipunctatus.*)
(*Gymnodactylus crucifer.*)
Galadi.

Two lines of dark spots down back; tail same length as body.

AGAMIDÆ (THE AGAMOID LIZARDS).

Ruppell's Agama (*Agama ruppelli*).

Curious thorny scales at sides of neck; tail longer than body. Length 13 inches. Head red; throat spotted with yellow; body and legs deep blue; white line along middle of back. These brilliant colours fade immediately after death.

The Agile Agama (*Agama agilis*).

Occipital scale of the head small; no rings on tail.

Agama (*Agama ruderata*).

East African Thorny-tailed Lizard (*Aporoscelis princeps*).

Length 7½ inches.

Broad Thorny-tailed Lizard (*Aporoscelis batilliferus*).

For figure and description of this curious form see pages 175, 176.

VARANIDÆ (The Monitors).

Large Tree Monitor (*Varanus ocellatus*).

Wardare.

This formidable-looking monster is to be found perched on the top of high thorn-bushes, and is perfectly harmless. Body dirty yellow and gray barred irregularly with dirty white ; tail gray and white in regular bars ; under parts dirty yellow-white ; long yellow claws. Length from tip of nose to end of tail, 3 feet 2 inches ; length of tail, 19¾ inches.

LACERTIDÆ (True Lizards).

Algerian Keeled Lizard (*Tropidosaura algira*).

No collar ; soles feebly keeled.

Common Fringe-toed Lizard (*Acanthodactylus vulgaris*).

Tail twice as long as head and body ; above bronze green, with two golden streaks along side ; under parts whitish. Length 10¼ inches.

Fringe-toed Lizard (*Acanthodactylus savignyi*).

Revoil's Lizard (*Eremias revoili*).

Dark snake-like markings down sides of back ; tail long.

(*Eremias lugubris.*)

SCINCIDÆ (The Skink Tribe).

The Eyed Skink (*Gongylus ocellatus*).

Muzzle wedge-shaped ; scales thin and smooth ; the tail conical and pointed ; toes rather flattened ; eyes guarded with distinct eyelids ; limbs stout ; ears small.

CHAMÆLIONIDÆ (The Chameleons).

The Common Chameleon (*Chamæleo vulgaris*).

Colour by day dark green, by night whitish-yellow, when on a bough or disturbed, purple-brown ; tongue very long. Length 10 inches.

(*Chamæleo kerstenii.*)

SNAKES.

Smith's Fierce Snake (*Zamenis smithii*).

Found usually on the ground and occasionally on thorn-bushes.

Colour dark straw, yellow on upper parts ; belly light yellow ; head darker. Length of one killed by me, 23 inches.

Tree Snake (*Psammophis biseriatus*).

Often found on low-lying thorn-bushes.

Colour : back dark gray-brown ; two thin lines of brown run down the sides ; belly blue-gray. Length of one killed by me, 22¾ inches.

Asp, or Egyptian Cobra (*Naia haie*).

This fine and dangerous snake was occasionally met with. On being suddenly surprised, they would retreat to a thorn-bush, and there rear themselves up in the well-known fashion, with neck flattened out, and hiss loudly.

Colour above, dark straw ; belly light straw yellow. Length of one killed by me, 4 feet 7½ inches.

FISH.

The Mud-skipper (*P. kœbrenteri*).

I noticed this extraordinary fish hopping from the sand into the sea as I walked along the shore at Berbera.

The Blue Shark (*Carcharias glaucus*).

Common in the harbour at Berbera. Length from 15 to 20 feet.

The Cromid (*Chromis spilurus*).

Found in water-holes near the Webbi Shebeyli and near Sheik Husein, West Somaliland.

Cat-fish (*Clarias lazera*).

Webbi Shebeyli.
(*Entropius depressirostris.*)
Webbi Shebeyli.
(*Synodontis geledensi.*)
Geledi ; Webbi Shebeyli.
(*Synodontis punctulatus.*)
Webbi Shebeyli.
(*Alestes affinis.*)
Webbi Shebeyli.

The Barbel (*Barbus byrni*).

Webbi Shebeyli.

African Beaked Fish (*Mormyrus zambaneizi*).

Geledi ; Webbi Shebeyli.
(*Cyprimodon hammonis.*)
Webbi Shebeyli.

Map of
SOMALILAND
showing

C. V. A. PEEL'S

1st Expedition –––––
2nd Expedition •••••

SCALE OF MILES.
0   50   100   150   200

INDEX.

INDEX.

THE END.